The Haynes
Welding
Manual

by Jay Storer
and John H Haynes
Member of the Guild of Motoring Writers

The Haynes Manual
for selecting and using welding equipment

ABC

Haynes Publishing Group
Sparkford Nr Yeovil
Somerset BA22 7JJ England

Haynes North America, Inc
861 Lawrence Drive
Newbury Park
California 91320 USA

Haynes Welding Manual

Acknowledgements

We are grateful for the help and cooperation of welding equipment manufacturers such as Airco, Daytona MIG, HTP America, Lincoln Electric, Miller Electric and the ESAB Group, for their assistance with technical information and illustrations. Thanks to FitzMaurice-Smith Racing in Ventura for assistance with cover photography. We also wish to thank the Eastwood Company, Maguire's Welding and Valley Vintage Rods for assistance.

A book in the Haynes Automotive Repair Manual Series

Printed in the U.S.A.

ISBN 1 56392 110 3

Library of Congress Catalog Card Number 94-74485

Contents

Haynes Welding Manual

1 Introduction

Welding is a process critical to our present state of civilization and technical advancement, yet little understood and most often taken for granted. Unless exposed to the building, machinery or automotive trades, the average person never realizes how much we depend on the welding process, which is a fundamental part of the process of building most of what we depend on daily, including vehicles, buildings, appliances, bridges and a great deal more. In fact, once you really start to examine the objects around us, it's hard to imagine our world without the welding process.

Architecturally speaking, we might all be living in one-room wood or adobe-brick houses if it weren't for welding. Certainly all large commercial and residential structures are built with a considerable "skeleton" of welded structural steel, and even most single-family, wood-framed houses are built using some welded components, even down to items like the electrical outlet boxes in the walls. Anyone who has watched the construction progress of a major highway improvement like a bridge or tunnel has seen the helmeted weldors, unsung heroes of the construction process, spraying a shower of sparks from high on a scaffold while they join metals to hold critical loads.

Sitting in an airport terminal recently with some time on our hands gave us something to think about. Virtually everything around us involved welding in some way. There was a large rack of telephone books in stainless-steel racks, each carefully TIG-welded and sanded, a post office box that was made of welded steel, the telephone stall had welded components, and the seats we were sitting on were part of a welded-steel structure that held eight seats. Everywhere you look in the modern world, you'll find examples of how widespread and important is the use of welding techniques and equipment.

Much of our Haynes audience is familiar with the automotive world, and here is a field where construction and repairs made by welding are absolutely essential, in fact essential to virtually all forms of transportation, from bicycles to cars, trucks, trains, aircraft and space vehicles. Even if we could go back before the "horseless carriage" was developed at the end of the 19th century, we would still need some form of welding to return to horse-drawn transportation, in welded brackets for harnesses and wagon components.

1.1 Welding had its ancient origins in the fires of blacksmiths, who could forge two white-hot pieces of metal together with hammer blows and patience. It remained for history to bring us to electricity and bottled gasses for welding techniques to develop any further. Modern-day farrier (blacksmith/horseshoer) Richard Heller illustrates the old ways.

1.3 The farrier of today works out of a truck, filled with equipment like a grinder, drill press and welder, all running on AC power when available; otherwise, horseshoes are shaped in a portable forge. Today's blacksmith has the advantage of tools like this MIG welder that speed up making special horseshoes.

1.2 Metal cutting in the old days was no easier. A white-hot piece of metal was laid over a hardy (like a wedge or chisel point) in the big anvil, and struck hard with a hammer, chopping the softened piece off. Final shaping of most items was by hand with stones and files.

Since we've established that welding is a technical process our present society can't live without, in this book we'll explore more about the process, removing the mystery, and examining the available equipment as it can be useful to us in fabricating with metal or repairing metal items. We'll show all of the most up-to-date equipment, describe the various welding types, make recommendations, show how welding is used in everyday situations, and develop welding projects that illustrate how you can build or repair automotive, farm and household objects.

Definitions of welding

At one time, the simple definition of welding was "joining metals through heating them to a molten state and fusing them together." As technical progress in welding processes has advanced, the definition has had to change.

There are now two basic forms of welding: fusion and non-fusion. The former is the most common, and it involves the actual melting of the parent metals being joined. Not all welding today involves melting. Non-fusion welding is most commonly represented by soldering and brazing, two processes of joining metals where the parent metal is heated, but not melted, and a second or "filler" metal is melted between them, forming a strong bond when all are cooled.

Pressure and friction alone can weld metals together, such as when a machinist turns down a piece of metal in a lathe. Often, pieces of the metal chips can become welded to the cutting

1.4 Under the center bridge column here are a welder (a machine) and a weldor (a person). He is welding up steel enclosures for the concrete columns, to retrofit more strength in California bridges to meet newer earthquake codes.

1.5 Wherever you see buildings go up, the basis for them is always steel, whether they wind up with wood, bricks or cement on the *outside*, it all began with the work of ironworkers and weldors.

1.6 The construction and repair of heavy equipment and farm machinery would be nearly impossible without welding. Arc welding is usually used, as here modifying the front of a dirt scoop on a John Deere, where welding is outdoors and on heavy plates.

tool, which is a simple example of a process that can be used in production work in joining metals. Other kinds of "cold" welding may today involve sound and light, as in sonic-welding or laser-welding.

Today, the term "welding" has even been applied to the processes of joining non-metallic materials, such as plastic-welding which sometimes involves a fusion of materials as a result of heat or chemical action. As kids, we have all played with plastic models that we constructed using "glues" that would react with and actually "melt together" the two pieces we were joining.

For today's definition of welding to be all-encompassing, it would have to read "the joining of metals and plastics without the use of fasteners." This definition covers a lot of ground, but, given the interests and needs of the majority of our readers, this book will concentrate on welding as it applies to metals joined by heat processes produced either by a flame or electrical current.

Semantically speaking, throughout this book we will be illustrating and referring to pieces of welding equipment and to the people who operate them. Sometimes the same term "welder" is used to apply to both the machine and the man, which can become confusing, so for our purposes, we will from now on refer to the machine as a "welder" and to the person operating it as a "weldor."

Development of modern welding

Welding can trace its roots far back in time to the first blacksmiths who heated and shaped metals. At that time, metals were primarily used for tools and weapons, both of vital importance in those days. The blacksmith was an important tradesman in any community, earning a little more respect than most, even by lords and kings who depended on weapons for maintaining power. The "art" of smithing was understood by a select few, and blacksmiths were accorded almost the fear-based respect of a low-level sorcerer. Given the traditional image

1.7 Welding is even used in many art forms today. Bill McKewen is a metal sculptor who works with rods, tubes, plates, wires and custom castings to create interesting works that combine hard metals with "organic" elements.

1.8 One of Bill's largest works is this 30-foot tall sculpture called "Organic Form 1", which is made entirely of stainless-steel and weighs over 1000 pounds.

1.9 In a close-up of the "transition point" in Bill's sculpture, we can see how the stainless tubing and solid rod is wrapped with stainless-steel oil field cable and welded to a large shape originally carved of foam and then sandcast in stainless and final-shaped with a body grinder.

of the blacksmith as a large, muscular man covered with soot who works in a fiery, smoky environment, hammering loudly and magically making useful objects out of nothing, it's no wonder he was treated a little differently.

The blacksmith heated metals in a wood fire (coal was used later on) and hammered them into tools and weapons, performed basic heat-treating to harden some areas, and ground sharp edges with a foot-powered stone grinding wheel.

There were times when an object couldn't be made from one piece of metal. Gradually, the techniques developed to join pieces of metal either with bolts, hot rivets, or welding. This first use of welding consisted of heating the objects to a certain color (fairly precise indicator of the temperature) and quickly hammering them together on the anvil. The heat and pressure joined the items, and the process has been called "forge-welding."

As history marched on, larger and larger items had to be made of metal, especially with the industrial revolution of the 19th century. Most machinery was made of cast metal, produced when molten metal was poured into a mold and

1.10 In high-technology areas like nuclear vessels, aviation and here, at a large race car-building shop, quality welding technology is critical to success with metals.

1.11 Not every welder and weldor works indoors. This is an oil field service truck with gas-welding/cutting equipment, arc welder and crane. Many welding shops have portable setups like this for remote jobs.

allowed to solidify. Repairing broken castings was a common procedure in industry and manufacturing. Cast metal is too brittle for forge-welding on an anvil, and the items were too large, so a process of "cast-welding" was developed in which the broken machinery was heated, a temporary mold bolted around the area to be repaired, and molten metal was poured in. Done right, the molten metal bonded with the parent casting and the goldrush mine or cotton gin was back in business.

As the 20th century dawned, electricity came into wider usage, especially for lighting. The early carbon-arc lamps made as much heat as they did light, and someone started using electric carbon-arc rods to fusion-weld metals. Soon after, the simple stick electrode was developed that is similar to arc-welding rods of today, and about that same time oxy-acetylene gas welding was also developing. It's ironic that gas welding also grew out of the advancements in lighting, since acetylene gas had been used for car lights up until just before W.W.I.

1.12 The back of the same oil field welding truck is built as a large, heavy workbench-away-from-a-shop. Big Lincoln ac/dc arc welder has its own engine power and generator to run lights for night work.

Speaking of W.W.I, anyone who is familiar with history knows that many technological advances have resulted from the accelerated development that, unfortunately, only seems to come from a wartime environment. W.W.I saw the further development of gas and stick welding, and soon after that the refinement of X-ray technology aided further industrial use of welding. The exacting inspection of welds made possible by X-rays speeded welding's acceptance.

The rapid development of the aircraft industry between the wars, and the increased use of lightweight metals to replace wood and fabric in fuselages and wings led to further advances in welding. W.W.II saw the burgeoning aircraft industry with increased requirements for joining light metals such as aluminum and magnesium faster, stronger and smoother than with drilling and riveting, as had been used before. Inert-gas welding was invented before the war, but the gasses were considered too expensive at the time, and it took a war-time environment to accelerate its development. After the war, because the lightweight metals were in demand for many military and civilian applications, TIG welding was further refined, and MIG welding was invented around 1948.

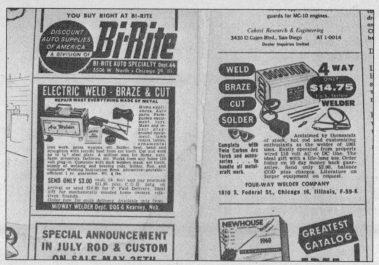

1.13 Back in the Fifties and Sixties, car enthusiast magazines were all advertising these "twin carbon-arc" welders, which were the original "Buzzboxes." While some of these did *work*, most of them were tried a few times and then put on a shelf out in the garage. Today they're collector's items from welding history.

1.14 Today's modern home/shop/garage welding equipment is likely to be a clean, efficient, safer welding system like MIG, or wire-feed, welding. Machines like this are getting less expensive all the time, and some models can be hooked to standard household 110V current, making them quite portable.

1.15 If you decide to purchase a welder, visit your local welding supply center to talk to the salespeople and find out what equipment best suits your needs and budget. A well-equipped store will have everything you'll need, from gasses to glasses.

Today

In the remaining decades of the 20th century, welding developments have come at a rapid pace, often closely tied to electronics development, as new and better methods of applying cleaner and more controlled heat have come along. In the past decade, we have seen the cost and complexity of welding equipment reduced in some areas, to the point where equipment that was once considered solely the province of the high-production professional shop is now found in garages and hobby shops around the country.

It's been good news for the automotive hobbyist, whether he is restoring an old car or building a race car, as well as good news for the small farmer trying to maintain and repair his equipment. Welders are now being purchased by metal-sculptors and other artists and craftsmen, as well as being used for the most everyday kinds of household jobs such as repairing a bicycle or garden tool, building a firewood storage rack or a barbecue, or even fabricating a small utility trailer at home.

Welding has been compared to playing a musical instrument. In the same way that anyone can pick-up a harmonica and start making sounds with it, most anyone with some mechanical aptitude can, with a little practice, start using popular kinds of modern welding equipment for non-critical jobs. But to make *music* with that harmonica, or good, strong, clean welds with a welder, will take time. As the hip musician once said when asked how to get to Carnegie Hall, "Practice, man, practice!" The more time spent consistently practicing with a welding setup, whatever the type, the better your results will be. If you use your welder only occasionally, don't just pick-up the torch and expect to lay a perfect bead the first time. There is a rhythm to find. Practice first on a scrap piece of metal of the same thickness as the work you intend to weld, and, when you have the rhythm down, repair or fabricate your job.

Though not considered with the same awe as the ancient blacksmith, a professional weldor today can still make a satisfying living, for it seems to be a skill that, far from fading out due to replacement technology, is seeing ever-increasing usage in business and industry. Weldors today find diversified employment in oil field and pipeline work, building construction, bridges and other infrastructure, automotive work from assembly-line welding to body shop repair to race car fabrication and antique auto restoration, to the nuclear-power industry, aviation and aerospace work, defense work, and manufacturing work building products from household appliances to huge boilers and construction equipment.

This book is intended as an overall introduction to the welding process, illustrating most of the common equipment and work techniques for both home and shop welding. While this is not a textbook for the would-be professional weldor, there is enough of an overview here to give a prospective welding student a basic understanding before delving into the more detailed professional textbooks on the subject.

Whether you plan to restore a vintage car, build a race car or experimental aircraft, construct your own wrought-iron fence, sculpt a metal art masterpiece, or go into welding professionally, you'll find this book of interest. The handy Source List and Glossary of Terms at the end of the book will be helpful for future reference.

Notes

2 Types of welding

If you are reading this book, chances are you have had some exposure to welding through watching a repair done such as having a new exhaust system put on your car, through some hobby interest in the metal arts/crafts area or through some industrial exposure to welding as used in manufacturing and building processes. Obviously you have become interested enough in learning about welding to purchase this book which we feel is an excellent introduction to a field where there are lots of involved textbooks for the person pursuing welding as a profession, but few *basic* books for someone getting started at the hobby, farm or home/shop level.

Perhaps your initial exposure to welding has sparked an interest in doing it yourself. If you are involved in automotive work, you already know how valuable the process can be in fabrication and repairs. Once you have seen it performed, you realize how *handy* this capability is. You can join pieces of metal to either repair something that was damaged and otherwise scheduled for replacement or build something entirely new, from a barbecue grille to a race car.

Once you have the basic skills and the right equipment, you'll find many more uses for welding than you had anticipated. Like a good truck or a specialized tool, once you have a welder, you'll wonder how you ever got along without it! You'll probably find yourself building a materials rack, stocking it with various sizes of tubing and plates, and actually looking for new projects to tackle, from building a workbench to last a lifetime, to storage racks, moveable shop carts, engine stands, shelving, and much more.

There are quite a few types of welding processes, and today there are a great many welders to choose from. There are so many, in fact, that just picking the process and the ma-

2.1 There are a number of choices today when shopping for welding equipment. The right choice for you depends on the kind of jobs you plan to do, where you plan to do them, your budget and how much time you can devote to training and practice before you become proficient at one of the methods we'll be looking at.

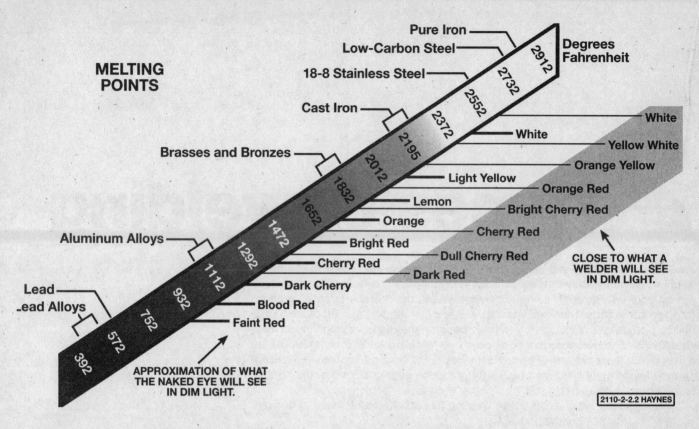

MELTING POINTS

Pure Iron — 2912
Low-Carbon Steel — 2732
Degrees Fahrenheit
18-8 Stainless Steel — 2552
2372
Cast Iron — 2195
White
2012
White
Brasses and Bronzes — 1832
Yellow White
Orange Yellow
Light Yellow
1652
Orange Red
Lemon
Bright Cherry Red
1472
Orange
Cherry Red
Bright Red
1292
Dull Cherry Red
Aluminum Alloys — 1112
Cherry Red
Dark Red
Dark Cherry
932
CLOSE TO WHAT A WELDER WILL SEE IN DIM LIGHT.
Blood Red
Lead
752
Lead Alloys
Faint Red
572
392

APPROXIMATION OF WHAT THE NAKED EYE WILL SEE IN DIM LIGHT.

2110-2-2.2 HAYNES

2.2 Welding is a process of *fusion*, in which metal parts are heated to the melting point and fused together, usually with a filler of the same material melted along with the "parent" metal. All metals melt at different temperatures, and this chart shows some interesting comparisons, as well as relating the heated metal's color to its temperature.

chinery which best suit your needs may seem a considerable task. This chapter will give you a brief overview of the various processes along with an analysis of the pros and cons for each type and how best to select equipment based on *your* needs.

How it works

The most basic principle of the welding process is joining two pieces of metal together (or at least two edges of the same piece, in the case of repairing a crack). This is generally accomplished by heating the metals to be joined until they become liquid or molten and the two edges fuse together. Most often, the complete joining of the two metal edges is accomplished by melting new metal into the joint at the same time. The new metal added to form a fused welding joint is called filler metal, while the original pieces being joined are called the parent metal. Together they form a welded "bead" of filler and parent metal that is usually thicker than the parent metal. Depending on the skill of the weldor and the type of welding, two pieces of metal can be joined in such a way that with a little filing or sanding of the bead, the joint is virtually undetectable, a particularly important aspect when making automotive body repairs. The first time you may have observed a professional weldor working, the process may have seemed like a sorcerer doing alchemy with a magic wand. With the proper equipment and practice, you can do a little magic yourself, a magic that can give tremendous personal satisfaction, as well as save you considerable expense compared to having the same work done at a professional fabrication shop.

2.3 The welding corner of this well-equipped race-car prep shop holds a variety of equipment, from a large TIG machine at left (with cooling unit on top), to a heavy-duty plasma cutter, oxy-acetylene cutting/heating/welding outfit, and two small plasma cutters. Not shown here are the two MIG welders in use elsewhere in the shop.

2.4 You will have to develop some new contacts once you get into welding, one of which will be a reliable local source for metals for your projects. This is ABC Metals (aluminum, brass and copper) in Oxnard, California. They have a lot of aluminum here at scrap prices, but it's more of a gold mine for the hobbyist or car-builder who needs relatively small bits and pieces and not a trainload. Knowledgeable salespeople at a metal yard can be very helpful.

It takes a tremendous amount of localized heat to weld metals together, and heat control is the key to welding properly. Every material has its own specific melting point, and to make a weld you need to heat the material to that point but not beyond it. Visualize an ice cube, which is solid material (when cold). If you heat it to the melting point (above 32 degrees F), the solid becomes a liquid (water), heating it further will vaporize it into steam and for your purposes the material is *gone*. The same changes happen to metal, although at much higher temperatures. Common lead solder such as you might use to solder electrical connections can melt at temperatures from 250-750° F (depending on the alloy), aluminum melts at just below 1250° F, and common mild steel melts at 2750° F.

The heat required to make metal molten enough to fusion-weld can be achieved in several ways, but the most common for home/shop situations will be generated either with a flame or some use of electrical current. The traditional source in welding has been the oxy-acetylene torch, while electricity is now used in most of the other methods, such as arc-welding, MIG-welding, and TIG-welding.

One thing that is common to all the forms of welding is that the filler material must be compatible with the parent metal, and all efforts must be made to make a "clean" weld free of outside contaminants that could weaken the joint. If you are welding aluminum, the filler rod must be aluminum, a stainless filler rod must be used for welding stainless-steel and steel rods are used on steel. In gas welding, the cleanliness of the weld is controlled by the correct adjustment of the torch flame and the cleanliness of the two edges of the parent metal. In electric welding, an inert gas "cloud" is formed right around the welding area that keeps outside oxygen or impurities from contaminating the weld. The shielding gas is generated in several ways, as you'll see as we further describe the various types of equipment.

Metal alloys

The melting point of the metal you work with will vary with the basic nature of the material (iron, steel, aluminum, magnesium, etc.), and the alloy of the metal. Most metals today are not in pure form, they are alloyed or mixed with another metal to give the new material special characteristics. Copper, lead and iron are basic pure metals that have been used by man for tools and other ob-

2.5 Non-ferrous metals like aluminum are generally marked with their alloy and heat-treat, such as here on this sheet of 6061-T6. If you need a specific metal for a project, you may have to buy new material rather than remnants, because the smaller scrap pieces may not have the markings on them.

2.6 Weldor Bill Maguire fabricated this recumbent bicycle for himself from 4130 chrome-moly thinwall tubing, which is very strong but light. The idea was to reduce the bike weight, wind resistance and pedal effort. Bill joined the thin tubing with TIG welding.

jects for thousands of years. Mixing various metals together can produce a new metal with new uses. Copper mixed with zinc will make brass, which has strength, reduced cost, and better suitability for machining and casting. The same base copper mixed with tin makes bronze, which was alloyed as far back as 2000 years to make weapons. Gold and silver, precious as they are in their pure state are seldom utilized in their natural form which is quite soft in comparison to other metals.

When alloyed with other metals which add strength or other characteristics, gold and silver can be used for jewelry, coins and many other uses. We commonly describe different gold objects by "carats." While pure gold is 24 carat, 12-carat gold is only half gold and half other metals, and the closer the carat-number is to 24, the more gold is in the object. The other alloys reduce the expense of the pure gold and make it more durable and useful. Were rings and other jewelry to be made of 24-carat pure gold, they would be too soft and not last in normal use.

Most of the metals you will be working with in your welding will be of two kinds, ferrous and non-ferrous. The former includes metals that contain iron, most commonly steel. The most commonly-welded non-ferrous metal is aluminum. Both steel and aluminum can vary considerably in the welding process depending on the alloy. By changing the alloy of either steel or aluminum, different properties can be obtained, to either make the metal more flexible (ability to bend without breaking), malleable (ability to be formed with a hammer), ductile (ability to be drawn out or hammered thin) or to improve its strength for a specific application. Steel is made from refined iron combined with carbon and other elements. How much carbon is added determines the properties of the steel alloy. Most of the steel we might use for projects is relatively low in carbon, called mild steel. With higher levels of carbon, you get medium-carbon steel (used for shafts and axles), high-carbon steel (used for automotive and industrial springs), while very-high-carbon steel is used to make files and sharp-edged cutting tools. The common mild steel we use most often is weldable by virtually all of the techniques described in this book, while the higher-carbon steels have special requirements. Other elements commonly alloyed with steel are manganese, tungsten, nickel and chromium. The latter two combine with steel to make

2.7 Get to know the personnel at your local welding supply store. They can be very helpful when it comes to choosing equipment, and they will have all the supplies you'll need in the future. Most stores carry several brands of equipment, all the safety items, and even the smaller home/shop machines.

2.8 The welding supply store should be able to tell you where to buy steel locally, which you will probably use for most of your welding projects. Most yards have a remnant section as shown, where you can buy short lengths of material at by-the-pound prices. Tubing for a trailer project is being weighed.

stainless-steel, a very useful material that requires somewhat different welding techniques. Anyone familiar with race-car and aircraft construction may have heard of 4130 chrome-moly steel, which is often used in these applications for its high strength relative to its weight. The four-digit number describes the alloy as containing molybdenum, and the amount of carbon. This alloy contains more carbon than mild steel, as well as chromium and molybdenum, both of which add properties of rust-resistance, strength and hardness. Even though this is a higher-carbon steel than mild steel, it really contains only 30/100th of 1% of carbon, which shows how scientific the alloying of metals really is. A tiny change in content can radically affect the properties of the final metal.

In steel and aluminum, not only are there different alloys, but different heat-treat processes. In the simplest terms, heat-treating is a scientific process of heating a metal to a specific temperature and then cooling it, either slowly or quickly, and with or without oil. The heat-treating can affect the hardness and other characteristics of the metal. When aluminum is purchased new in sheets or tubes, it is generally marked with its alloy and heat-treat, such as 3003-T3, which is a sheet aluminum that is considered "half-hard" and is commonly used in making race-car bodywork, where it has to be somewhat strong, but also able to be bent, welded and hammered. On the other end of the spectrum, 7075-T6 aluminum is very hard and strong. Called "aerospace aluminum" in the vernacular, it is often used in making machined aluminum parts and applications where very high strength is required. While it is strong and hard, it doesn't bend. There are volumes of scientific books on the alloying and heat-treating of metals, but, for your purposes as a home weldor, just remember to find out what kind of metal you are welding, and when making a project ask a metals expert to recommend the most suitable material. In general, the higher the carbon content in steel, and the higher the heat-treat on aluminum, the stronger the material will be but tougher to form into a shape, and the tougher metal alloys can be more brittle.

If you do decide to purchase a welder, you will eventually get to know the people at your local source for welding equipment, and they should be of considerable help in answering your questions and getting your setup working well. They will also be able to tell you where locally to purchase the metals you need for your projects. Most metal supply houses have a "scraps" section where you can purchase cut ends, small plates and short lengths of various tubes, all at about half the price of prime material, which is usually sold in large, unwieldy sheets or 20-foot lengths of tubing. Use the scrap pieces for all your experimentation with various types of welds, until you are doing pretty well. You may even be able to build small projects, like a welding cart, using the short lengths of tubing or angle-iron from the scraps section. Once you get to know the people at both the welding supply house and the metal yard, you'll have experts to wade through the technical jargon of alloys and heat-treats, and help you sort out the right material for your future projects.

Oxy-acetylene gas welding

This is perhaps the oldest and most versatile of welding setups. For a long time, it was the only setup recommended for the home/shop use, and has been among the least expensive to get started with. The basic combination in a typical gas-welding package are two high-pressure cylindrical tanks, one for oxygen, one for acetylene, a set of gauges and regulators to control the gas flow out of the tanks, a pair of hoses, and a torch. The torch usually comes with a variety of tips, tip cleaners, a spark lighter, and good sets may include a helmet, gloves and often a cutting-torch.

The latter is what really makes the oxy-acetylene system so versatile. It is one of the few welding systems that can do *cutting* as well as welding. This can be invaluable in both repair and fabrication work. Cutting away damaged or unwanted material is easily done with a properly-used cutting-torch attachment, and you may have many projects where you need to cut an *irregular* shape out of steel plate. The bulk of tubing and angle-iron cutting is usually done with some kind of saw or an abrasive cutoff wheel, but these tools can only make a straight cut; they can't go around corners. If you need to cut out a circle from a steel plate, you can draw the circle on the plate with a compass and a special hard crayon called a soapstone (which leaves a line you can see even when welding), then use your cutting torch to follow the line and you have your part. Any shape can be cut out. If you make up a cardboard template of the piece you need, trace around the pattern with your soapstone onto the plate, and make it.

Cutting with a torch takes skill to closely follow a line, and even then the edges of the metal will require some grinding, filing or sanding to get a smooth edge. Most experienced weldors know just how much to cut *outside* their pattern

2.9 Gas welding with oxygen and acetylene gasses is one of the oldest forms of welding, and is still used today in construction, muffler shops and farm repairs. Its versatility lies in the ability to cut *and* weld, on thick and thin materials, and to do braze-welding as well. The flux shown is only used for brazing. Note the different size and shape of the two gas cylinders.

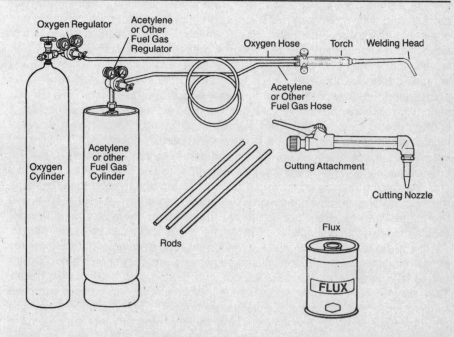

2.10 You'll need a safe area to practice your gas welding. Fire bricks like these are safe to weld on and don't suck the heat out of your parent metal as you weld. The skills you'll have to learn with gas welding are torch movement, even feeding of filler rod with your other hand, and steady, small circles to make consistent puddles.

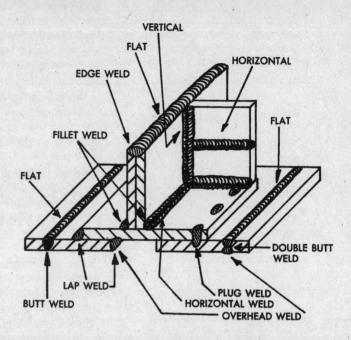

size to have an exact-size piece after cleaning up the cut edges with a grinder.

The oxy-acetylene setup is still the least expensive welding system if you buy the torches, gauges and hoses, and *lease* the gas cylinders. The tanks are expensive to purchase outright, but can be leased from your local welding supply store with a deposit down and a small monthly fee. Many shops today will take a credit application in lieu of a deposit, and you will open an account there, assuming your credit is good.

2.11 This illustration shows virtually all of the basic weld types and positions. With each type of welding you practice, you'll first learn to make a steady bead on a steel plate, then do flat butt-welds, then move on to corner welds and tougher ones like overhead and vertical welds. If you first learn torch control with gas welding, you'll be able to pick-up any other welding method more easily.

2.12 Oxy-acetylene torch flames can be put to some sophisticated uses. This is a mechanical gas pattern cutter (ESAB Silhouette 500), which can follow a pattern under the stylus and cut out two identical copies with the torch heads at right. Intricate parts can be cut out repeatedly, and with very clean edges because the torch movement is motorized and very smooth.

Leasing tanks is an inexpensive way to get started, but if you do only a small amount of welding infrequently, it may not be a practical arrangement for you. After you have been paying rental fees for a year or two, you'll realize you could have purchased the tanks outright for the same amount of money. If you knew you only had to do some gas-welding for a few months, then the leasing deal would be better.

When welding with oxy-acetylene equipment, the basic procedure is to set the proper gas flow to the torch with the regulators, crack open the valves on the torch, light the flame with a friction-sparking lighter and then adjust the ratio of oxygen to acetylene to achieve the proper flame. Changing tip sizes makes a bigger or smaller flame, so you suit the tip size to the thickness of the parent metals you are welding. A smaller flame is used for thinner metals. The torch is brought down to the work area (the weldor is wearing his dark-lensed safety goggles) and the flame is used to heat the two edges to be joined, while your other hand feeds a piece of filler rod into the molten puddle as you move along the joint. Weld joints can be made with or without a filler rod, but a filler rod is used most often.

This is a very simplistic description of the process of gas-welding. It takes considerable practice and good hand/eye coordination to master. Once learned, the skills can be very useful, but it is a process rather difficult to learn from a book. Taking a class or having an experienced friend take you through the process will ease the learning curve considerably.

Besides the versatility of doing both welding and cutting, oxy-acetylene equipment also has many other shop uses in supplying a lot of localized heat. You may have projects where you need to bend a piece of metal. Thin sheet metal can be easily bent with pliers, vise-grips or put into a vise and bent over with a hammer, but thick metal may crack when bent cold. If you have a 1/4-inch-thick steel bracket you need to bend at an angle, cold-bending with a hammer and vise may require so much hammer force as to distort the part out of shape, as well as mark the surface up or even damage the vise. If you closely examine the piece of thick plate after a cold bend, you may see the metal in the corner of the bend looking crystallized, which weakens that spot. Heating the metal to the right temperature with a torch before bending it, along the line where the bend should be, allows an easy bend with less disturbance of the metal's integrity along the bend. Another use of gas welding equipment is for brazing ferrous and non-ferrous metals such as copper and brass. In brazing, the parent metal is not made molten, it is heated enough to melt a brass filler rod, which attaches to both pieces of parent metal, making a firm joint.

Besides heating metal for bending, gas equipment is also used in many automotive shops for freeing frozen parts. Metals expand when heated, and when a rusted nut on a fastener is heated, the nut expands and breaks the bond, so the nut can be removed. When working under a car that has seen winter road salts, or when disassembling an old car for restoration, a gas torch can be very handy for getting off rusted nuts without busting your knuckles when your wrench rounds off an old nut. Many a mechanic on older cars would not be without his faithful "smoke wrench." Machine shops also use a torch to heat and expand parts that have a press fit. A gear that fits on a shaft may be heated with a special "rosebud" tip that spreads the flame around a wider area, and when the gear has expanded, it is picked up with tongs and slipped onto the unheated (and not expanded) shaft. When it cools off and contracts, the gear is securely fastened to the shaft, but can be removed at a later time just by reheating it again.

Despite the versatility of the gas-welding equipment, it may not be the ideal equipment for you, depending on your needs. If you have other uses for it besides just welding, then it is definitely a must have, but, if you just need to occasionally weld various thicknesses of steel together, some of today's electric welders may be more suitable for you. Gas welding is harder to learn, there are more safety problems in the shop when using a gas torch (especially when cutting), welding thick metals takes good skills and it is easy to distort the parent metal when welding thin sheet metal. Automotive body men today are using a torch less and less when doing repairs on thin metal. However, one of the advantages of gas-welding equipment over any electric-welder is portability. Your gas welding cart can be moved around anywhere without wires, even carried (when properly secured) in your pick-up for welding at a remote site.

If you have the budget and the need for gas-welding's versatility and portability, then your ideal shop setup would include both an oxy-acetylene rig *and* some kind of electric welder.

Arc welding

Like gas welding, electric arc welding has been around for almost 100 years, and the fact that it is still around today illustrates its continued usefulness. The official acronym for arc welding is SMAW, which stands for Shielded Metal Arc Welding. The basic components of the setup include the machine (the power source), a ground lead you clamp to the work anywhere except where the weld is to be made, an electrode lead which runs from the machine to an electrode holder, which is a handle with a clamp that holds consumable electrodes. The electrodes are metal rods covered with a coating.

In use, the weldor strikes an arc against the parent metal with the electrode, which completes the circuit between the two leads and causes a bright light and concentrated heat. Arc welding uses considerable amperage of electricity to generate the intense arc, which melts the parent metal. The central metal core of the electrode melts as the work progresses, becoming the filler metal, while the fluxed coating produces a shielding gas around the welding area that protects the parent and filler metal from impurities in the air. Arc-welding produces *slag* as you proceed, a thick coating of impurities and deposits left from the rod's coating. This slag must be chipped off with a chipping hammer, which is usually included with the machine.

There are a wide variety of welding rods (electrodes) available to suit almost any purpose. The 12-14-inch-long rods are also called "sticks", and you may often hear arc-welding referred to as *stick* welding. The rods vary in thickness, according to the thickness of the metal you are welding, and also in alloy and flux-coating content. There are many special-purpose rods, and, because of the variety, rods are usually marked with a number at the beginning of the flux coating, and different colors may also be added to the fluxes for quick identification.

Rods are usually sold in boxes or cans of fairly large quantity, which can be a problem for home/shop use where the welding is infrequent. The coatings on arc-welding rods are very susceptible to moisture in the air, and must be stored in very dry, secure containers to remain effective. You may have seen welding filler rods in gas-welding outfits stored in simple lengths of pipe welded to the welding cart, but this is not suitable for arc rods. If you do purchase an arc machine, invest in several airtight metal containers to store the rods, even using bags of desiccant (moisture-absorbing crystals usually found in small bags packed with cameras or sensitive electronic equipment) in the cans.

2.13 In farm and construction equipment repair, most work is done with oxy-acetylene cutting and arc, or stick, welding. Arc welding is not affected by wind outdoors, and is able to join or repair very thick materials.

2.14 Two endeavors you wouldn't think of together, art and welding, combine today as many sculptors and artists are now working in metals. Small works are usually torch or TIG welded, with larger works like this one utilizing arc or MIG welding equipment.

There are two basic types of arc-welders, relating to the polarity of the electricity they produce, AC or DC. The DC machines are generally larger, industrial units found in production shops, where they are hard-wired in, or mounted in conjunction with an engine for truck-mounted use in mobile field welding. Most shop-type DC machines require shop-type electrical input, such as 440V or *three-phase* 220V, which you will not find in any standard home. They are designed to operate day in and day out without overheating, and are considered the best choice for welding really thick materials, so that is why we see DC arc machines in use building bridges, buildings, ships, etc. There are a few small DC machines for home use, but they have limited amperage and should be used on lighter materials. There are even combination AC/DC machines, but these are usually expensive shop machines.

By far, the most basic and practical home/shop arc-welder is an AC machine often called a "buzz-box" because of the sound it makes when you are welding. This is the least expensive single welding system you can buy, with a good name-brand buzz-box costing about the same as a set of oxy-acetylene torches. However, the arc machine comes with rods and everything you need, while the gas setup also requires filled cylinders which make a ready-to-weld gas setup about twice as expensive as a basic arc box.

The wiring you have in your house or shop will be a factor in choosing the type of equipment best suited for your purposes. To use an arc machine, you'll need 220V availability. If you already have an electric stove in your house (or the house had at least been wired for this) or an electric clothes dryer, you're probably in good shape because many electric stoves and dryers use 220V current. However, unless your dryer outlet is already out in your garage, you may have to have a qualified electrician run this 220V power out to where you'll be doing your welding. If you don't already have a 220V outlet, the cost of running new service to your garage may double the total expense of setting up to do arc-welding at home.

Also, welders do not just plug into the same outlet as your appliances. The welder has a different arrangement of prongs on its plug, and an adapter is required to plug into a 220V appliance outlet. The outlet you use should also have a good 20-30-amp circuit breaker as well. Note that there are some small buzz-boxes that plug into ordinary household 110V power, but they aren't recommended for anything but light and occasional work.

A stick-welder is relatively easy to use. Unlike gas welding, where you have to operate the torch with one hand while feeding the filler rod with the other hand, there is only one piece to control with arc-welding, the rod-holder. However, the rod starts out 12 to 14 inches long but is used up continually (gets shorter) as you weld, making it tough to maintain an exact distance of rod to workpiece, which is critical to a good arc weld. With the rod too close, you burn holes in the metal, and too far away you can lose the arc entirely and have to restart. So the trick in arc welding is control of the tip of the rod, and, because it is always getting shorter, you have to "fine-tune" your wrist movement in the hand working the electrode-holder. For this reason, most arc-welding is done with two hands, especially when learning. Use your other hand to steady and help control your wrist action on the "working" hand. Professional weldors use arc-welding upside down, laying on their back, hanging from scaffolding, or even underwater with special equipment, but for the novice, a comfortable body and hand position is very important to making good welds.

An AC arc-welder is well-suited to working on heavier steel materials, from 1/8-inch to 1/2-inch thick, but is difficult to control on thinner materials. The machine will have an amperage knob, with settings from 30-230 amps (depends on make and model), which you suit to the rod and the work material and thickness. Some of the more expensive shop machines have settings that go as low as 4 amps for light materials, but gas, MIG or TIG welding is more popular today for thin metals such as most automotive work. For fabricating shop equipment, building a utility trailer, frame repairs or farm equipment maintenance, the buzz-box works fine.

To sum up the pros and cons of an AC arc-welder, the advantages include the low initial cost, easy operation (with practice), versatility (it can be used indoors or out) and it offers a high level of dependability (no moving parts) and quietness of operation. Disadvantages include: it's less practical for thinner metals, your shop may require rewiring to accommodate it, the home arc-welder usually can't be used for welding long seams all at one time, you are restricted to the limits of your power-cord length (as with any electric machine except the generator-driven type), the welds may have considerable spatter and not look as "clean" as other types if that is a consideration (such as in art projects, metal furniture design or street-rod fabricating), and there is the safety consideration of potential skin burns. Compared to gas welding, arc-welding poses more danger due to burns, not just from little spatters of hot metal, but from any skin that is exposed to the UV and infra-red rays. You can get a severe sunburn from exposure (pro weldors wear heavy leather protective clothing) and observing an arc-weld in progress without a helmet on, even for just a second or two, can cause headaches and eye irritation.

The buzz-box was once the most practical home/shop welder, but increasing availability and affordability of home MIG machines in the last ten years has put up a serious challenge to that title.

MIG (wire-feed) welders

This category of welding system has become one of the most popular for today's home/shop use. The initials stand for Metal Inert Gas, but is also listed in technical descriptions as GMAW, for Gas Metal Arc Welding. The basic elements of the setup include a power supply (machine), a torch with a large-diameter cable, a ground wire with clamp. and a bottle of compressed shielding gas. Inside the machine is a roll of relatively-thin wire and a motorized transport system for this wire.

In practice, you weld almost like arc-welding, but the electrode (wire) is constantly fed through the cable to the gun and consumed at the weld. When you pull the trigger of the MIG gun, you start the supply of amperage (when the arc starts on your work), the feeding of the wire electrode, and the flow of shielding gas, which is also routed inside the gun's cable and comes out of the tip all around the electrode, preserving the integrity of the weld like the flux coating does on arc rods.

The advantages of the MIG system includes a much cleaner weld than either gas or arc, good versatility in materials with the ability to do very well on thin metals, and there is no electrode or filler rod to keep replacing. Control is easy because you can set the amperage on the machine and also infinitely adjust the speed of the wire com-

2.15 Anyone who is a fan of auto racing is familiar with various types of welding. In the immaculate shop of Larry Smith Marketing, a crewman is putting a final MIG weld on a complete NASCAR chassis for a car like the Matco Tools entry at left. Race car shops use a variety of welding techniques, from gas to MIG and TIG.

2.16 Small, portable wire-feed, or MIG, welders have become one of the most popular welding machines for home/shop use. Easy to set up and simple to operate, they produce very clean welds, and models from 100-amp to 140-amp can be operated on household 110V current.

2.17 Most MIG machines operate with a bottle of shielding gas, but some are equipped to run with flux-cored wire which makes its own shielding gas as it arcs, making the process more suitable for outdoor and drafty situations. This home/shop-sized unit shown is a combination machine that can operate with gas shielding/solid wire, or the flux-core wire.

2.18 At the professional shop level, MIG welders are all 220V machines, and offer power up to 250 amps, which is enough to weld most anything. This Millermatic 250 is a popular machine in fabricating shops and automotive shops. There is even a model of this machine with a small computer in which you can store the welding parameters of up to nine different jobs, in five different languages.

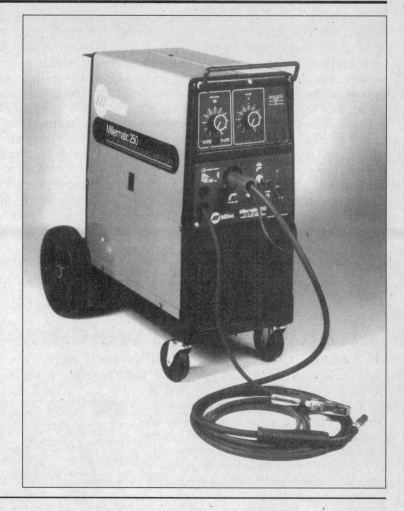

ing out of the gun. Various-diameter steel wires are available to weld material from the thinnest sheet metal to 1/4-inch and 3/8-inch, as well as stainless-steel and aluminum wires to weld those materials with. The weld from a MIG gun is much cleaner than arc welding in terms of spatter, and there is no slag coating to chip off.

Originally, wire-feed MIG machines were developed strictly for the professional shop doing long-duration production welding. A roll of wire in one of these machines can last for an entire eight-hour shift without the weldor ever stopping for a new electrode. Because the wire is machine fed into the weld puddle, the heat and wire-feed rate can be tuned so that production welds can be made much faster than with other systems. The MIG machine has been an expensive piece of equipment in the past (and heavy-duty, big-shop models are still fairly expensive), so it never used to be recommended to anyone for home/shop use. However, less-expensive MIG machines have become widely available in the past 5-10 years that have made these an excellent choice for the hobbyist, particularly the automotive hobbyist. These newer machines, mostly imported and built with a few less features and a lower duty-cycle than would be required in a production environment, have not only become very popular with the hobbyists but are also are finding their way into more small fabricating shops, muffler shops and race-car fabrication shops as a less expensive alternative to the big machines, yet with better speed and weld quality than arc or gas.

MIG machines range in size and features from "pocket" machines to large, full-featured machines for shop environments that require 100% duty-cycle. There are a number of smaller machines available today that operate on 110V household current, which makes them very portable, and no garage rewiring is

2.19 If you're lucky, the welding store near you will have a demonstration area, such as here at Altair Gasses & Equipment, Oxnard, California. Here a portable MIG unit is being tested where customers can watch through a large safety lens (behind operator, at right). You can get a feel for different equipment before you decide what machine best suits your needs.

2.20 If you are interested in cars as a hobby, whether it be kit cars, street rods, race cars, or antique restorations, you should become familiar with various welding techniques, and perhaps buy a system. When fabricating parts at home, it's a lot easier if you have your own welder, even if all you do is tack parts together and bring them to someone else for final welding.

necessary. These smaller wire-feed machines usually have 4-7 heat range settings from 30 to 110 or 140 amps, and can handle light sheet metal such as auto body material up to metals as thick as 1/4-inch or 3/8-inch (less maximum thickness is possible on aluminum). They either have wheels on the bottom or have optional, wheeled carts that make then very easy to move around your shop or garage. Many beginning weldors like to build their own welding cart as their first project with a new welding machine.

The shielding gas used with MIG machines can be CO_2, Argon, or a mixture of the two, depending on the materials you are welding. The basic gas used most often is straight CO_2, because it is the least expensive. Various sized gas bottles are available from small, very portable 20-cubic-foot bottles (about two feet high), to 120-cubic-foot bottles (four foot high, six-inches in diameter) that can supply enough gas for eight hours of continuous welding. The small bottles are fine for occasional home/shop use where long seams are not welded regularly.

One of the factors that has made MIG welders so popular with home/shop users is the relatively easy learning curve associated with using them. Given a little instruction and practice, most people can be up and welding a decent bead in an hour or two. We're not suggesting that that person would then be ready for a full-time job as a weldor, or that his/her first welds would pass rigid specifications for nuclear reactors, but the wire-feed machines are easier to learn than most other systems. One of the factors that makes it easier is of course not having to deal with feeding the filler rod in with your other hand. In automotive body work this can be particularly helpful when you have to hold something with your left hand, like the alignment of two pieces of sheet metal, while you tack them together with the one-hand MIG torch. Torch position is very important in all forms of welding, and the fact that the distance of the MIG tip from the work is constant (in many cases the nozzle is actually touching the work to steady it) makes controlling the weld much easier.

After selecting the proper heat setting based on the thickness of the material

2.21 Typical home/shop projects such as a utility trailer, race-car trailer, metals rack, shop cart, engine stand, hoist and much more can be built at home with either MIG (shown) or an AC arc welder.

2.22 Street rodding and antique car restoration frequently require welding on old, even rusty sheet metal body panels. Here the lower portion of a '32 Ford cowl has been patched with new steel to replace rust-out area. The panel was MIG-welded in with a 110V welder, ground down with a body-sander, is ready for finishing and another 60 years on the road.

you are welding, the only other variable to control is the speed the wire is fed into the weld puddle. If the speed is wrong, there will be a lot of sputtering and uneven welding and penetration. Most MIG weldors tune the wire-speed in by *sound*, They set up on a scrap piece of metal with a wire speed that may be too slow or too fast, then pull a bead while adjusting the speed. When the right speed is reached, the MIG welder gives a distinctive crackling sound to the procedure. The steady crackling sound means you have the right wire speed.

There are three basic types of small MIG machines. Those that use plain wire with a bottle of shielding gas, those that use flux-coated wire and no gas bottle, and combination machines that can run either fluxed or plain wire. The flux on the wire functions the same as the coatings on arc rods, creating a shielding gas as the wire is consumed. The bottled-gas-shielded MIG welding is the preferred method for indoor welding where clean-looking weld beads are desired. However, the shielding gas around the weld process is subject to being disturbed by air currents, so for outdoor welding (such as farm equipment repair, fence construction, etc.) the fluxed-wire machine is better. The weld isn't quite as clean as with the gas, and fluxed wire doesn't do as good a job on thin sheet metal (under 18-gauge) but these machines are more practical for the outdoor work, which is usually on heavier materials anyway. Also, the fluxed-wire machine never need to have a bottle refilled, so as long as you have plenty of wire inside the machine, you can't have your work delayed by running out of shielding gas.

Considering all of these factors, the modern MIG machine may be the most practical type of machine for many do-it-yourselfers, particularly the automotive hobbyist, who has to make very clean welds, both with thin sheet metal as well as heavier chassis work. The ease of operation, maneuverability around the shop (with the 110V machines), one-hand torch operation and the gentle learning curve have combined to make many first-time MIG weldors tackle their projects with confidence.

TIG (heli-arc) welding

This is unquestionably the "Rolls-Royce" of the welding processes in many ways. The lettering stands for Tungsten Inert Gas, but many weldors refer to it as

2.23 Basic components of a TIG-welding system. Very similar to operating a gas torch and using your other hand to feed filler rod, TIG produces the cleanest welds with the least amount of material warpage, and is the best system for thin, high-strength material like chrome-moly as well as aluminum.

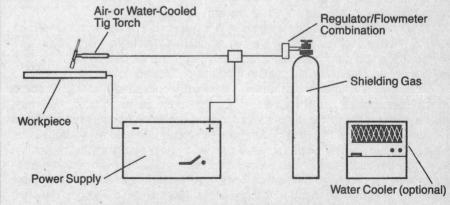

COMPONENTS OF A TIG WELDING SYSTEM

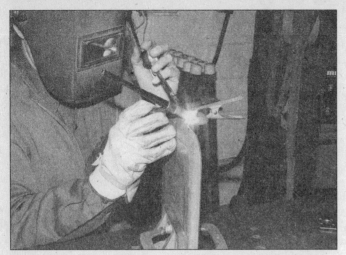

2.24 While TIG or heli-arc welding is considered by many to be the most *controllable* welding technique, it takes more practice than any other. You have to learn to manipulate the torch with one hand, the rod with the other, and the amperage control with your foot on a pedal. There are no sparks, spatter or slag. Here an aluminum frypan's handle mount is being repaired. The heli-arc welding didn't even bother the non-stick coating on the other side!

2.25 Where TIG welding really shines is in two tough situations in one job, like thin materials *and* aluminum, such as this part that looks like something from a space ship. This wound up being a belt-pack of controls for a big piece of machinery - the operator strapped this to his waist. Aluminum is tougher to weld than steel because it doesn't change color as you heat it. When it melts it turns shiny, but tarry a little longer with the torch and the material has holes in it. Don't tackle a project like this until you have mastered the process.

heli-arc welding, though this is a trade name established by the Linde Corporation many years ago. The name refers to the fact that back then, helium was used as the shielding gas for the process, though today argon is the most commonly used gas for TIG welding. Either shielding gas has the capacity to exclude foreign materials during the welding process, as well as being unable to combine with other elements to form chemical compounds detrimental to the weld integrity. The process can also been seen abbreviated as GTAW, for Gas Tungsten Arc Welding.

The basic components of the TIG process include a welding machine, a torch with a tungsten electrode, a ground cable, a foot-operated amperage control pedal and a bottle of compressed shielding gas such as argon. It differs basically from stick welding and MIG welding in that the electrode is not consumed, and filler rod is separately hand-fed into the weld puddle when needed. In operation, the machine is turned on, the weldor brings the torch close to the work and depresses the foot pedal to start the arc. Current flows through the tungsten to the workpiece, creating an intense but concentrated heat that melts the parent metal, with the operator controlling the amperage with the foot-pedal while welding, and feeding the appropriate filler rod to the puddle as needed. The tungsten electrode has a very high melting point and is not consumed.

What makes the heli-arc different in practice from other systems is the higher operator skill required, since the weldor has to coordinate with both hands and the foot pedal, all of which affects the quality of the finished weld. Unless you are already an accomplished weldor with an oxy-acetylene gas-welding torch, you'll find the TIG process takes a *lot* of practice.

TIG welding produces the cleanest, flux-free and spatter-free beads with virtually no contamination. For this reason, it is the method of choice for such critical applications as race cars, aircraft, missile construction and nuclear reactor welding. The TIG welds are strong, ductile and corrosion-resistant with virtually no cleanup required, making it popular for welding of surgical, medical and food-service equipment, especially on stainless-steel. There is little smoke produced during TIG welding and no flying sparks, and without the smoke and sparks the weldor can more critically observe the welding action as he goes.

While there is a lot of skill required in TIG welding, its ability to handle all kinds of metals of varying thicknesses, the ability to reach into corners and hard-to-access areas to weld and its outstanding ability to mate thin metals without putting excessive heat and distortion into a wide area on either side of the weld has made the heli-arc method particularly useful in race-car and other critical construction applications. The types of metals that can be welded with TIG machines include: all steel alloys, aluminum alloys, aluminum castings, stainless-steel, copper and nickel alloys, magnesium and exotic metals such as titanium and zirconium. It is one of the few systems that can tackle welding dissimilar metals and joining metals of different thicknesses. It's been said that a skilled TIG weldor could join a razor blade to a railroad track, though there isn't much call for that.

The torch for TIG welding is smaller and lighter than most other welding torches, allowing for greater weldor comfort when welding for long periods. For production welding, most TIG machines are equipped with a water-circulating system to keep the torch cool. In use, a water pump circulates filtered water from a storage tank out through the main cable to the torch head and then returns the heated water back to the tank. Many cooling units employ a small radiator and electric fan to cool the water. Where lots of production welding is done, a large water storage tank is used, or the water is fed in cold from the shop's plumbing and the heated water is plumbed back into the drain system, so heated water is never circulated back through the torch. The TIG machine requires shop-type current input (230V/460V/575V single-phase or 230V/460V three-phase) and connections to and from the water-cooling equipment, making it one of the least portable of welding systems.

Because of the electrical requirements and other hookups, the steep operator learning curve, and the considerable expense of the most shop-type TIG machines, this has never been a system that has penetrated much into the home/shop and hobbyist market. Rare and proud is the automotive hobbyist or racer who has a heli-arc machine at home, and who knows how to use it to its capacity. The process has assumed an almost "mystical" aura to automotive fans because of its use in race-car construction, and even otherwise skilled home weldors will bring certain components like critical steering gear to a professional to have the parts TIG-welded. Street rod builders love it for the quality of weld, which is often cosmetically appealing enough to require no grinding or filling to make the welded part ready for painting or even chrome-plating.

Shops with TIG machines rarely take advantage of this, but most TIG welding machines are capable of also performing stick welding if the job should require it. TIG welding is ideal for thinner materials, but if a job required joining some one-inch-thick plates, the stick-welding mode would be much faster. The arc capability would also come in handy if the job required some welding outdoors or near a drafty doorway, where the draft could blow the argon shielding gas away and cause an erratic weld. Switching to the arc mode simply requires a switch on the machine be thrown to the correct current position for arc, and the arc "torch" electrode cable plugged in. When in the arc mode, the foot control is deactivated and the weldor sets the amperage on the machine with a knob, like a straight arc machine.

While most production shop TIG machines are large, expensive, heavy-duty machines with water-cooling systems for the torch, there have been strides in the past ten years at making a more affordable TIG machine. Today there are several to choose from which are air-cooled instead of water-cooled, reducing cost and complexity, that feature straight 220V, single-phase input connections for simplified electrical hookup, and have lighter-duty, less-expensive internal electrical components. These new machine are one-half to one-third the cost of their bigger conventional TIG brothers.

Because of these factors, there are more small shops that today can afford the benefits of TIG welding, such as high-quality welds on thin materials, and the ability to weld beautifully on non-ferrous materials like aluminum, even cast aluminum. The are often seen in large engine rebuilding facilities and automotive machine shops, where they serve their time repairing cracks in aluminum blocks and heads, expensive parts that would otherwise have to be replaced if such repairs could not be made. However, these "economy" TIG machines can't do everything the big ones can, particularly when it comes to torch cooling. If long welds are to be made, the air-cooled torch will get too uncomfortable to hold. Also, the smaller, less-expensive electrical components inside will not have as long a duty-cycle as the big machines (more on duty-cycles later), but in a small shop fabricating race-car or street rod parts and doing precision chassis work, long, continuous welds are not often encountered.

Some welding machines today offer "convertible" adaptability. Kits can be added to some MIG machines to add heli-arc capability, and there are kits with a different torch and a separate wire-feeder to use the output of the bigger TIG machines as a MIG machine, but this convertibility usually puts the machine out of the home/shop price range.

Even with the introduction of this new generation of more-affordable TIG machines, this is still a system that isn't practical for the average home/shop weldor to get into. As with oxy-acetylene gas welding, the practice time it takes to be good with a heli-arc torch requires consistent, daily operation, and most occasional weldors just can't get enough time on the machine to really do well. Most basic home/shop fabrication and repair projects do not require the "reactor-quality" welds and superior cosmetic appearance of TIG welding, and even the economy TIG machines cost more than twice what other starting welder setups cost, making the gas welder and small MIG machines still the most versatile equipment for home use. A drawback of TIG welding is that it is a *slow* process, so for a project like building a utility trailer, a typical home MIG machine would be much faster.

Duty-cycles

In any discussion of electric welding processes, the term duty-cycle comes up and is a source of some confusion to the beginning weldor. Basically, the bigger, heavier and more expensive pro-shop type welding machines have transformers and other internal electrical components designed to operate for long periods of time without overheating. Smaller, home-type machines can't operate as long, because the internal components had to be made less expensive in order to reduce the overall costs to a "consumer" level.

The official quantifier of such work capability is called the duty-cycle. It is expressed as a percentage, such as a "40% duty-cycle." What this refers to is a ten-minute period in a laboratory welding test. At a 40% duty-cycle, a particular welding machine is capable of welding for *four minutes out of ten*. In other words, if you welded non-stop for four minutes straight, you would have to let the machine "idle" for six minutes before resuming welding, allowing the internal components to cool off. The maximum current that a welding machine can draw from its components is limited by the temperature rise of those parts, and the temperature goes up with the square of the current draw.

Bigger, more professional and more expensive welding machines will have higher duty-cycles because of the nature of the work they have to do. There are some cases where a robotic or machine-driven automatic welder must be capable of 100% duty-cycle because it is operated continuously, but this is unusual.

The advertised duty-cycle of a welding machine is *usually* given at the maximum current draw of the machine, the highest amp setting. This setting of course is required only when welding the thickest material the machine is capable of. As the amperage setting of a welding machine is reduced, the effective duty-cycle is *increased*, so that there is somewhere on the welding machine's "curve" a point where the duty-cycle is close to 100% at some amperage setting.

For the home/shop user who is rarely welding anything thicker than 1/4-inch or 3/8-inch mild steel, the duty-cycle is not a problem. However, it's important to know what the duty-cycle for your machine is at various amperages, and especially to understand the term when shopping for a machine. For instance, one popular introductory-level 110V MIG machine has an amperage range of 30-110 amps. Right away, you know that such a machine is not really designed for long welds on heavy materials, because the maximum amperage is only 110. Further, the advertised duty-cycle for this machine is 95% at the 30-amp setting, but 25% at the highest amp setting, showing the difference in how the current-draw heats up the components. Depending on your average welding needs, such a machine may be just fine, handling short welds occasionally on 1/4-inch steel, and longer periods on thinner material. Most automotive sheet metal, for instance, seldom requires an amperage setting above 30, and even the small MIG machines have a long duty-cycle at this setting.

Generally, welding machine price goes up with maximum amperage and duty-cycle. You can roughly compare the performance of the machines being considered by comparing their duty-cycle at the amperages you will most often be using. A feature to look for on some of the better machines is an "overheat" protection circuit and warning light, which may save you the cost of a burned-out component. Some machines automatically shut down when the overheat circuit kicks, and in others an internal electric fan comes on to speed the cooling process, but like most "bells and whistles" these features usually cost a little more.

Plasma arc welding and cutting

This is another welding/cutting process that has developed in the recent past that was once considered exotic, yet is now filtering down to lower price levels in the welding marketplace. The nomenclature refers to the plasma state of a gaseous material, in which the material is heated so much that the gas conducts electricity. What makes PAW (Plasma Arc Welding) so different is that the flow of superheated *gas* actually makes the welding arc, with the metal electrode

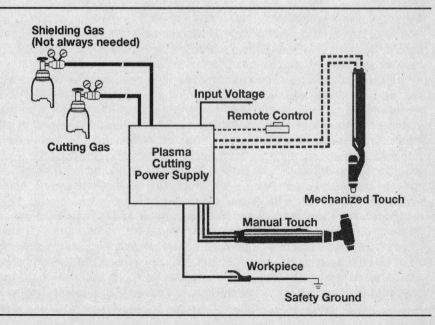

2.26 Plasma cutting is rapidly replacing oxy-acetylene cutting in many home and shop applications. Used either as a mechanized cutter or by hand, the system is simple to operate, and makes a faster, cleaner cut with much less sparking and less heat induced into the parent metal.

safely hidden way up inside the torch body away from the welding action.

The plasma welder makes a hotter and easier-to-control arc than even the much-touted TIG welder. The arc becomes a narrow column of heated gas (usually argon or nitrogen) that can be directed as precisely as a surgical laser. A second gas is plumbed through the torch to maintain a gas shield over the weld area, as is done in most electric welding. The extremely-high temperature of the plasma arc means that higher welding speeds can be used in production applications, and where there is a close fit of the two edges being welded, as is usually the case in a production situation with newly cut materials, often the plasma weld is accomplished with no addition of filler material when welding thinner stocks. This has made it a preferred system for some industrial applications.

In operation, the plasma equipment looks much like TIG equipment, except that there are two bottles of gas, and the torch is designed differently inside. The very dense, very hot "flame" does not require as precise an arc-starting-distance of the torch to the material, making plasma equipment somewhat easier to operate than TIG, especially on projects where no filler metal is needed. In TIG-welding, the weldor must strike an arc with his tungsten electrode With the plasma method, however, the electrode is too far up inside the torch head to get near the parent metal, so most of the plasma machines have high-frequency arc-starting circuitry that makes them easy to get up and running, using the hot gas column to start the arc, after which the proper torch-to-work distance is easily established by the weldor.

While there are specialized applications where plasma-arc welding is the preferred method, its widest area of usage today is in *cutting*. The column of plasma-stage-heated gas is hot enough to cut through virtually any material at almost any thickness. On thin materials, the plasma cutter goes through as fast as the operator can move the torch (speeds up to 100 inches per minute), and even on 1/2-inch-thick steel the moderate-size cutters can cut at 15 inches per minute, which is about one inch every four seconds!

While the speed of the plasma cutter is exceptional, it is the quality of the cut that has made it so popular today in many applications like automotive, duct repair and fabrication, and medical or food-service equipment work. The plasma cutter will cut virtually any ferrous or non-ferrous material with equal ease, even on aluminum and stainless where ordinary torch cutting is difficult without considerable pre-cut and post-cut cleaning.

Since there need be no direct contact between the torch and the work material, plasma cutting doesn't involve a lot of spatter getting into the torch head, and most materials can be cut with no pre-cut cleaning. This is especially important to automotive users, who can make clean, fast cuts in sheet metal, whether it's painted, rusty or dirty. The concentration of the narrow cut and the speed the plasma torch can travel means that the cut edges are many times cleaner than even a machine-cut edge from an oxy-acetylene torch. There may be little or no cleanup of the cut edges required, depending on the job requirements, and the cut edges are not only smooth but uncontaminated, so that plasma-cut edges can generally be welded together much easier that edges cut with a gas torch where oxidation must be ground off before welding.

Plasma cutters have become particularly popular in machine-cutting operations where the torch head is mounted on a machine that has a pantograph arrangement. The weldor moves an arm around a wood, paper or metal template and the cutting torch cuts that exact shape out of metal. Sometimes, several cut-

2.27 In fabricating shops, a large 220V (or higher current, three-phase) plasma cutter is used, capable of cutting thick materials and traveling at fast cutting speeds. Most plasma cutters are used without shielding gas, using air from the shop air compressor to cool the torch and form the ionized gas column under the tip that creates the arc.

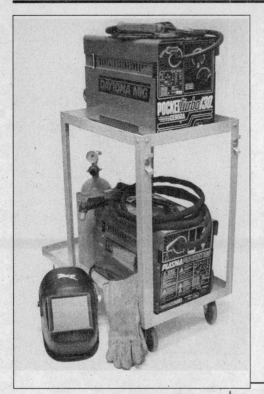

2.29 Eventually, you will find yourself at a steel supply store, shopping for plate, angle-iron or tubing for a project. Steel is usually sold in 20-foot lengths, but it's often cheaper to buy steel here than at a home/lumber type store.

2.28 Where the really complete home/shop setup was once an AC arc welder and a set of gas torches, today more shops utilize a MIG welder and plasma cutter. This welding cart features a gas-shielded 130-amp MIG and a plasma cutter capable of cutting up to 3/16-inch material, and both machines operate on household 110V current.

ting heads are operating on a large sheet of metal plate, cutting three or four copies of the template out at the same time. The clean plasma cuts mean less labor is required to make a finished part.

Metal cutting has been done for decades with oxy-acetylene equipment, but, besides the clean-cut edges, a plasma cutter has one other major advantage over the oxy-acetylene torch. Since the main component of the air around us is nitrogen, which make a good inert gas to superheat into a plasma flame, common air can be used as the cutting gas. This is usually supplied simply by hooking the welding machine up to a standard shop air compressor making 75 psi. Not only is the compressed air virtually free, with no bottles to fill, but plasma cutting involves no flammable gasses in dangerous high-pressure cylinders. There is a major savings in bottled-gas costs, convenience, and shop safety.

The nature of the plasma-cutting process is such that very little spark spray comes from the cutting action, and there is virtually no discoloration or distortion of the cut edges. It is almost like "cold" cutting. These attributes make the plasma system the method of choice now in automobile wrecking yards for cutting up cars for dismantling. It's much faster than a gas torch, and the chance of fires starting from flying sparks and droplets of molten metal is greatly reduced. Plasma cutters have been operated in such situations with torch hoses as long as 234 feet, with the welding machine kept indoors in a shed and the operator wandering around the yard with the torch, not having to transport a heavy cart with bottles of compressed gasses. Body shops love it for its clean edges and the ability to cut an exterior body panel with less chance of igniting undercoating, paint or burning a hole in an interior panel with a stray blob of molten metal.

Although the technology sounds complicated, plasma equipment is perhaps easier to maintain than gas, MIG or TIG equipment, and the learning curve is not as steep. As with the modern MIG and TIG machines, recent years have seen the price of plasma-cutting equipment come down considerably, and this has put the technology in the hands of many automotive shops. Most home/shop users will not have enough cutting work to do to justify owning a plasma cutter, but when a lot of cutting needs to be done, and done more safely than with traditional gas, this is definitely the way to go. If you are around a body shop or fabri-

2.30 If you can't carry a 20-foot length of steel home with you, steel houses will generally make one "courtesy" cut for a small fee. Any cuts after that are expensive, so it's best if you have some method at home for cutting the metal for your projects.

2.31 This steel supply store has a neatly-organized rack for materials, in which each different thickness of material is identified by a different color of paint on the ends, which makes shopping a lot easier for hobbyists without a micrometer.

cation shop that has a plasma cutter, see if they will demonstrate it to you. You'll find it amazing when you see how fast it cuts, how little spark spray there is, and how clean and relatively *cool* the cut edges are.

Practice and training

When it comes to hand-eye coordination, everyone has a little different skill level to start with. How easily each person can pick-up a welding machine, read the instructions and begin joining metals together will differ with that person's mechanical background. Some people seem to flow into the work intuitively; others require considerable practice and often a little coaching from someone who can weld already.

Each of the welding systems we have discussed in this chapter requires a different amount of practice and skill to master, but rest assured that even if you have never done anything like this before *you can learn to weld*. Millions of men and women have learned to do this in the past. During the domestic manpower shortages of W.W.II, there were many housewives who went to work in the defense plants, and even though they had never done anything mechanical they were there riveting, metal-shaping and welding on aircraft, tanks, ships and many other critical projects.

The first step in deciding what kind of equipment you need is to accurately assess the kinds of projects you would do most often if you had welding equipment in your home/shop. The thicknesses of metals you want to work with, the types and alloys of metals, the kind of electrical power you have available and the length of the welds you may need to perform are all factors in choosing the right machine. We've given you enough of a brief outline of the advantages and disadvantages of each type of equipment to aim you in the right direction. You may also want to consult with your local welding shop and local welding supply store before making your decision. If you know someone who already has a welder at home, ask his advice and even see if he will let you try out his equipment on some scrap pieces.

Most people who are serious about picking up welding skills and doing it right can benefit from actual training. Your local community college may have adult evening courses in basic welding, or there may be a trade/technical school nearby. Courses offered at publicly-funded community colleges and trade schools are usually inexpensive, and the hours are often built around a working person's schedule. There is a real difference between a weld that *looks* good, and a weld that *performs* well. If you practice welding on your own, you may achieve welds that look OK to you, but which may fail in actual use. One of the valuable parts of the training you will receive in a legitimate course is the critique from the instructor. He can show you how to test various trial welds for strength and let you know when you're getting it right. We think such training is invaluable if you plan to do anything more involved than repairing a bicycle or garden tool. Good training shortens the learning curve dramatically, and we recommend it to any readers who have it available in their area.

3 Oxy-acetylene gas welding/cutting

Perhaps because of its history going back to the turn of the century, or perhaps due to its appearances in films and other popular imagery, gas welding/cutting has the most "romantic" image of the various welding systems we'll deal with in this book. When most people conjure up a vision of a weldor, it is of a perspiring, leather-clad man wearing dark goggles and wielding a flaming torch with sparks flying everywhere. In truth, this is more likely a picture of someone *cutting* with a torch rather than welding, but it points out the ubiquitous nature of the gas equipment in the overall welding picture.

Although losing some ground to modern electric welders in the most recent decade as the welding system of choice for the average home/shop user, oxy-acetylene equipment is still unarguably the most versatile setup for home, farm or shop. Besides its function as a fusion-joiner of metals, gas equipment also of course is extremely valuable as metal *cutting* equipment, and can also be used for non-fusion metalwork such as brazing, soldering, and the dying art of automotive body lead work. It is also useful equipment in any automotive shop for freeing rusted fasteners, heating machined parts that require a hot shrink-to-fit connection (like a gear on a shaft) and heating metal parts prior to bending them. It requires no water or electrical connections, making it one of the most portable of systems, you can load it into a pick-up truck and take it to any remote location. If the gas hoses are long enough, the weldor can climb up a pole or down a shaft to perform welding or cutting, a flexibility few other welding systems can match.

The basic gas process

When gasses are used in other types of welding, they are usually of the inert kind, like argon, CO_2 or helium, which are involved in the welding process only to keep the molten weld puddle clear of impurities from the air during formation. In oxy-acetylene welding/cutting, however, the

3.1 Versatile gas-welding equipment has been a mainstay of metal fabricating for most of the 20th century, and little has changed with procedures or equipment. The basics, fusing metals at their melting point, are still valid for many uses in farm, industry and home/shop hobby applications.

3.2 You'll find helpful people at your local welding supply store that can set you up with torch equipment, oxygen and acetylene bottles, and other supplies you'll need.

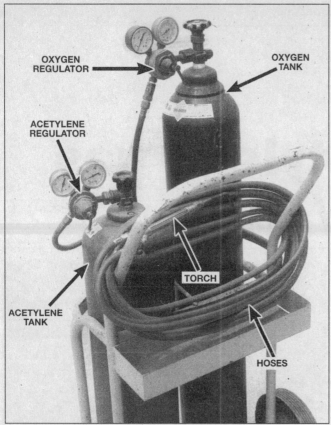

3.3 Look in the corner of almost any automotive or fabricating shop and you'll a setup just like this, with bottles, regulators, hoses and torch neatly corralled in a portable welding cart. Carts can be readily purchased, but most beginners like to make their own cart as their first project.

3.4 This is typical of a good, general-purpose welding, cutting and heating set, ideal for automotive, muffler shops, farm and trade schools. Starter sets have smaller torches and 10-12 foot of hose, bigger sets have larger torches and 25-foot hoses.

gases are what make the flame itself. Acetylene gas is quite flammable, and combined with oxygen, which by itself does not burn but speeds up the oxidation or burning of any other fuel, makes one of the hottest possible gas flames (5600-6300° F),suitable for the rapid welding, cutting or heating of most ferrous and non-ferrous materials. Although all compressed gasses pose some shop hazards because of the pressure inside the bottles, oxygen and acetylene are considerably more dangerous to work around, and require much more caution and close attention to safety rules.

Oxygen, while not exactly flammable by itself, is the gas necessary both for us to breathe and for any type of combustion to take place. Combustion is really nothing more than very rapid oxidation, and if pure oxygen is directed at something flammable, a fire can start very easily. Some inexperienced weldors have been know to dust off their work clothes with their unlit gas torch, but the extra oxygen that gets into their clothes can make it so flammable that any tiny spark could start the clothes on fire. Likewise, oxygen gas must be kept away from things like oily rags or any petroleum products. Oxygen as used in welding equipment is generally stored in high-pressure, 1/4-inch-thick-walled steel cylinders at 2200 psi. While oxygen may be important for our lungs to work, it can still be dangerous if too much is introduced to the bloodstream. For this reason, oxygen gas should be kept away from open cuts such as you might have on your hands.

Acetylene gas, on the other hand is flammable to the point of being explosive, and is also mildly poisonous, causing nausea and headaches if you breathe much of it. Older readers may remember using a "carbide cannon" on the 4th of July when they were kids. A small quantity of pellets were put into a small metal cannon which held some water. A gas was produced inside that was lit by a flint-sparker mechanism on top, and the result was a tremendous bang. The pellets were calcium-carbide, and the gas produced was acetylene.

Pressure in the acetylene gas cylinder is much less than with oxygen, at 250-325 psi, but the construction of the cylinder is different. Acetylene cylinders are shorter and fatter than oxygen bottles, and are constructed in two halves. Because acetylene is unstable at high pressures, the only way to get sufficient quantities into the standard bottle is to dissolve the acetylene in another medium. In welding tanks, the two halves are filled with an asbestos/cement mixture and then welded together. After baking, the material forms a honeycomb inside the tank. Liquid acetone is put into the tank because it will absorb 25 times its own volume in acetylene gas, thus stabilizing the acetylene.

Because of the differences in chemical action and storage of oxygen and acetylene, there must be no mix-ups between the two. For this reason, the tanks are made in different proportions and different colors; the acetylene bottle has only left-hand threads, and the hoses for each bottle are different, i.e. red hose for acetylene, green hose for oxygen **(see illustration)**. Both bottles have a threaded top for filling and connection of the regulators, and due to their high internal pressure, especially the oxygen cylinder, gas bottles should always be stored securely. If a bottle were to fall from a truck onto concrete, for instance, the regulator could be knocked off, suddenly releasing enough gas to propel the heavy bottle around like a kid's balloon, except with potentially deadly force. In addition, the acetylene bottle should always be stored in an upright position. If stored laying down, some of the liquid acetone inside could be drawn out of the bottle into the welding supply, ruining the weld.

The equipment

Besides the two gas bottles, there are gauges/regulators, hoses and the torch itself **(see illustration)**. Each gas tank has it's own set of two gauges mounted on a regulator body designed to reduce the high cylinder pressure down to a useable pressure for the torch. On each tank, there is

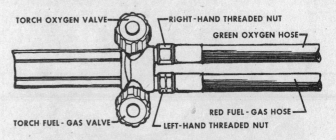

3.5 There must be no mix-up of gasses, so oxygen hoses are colored green, acetylene hoses red, and the acetylene hoses have left-hand threads, identified by a groove cut around the fittings.

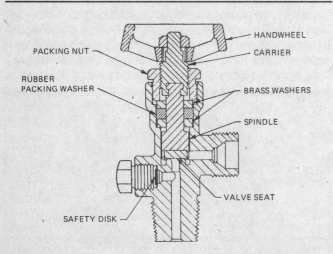

3.6 The gas bottles are fitted with valves, to which regulators are attached. This is a cutaway of an oxygen cylinder valve, showing the way the valve seals internally. Oxygen cylinder valves seal best when either closed or fully open.

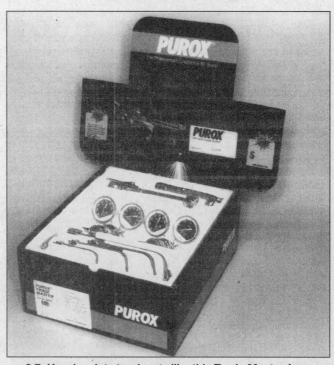

3.7 Heavier-duty torch sets like this Trade Master from L-TEC have torches capable of welding up to 3/8 steel, cutting up to 1 1/2-inch steel, and heating capability of 103,000 BTUs per hour.

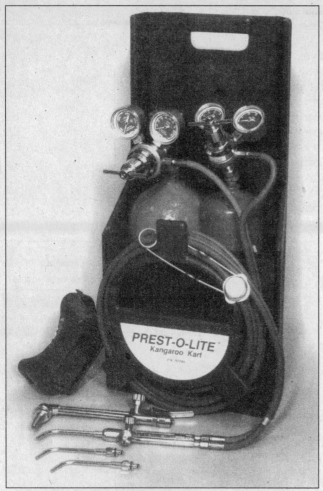

3.8 Highly portable "Kangaroo" outfit has everything you need in a small package, including a polypropylene carry cart. This doesn't have a lot of welding-time capacity, but is popular for maintenance work, metal sculptors, and automotive shops that don't use a torch too often.

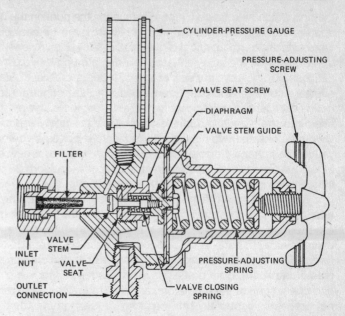

3.9 Cutaway of a single-stage regulator shows how the cylinder pressure is adjusted down to a usable range for welding. There are two gauges attached, one shows the total pressure left in the cylinder, and one shows the adjusted pressure supplying the torch.

one gauge to indicate the pressure in the tank, while the other gauge reads the pressure *after the regulator*, which is the pressure delivered to the torch and a very important adjustment in oxy-acetylene welding.

There are two basic types of regulators found on gas welding setups, single-stage and two-stage. The former type reduces the cylinder pressure to a working pressure in just one step, say from oxygen's 2200 psi to 3 psi for the torch **(see illustration)**. In the two-stage regulator, the first stage reduces pressure to about 30 psi; the second stage adjusts pressure from there down.

A great portion of the expense in a gas-welding setup comes from the gauges/regulators, and better ones simply cost more. The simpler-to-manufacture single-stage regulators cost less and are therefore commonly found on the less-expensive kits for oxy-acetylene welding **(see illustration)**. They work fine for most purposes, and their only drawback is

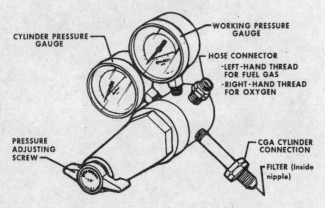

3.10 The gauge/regulator setup screws onto the tank's cylinder valve, and has a fitting for attaching the hose leading to the torch.

3.11 Connectors are available to add more hose onto a starter set for a longer working distance if you need it. These screw into your hoses and the extra new hoses screw on the other side.

that the regulation depends heavily (excuse the pun) on the pressure inside the tank. As the tank pressure goes down as the gas is used up, the regulation changes and must be adjusted again. Also, when doing a job that requires a lot of gas flow, such as large welds or cutting/heating thick plates, the single-stage regulator may not be able to keep up. The more expensive two-stage regulators maintain gas flow to the torch with less fluctuation, which is important in a professional welding operation but may not be a big factor in home/shop welding if you don't work on heavier materials. Obviously, gas-welding sets with two-stage regulators will cost more initially than the single-stage kits.

The hoses for a gas-welding setup are specially-designed to carry the oxygen and acetylene gasses. While they do not handle the very high tank pressures, they are built in three layers to withstand the *regulated* pressures for many years with proper care and maintenance. As mentioned above, the hose for carrying acetylene is red, while the oxygen hose is green, and the acetylene hose has left-hand threads on its fitting, so there is no chance of mixing them up when making connections (**Note:** *Left-handed fittings generally have a groove cut in around the fitting, to differentiate them from normal, right-hand fittings*). Doing so could be disastrous, since any residual flammable gas or other material in a hose connected to pure oxygen could cause the hose to ignite or explode. For this same reason, it is important that no lubricants or chemical compounds of any kind be used on the hoses or fittings. Gas-welding packages may contain hoses around 10-12 feet long in the economy or light-duty kits, and 20-25 feet long in the heavier, more professional sets. Extension hoses can be added to your starter set if you need to reach areas further from your tanks (**see illustration**).

3.12 In industrial situations, like this oilfield service truck, gas welding setups may be equipped with large cylinders and 100 feet of hose, to handle any situation.

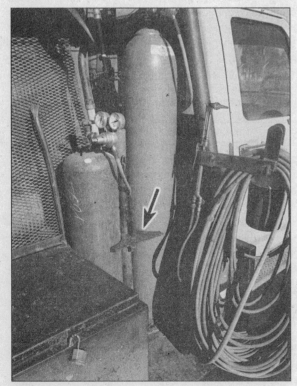

3.13 In this clever setup, the hoses and torch are attached to a swingaway arm for access to the tanks for servicing. Arrow indicates retaining plate with a simple steel wedge rod. Tanks are held securely but can be changed quickly without wrenches.

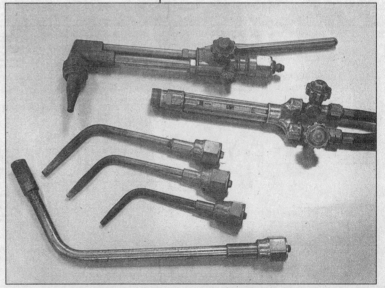

3.14 Basic torch sets include, from top: cutting torch attachment, basic torch head, a variety of welding tips sized for different thicknesses of material, and at bottom a rosebud tip for heating large areas.

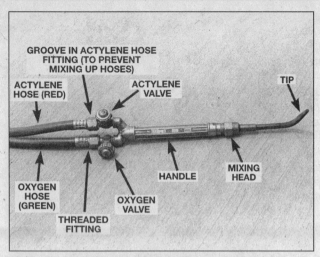

GROOVE IN ACTYLENE HOSE FITTING (TO PREVENT MIXING UP HOSES)

ACTYLENE HOSE (RED)

ACTYLENE VALVE

TIP

OXYGEN HOSE (GREEN)

THREADED FITTING

OXYGEN VALVE

HANDLE

MIXING HEAD

3.15 When assembled with welding tip and hoses, this is what an oxy-acetylene welding torch looks like. The two gasses are controlled by separate knobs, and are mixed inside the torch body.

The torch for oxy-acetylene welding is a precision-made tool, usually constructed with a forged brass body, two knobs controlling the gas flow, and copper tips of varying size **(see illustration)**. In use, the two gasses flow through valves controlled by the knobs, and mix inside the torch with the combined gasses coming out of the tip in an oxygen-to-acetylene ratio controlled by the weldor. The weldor changes tips, each of which has a carefully sized opening, to suit the gas-flow and flame shape required for a particular job. The makeup of the cutting torch is different from the welding torch and will be discussed later on.

Gas welding sets can be purchased three ways: as a welding-only setup, a cutting-only setup or a combination set with two torches. The type you choose will depend on your needs. If all you need to do is weld up animal corral fencing made from steel pipes, you may use a cutting-only gas set for cutting pipe to length and shaping the cut ends to fit against the next pipe, and use a generator-driven arc welder on your truck for joining the pipes. However, if you are doing automotive sheet metal work or metal sculptures with relatively-thin materials, you will probably do most of your cutting with an electric shear, hand tin snips, hacksaw, etc., and only require a torch for welding, brazing and occasional heating. A combination set is of course the most versatile. Most sets that you buy can be fitted with a different torch at any time, so if you decide to buy a welding-only setup, you can purchase a cutting torch later on if your need to.

After you purchase your welding package, you will have to buy or rent tanks. The standard-size oxygen and acetylene tanks will hold enough gas to last the home/shop user for a long, long time. The tanks must be *hydrostatically-tested* periodically, which involves filling them with water to a certain pressure to test for safety. When the test is due, your local gas supply cannot refill your tank until it is tested. When you buy new tanks outright, you then become responsible for the testing costs and any cylinder-valve repairs, while if you lease the cylinders, the gas company takes care of that as part of the lease agreement. Leasing the cylinders allows you to get started welding with the minimum investment, because outright purchase may be expensive. However, if you add up the monthly rent

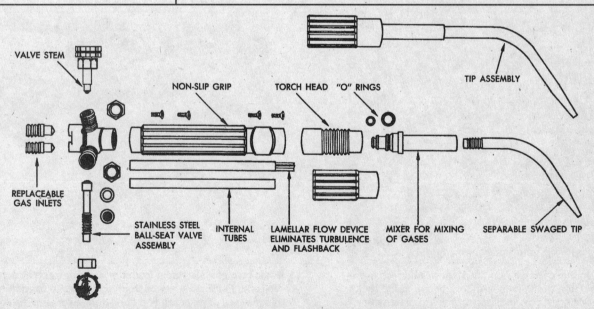

VALVE STEM

NON-SLIP GRIP

TORCH HEAD

"O" RINGS

TIP ASSEMBLY

REPLACEABLE GAS INLETS

STAINLESS STEEL BALL-SEAT VALVE ASSEMBLY

INTERNAL TUBES

LAMELLAR FLOW DEVICE ELIMINATES TURBULENCE AND FLASHBACK

MIXER FOR MIXING OF GASES

SEPARABLE SWAGED TIP

3.16 You'll never have cause to disassemble your torch this far, but these are the internal components. Some torches require wrenches to change tips and heads, while others have knurled, hand-tightened connectors.

3.17 Each of these little "flea circus" figures are welded up completely of thin welding rod and tiny blobs of molten metal. The artist works with a very small welding tip and tremendous patience, showing what can be done with skill and imagination.

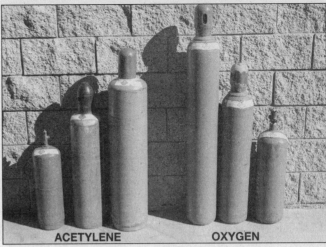

ACETYLENE   OXYGEN

3.18 The small, medium and large welding cylinders contain 80, 150 and 275 cubic feet of gas, but some manufacturers label theirs by a letter designation. Ask your welding supply shop approximately how long each size would last in terms of welding, and choose according to your needs.

charges, you'll find that after two years of leasing you could have purchased the tanks outright for the same money. Most leases run from 5-99 years, but if you move to another area where a different gas company is located, you may be able to return your tanks to the original location where you leased them and get back a pro-rated portion, then begin a new lease account in the area you move to. Look in your local telephone Yellow Pages under "Gasses, Industrial" or "Welding Supplies."

There are usually three sizes of tanks, small (80 cu. ft.), medium (150 cu. ft.) and large (275 cu. ft.). The small tanks are the easiest to store and maneuver around the shop and are fine for most occasional users. The medium tanks will be more than enough for most any home/shop use, lasting more than a year under normal use. The largest tanks are heavy, and more difficult to move around the shop.

Getting started with oxy-acetylene

Thoroughly read all the directions that come with your gas-welding setup before you do anything. If you have purchased a used welding set from someone, make sure the instructions are included, or have an experienced person help you get set up. Compressed gasses are dangerous; so is the welding process, and there are many more safety considerations to understand than we can cover here in this book. Obviously, since we are dealing here with a very hot flame and the promise of flying sparks, you should have a clean work area away from any flammable materials and a good fire extinguisher should be handy, as well as a source of water. If a spark gets onto your shoe, don't waste your extinguisher on that. Use a water spray bottle, which is also handy at times for cooling off a piece of metal.

Follow your set's directions for attaching the gauge/regulator sets to your filled bottles of oxygen and acetylene **(see illustration)**. The bottles should be secured with a sturdy

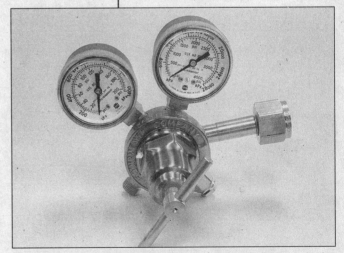

3.19 Most home/shop users of oxy-acetylene will have single-stage regulators on their torch sets. Unless you do a lot of welding/cutting, these are just fine, though you have to readjust the output pressure more frequently than with the professional, two-stage regulators.

3.20 Gas flow is regulated on the oxygen cylinder to 1-5 psi for welding, depending on the thickness of the material to be welded, and the acetylene pressure is adjusted the same. Higher pressures are set when performing cutting, but acetylene must never exceed 15 psi to the torch.

chain to either your bench or a welding cart that has provisions to keep it from tipping over easily. Before the regulators are attached, blow any dust out of the cylinder valves by *cracking* them. You should stand to the side of the cylinder when doing this, with the outlet pointed away, and very quickly open the valve slightly and close it again. Just a little blast of gas will ensure that the connection is free of dust.

Use a proper-fitting wrench (not an adjustable) on all your regulator and gas hose connections, which are usually brass fittings, and remember that the acetylene connections are *left-hand* threaded. Blow out the regulator by slowly opening the cylinder valve when the pressure-adjusting screw (usually T-shaped) is turned out all the way. One gauge will show you the cylinder pressure, and the other the hose/torch pressure. Attach the hoses and blow them out with a blast of gas. Adjust the regulators to provide 2-3 psi working pressure from each bottle **(see illustration)**. The cylinder valves should always be opened slowly, with your body away from the ends, and the oxygen valve should always be opened all the way. It is of a type that seals best either fully closed or fully open. The acetylene valve should be opened only about 1-1/2 turns.

Connect the hoses to your torch with the gas cylinder valves closed. In most cases this involves wrenches, but there are some professional sets that have snap-on connections (like air line hoses) to make quick, wrenchless work of changing torches **(see illustration)**. Select a medium tip from your set (your set's instructions will recommend what gas pressure works with which tip and what thickness of metal they are suited for) and attach to the torch. After everything is assembled, you can test the connections with soapy water for leaks.

You will need something to light the torch flame, and a wire-framed metal striker should have been included with your set **(see illustration)**. Never use open flames such as a cigarette, cigarette lighter or match to start your torch! Your fingers need to be well out of the way. You should be wearing leather gloves and heavy clothing with leather shoes or boots. Do not tuck your pants into your boots, or you could create a pocket there that could collect sparks. Likewise, do not wear pants with cuffs, for the same reason. Have your colored welding goggles on your head, but not yet over your eyes.

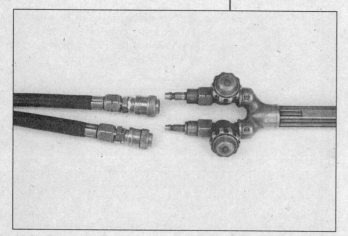

3.21 Some torches are equipped with quick-release fittings as usually seen on air-compressor hoses, making for quick, easy changes.

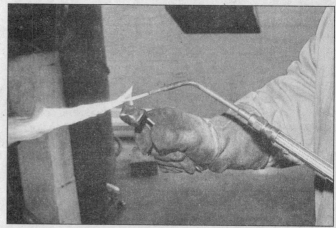

3.22 To start a torch, open the acetylene valve 1/2 turn and light immediately with a striker like this. Never use a match, cigarette or lighter, you could easily burn your hand. Once the sooty acetylene is lit, gradually add oxygen until you achieve a neutral flame.

Flame adjustment

This is a very important step in gas welding, and one you will be making every time you pick-up the torch to weld, braze, cut or solder, so you'll have to practice this to the point where it becomes second nature. Open the cylinder valves slowly as described before, and make sure the regulated pressure is set correctly. Hold the torch in your operating hand (right, if you are right-handed) and the striker in the opposite hand. Both valves on the torch are closed. Open the acetylene valve on the torch about a half-turn and operate the striker near the torch tip. There should be a flame with some sooty flying particles. Quickly add some oxygen and the soot should disappear. Study the illustrations of flame type. What you have right now is a *carburizing* flame, which is overly-rich in acetylene. As you add more oxygen, the flame characteristics will change. While the rich mix gives you a wide, flared-out yellow flame, adding oxygen will make the flame narrower and brighter.

The ideal flame for most gas welding is a *neutral* flame, which is neither carburizing nor oxidizing (too much oxygen). When you have adjusted the torch properly, there will be a large flame graduating from blue at the end away from the tip down to white near the torch and with an inner cone that should be light blue. If you add too much oxygen, the inner cone will be smaller, pale in color, and there may be a hissing sound. You'll need to practice achieving the neutral flame, and when you start welding, you'll see what happens to metals when the flame is incorrect.

The proper method of shutting off the torch is equally important. Close the acetylene valve on the torch first, then the oxygen. If you do it the other way around, there could be a small amount of gas left in the tip that could ignite. If you are through welding for some time, it is good safety practice to then close down the gas cylinder valves as well, but if you are going to weld again in a short while, just shut off the torch valves only.

Gas welding

You'll need a lot of small pieces of clean scrap metal to practice on, of varying thicknesses. Even if you only intend to do light sheet-metal welding, start by practicing with thicknesses up to 1/4-inch to become familiar with different tip sizes and flame adjustment. The cleaner the scrap pieces, the

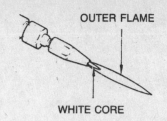

Neutral Flame

OUTER FLAME

WHITE CORE

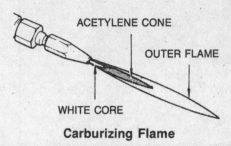

ACETYLENE CONE

OUTER FLAME

WHITE CORE

Carburizing Flame

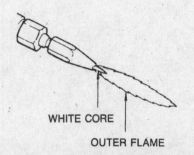

WHITE CORE

OUTER FLAME

Oxidizing Flame

3.23 The oxidizing flame has too much oxygen, and a feathery blue flame with small white inner flame. The carburizing flame is acetylene rich, and features a large flame, with a large blue inner cone and a longer, colored cone around that. For welding, adjust for a neutral flame.

3.24 You don't have to worry about grounding with gas equipment, but there is a dangerous flame involved, so your welding projects and practice sessions are best done over some firebricks like this, which you can get at your welding supply store.

better your welds will be, and this applies to any type of welding, gas or electric. You should sand or grind the areas to be welded to remove any paint, coatings or rust. You should not use for testing any metals that are galvanized or coated with zinc, or any kind of plating. Not only will welding be dirty and difficult, but the coatings may cause harmful gasses when vaporized in the weld.

Start your first exercise with a piece of steel on a level, non-flammable surface, not a wooden bench. The ideal work area would be a steel table (not just a wooden bench with thin sheet metal nailed onto it) with some firebricks on top. The firebricks can be obtained at your welding supply center, and, in addition to being non-flammable, they do not suck the heat out of your welding sample like a steel table, and there's no chance you're going to weld the sample *to* the brick. It can be very embarrassing when you practice on a steel table and you have various scraps welded - stuck to your table.

With your torch adjusted properly, pull down your goggles and put the torch tip about one inch from the steel and just try to make a long weld puddle of molten metal. The torch should be leaning back at a 45-degree angle, with the flame pointing in the direction the bead is going. When the steel starts melting into a small pool where you started, move the tip along and give it a rhythmic motion of an oval shape as you go, trying to follow a straight line, blending the newly-heated edge of the puddle with the back edge of the puddle. The process will leave a line of rippled ridges. If you are burning holes in the metal, there may be too much oxygen, the torch may be too close to the metal, the tip could be too large or you are possibly advancing the torch too slowly. If you go too fast, have the torch too far away or the tip is too small, your puddle will be very small and it won't penetrate the metal very far. The more the torch is pointed straight down at the metal (no angle) the deeper the penetration will be, and vice-versa. Practice at different angles until you can make a bead like our illustration, with even ripples and proper penetration.

Of course, not all of your welding will be done this way, in fact almost all of your real welding will involve adding filler rod, but for now you need to learn torch control and rhythm. Many of the projects you encounter will involve welding along an irregular line, especially in repair work, where you are welding up a crack. To become more familiar with making a bead along an irregular line (still without filler rod) draw a zigzag or curved line on the steel with soapstone and practice making a good bead. Proper hand control is everything in gas welding. Your hand must be comfortable and steady at all times. In welding classes, students are often challenged to write their first name in script with welding bead on a piece of metal, which challenges you in handling changes in bead direction.

When you are successful with these experiments laying down a good bead on the metal, you're ready to try joining two pieces using a filler rod. This requires not only good torch control, but control of your other hand as well with the filler rod. Generally, the filler rod should be the same material as the base or parent metal for good fusion welding. If you weld aluminum, the filler rod must be aluminum, and steel rods are used on steel. The steel filler rods are coated with copper to keep them from rusting and to make cleaner welds. As a basic rule, select a filler rod that is the same diameter as the thickness of the metal you are welding. Most light metals are welded with 3/32-inch, 1/16-inch or 1/8-inch rod, and you will probably never gas-weld with anything bigger than 1/4-inch rod. To weld thick materials, several passes are required to make a good fusion, and various forms of electric welding are usually much faster than a torch at making multiple-pass seams.

3.25 Heat in gas welding is controlled by matching the gas flow and tip size to the thickness of material. Your welding travel speed and tip-to-work distance will control the puddle size and penetration. With all things right, you should be able to heat your first puddle molten in about six seconds, then move along to make your bead. At left is a bead run too cold (bead stands up), at center is one run too hot and too fast, and at right is a better bead with good width and penetration.

Welding with filler rod

Let's say that you need to join two pieces of 1/8-inch-thick metal in a straight bead from right to left. Position the two pieces such that they are butted together where they are to be joined, and that you have something blocking or clamping them in place so they won't move as you weld. Start your weld puddle at the right end of the seam, and as the puddle develops, use your left hand to insert the tip of the filler rod into the center of the hot puddle, then pull it out right away. Set up a rhythm of alternately putting in the rod and taking it out as the bead progresses to the left. When we describe the puddle, the edge of the puddle closest to the direction you are traveling is the *front* edge, while the part of the puddle you just finished is the rear.

If you have ever done any soldering, you may have a bad habit of heating the solder with your torch or soldering iron and letting the molten lead drip onto the joint. This is a bad habit and one you shouldn't bring with you in your welding practice. The molten puddle should melt the filler rod, not the torch. If the rod sticks, then you are not keeping the puddle molten enough, or you are adding filler rod too fast, either of which will result in a low-quality weld.

This skill of making a good bead, with evenly overlapping ovals and good penetration will take considerable practice, but if you learn two-handed gas-welding techniques well, any other welding system you pick up later on will be considerably easier to learn. Most of the welding you will do will be *forehand* welding, in which you angle the torch so that the flame is aimed somewhat toward the direction of the desired weld bead. This preheats the metal as you go and makes addition of filler rod to the front edge of the puddle easier because it is truly hot. Sometimes it seems like keeping the proper torch distance, moving at the right speed, circling or ovaling the tip and dipping the rod in at the right time is just too much to concentrate on at one time, but you *will* get the hang of it. This isn't "brain surgery" and millions have learned before you. After a good long practice session, begin to examine things around you that are of welded construction and you'll get an appreciation of the practice it took to lay down those beautiful beads that look like they were done by some machine instead of human hands. Indeed there are some kinds of welding that are done with largely robotic welding machines, but a good weldor can make virtually perfect joints that are stronger than the parent metal.

We mentioned before that cleanliness is critical in making good welds. The two edges to be joined need to be sanded or ground clean to bright metal and should fit as closely as possible. Small gaps are inevitable in some kinds of work and can be bridged with filler rod, but gaps should be kept to a minimum. On thicker materials, you will find that it is easier to make a clean weld with good penetration if the edges of the two pieces are beveled before you weld. This can be done with a file or grinder. Thin materials have their own idiosyncrasies, mostly to do with keeping the two edges in alignment. As you progress with your weld bead, more and more heat travels out into the parent metal, so that after welding for some distance, the metal you now encounter is hotter than the metal you started on, so you may have to adjust the torch away slightly to compensate for the puddle forming faster.

Another problem with thin materials is that the parent metal tends to *distort* with the application of heat. Metal expands when heated, and two edges that were parallel when you started welding probably won't stay that way. Usually, the edges pull away and you have a gap to bridge that wasn't there when you started. The solution is to *tack-weld* at intervals before applying too much heat. A tack-weld is

3.26 When practicing basic butt welds, tack the near corner first, then tack the top corner with a slight gap between the parts. This will close up as the plates grow from welding heat.

3. 27 Start your bead about an inch beyond that first tack, and proceed toward the end, keeping the torch steady and dropping molten beads off the filler rod by dipping into the puddle quickly and evenly as you go, building an overlapping series of puddles.

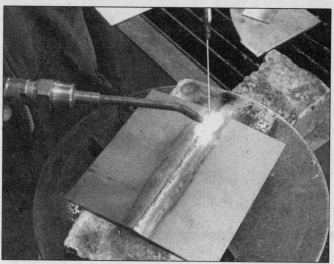

3.28 Before you are done, you will notice some movement or warping of the sample plates. If you plan to do automotive body work with a torch, you'll have to practice a lot on thin metal to get the hang of welding without burning holes or warping the work. Gas welding is not suited to the thin, high-strength body steels used on today's unibody cars.

simply a bead only one or two puddles long, done quickly. To join a long seam in sheet metal, tack the ends first, then the middle, and then put tacks every few inches apart, while alternating the ends you tack **(see illustration)**. When you go along later to do the final, full seam welding, the tack puddles can be melted into the main seam as you go, and the pieces will stay aligned the whole way. This is particularly important when joining long sheet-metal seams like welding a new quarter-panel onto a car. In auto bodywork, you need to keep the warpage to a minimum. In some cases when doing the final seam after tacking sheet metal, you may stop after a few inches are welded and quickly apply a body dolly to the backside of the weld area and hammer on the weld area on top with a body hammer. This "hammer-welding" (alternating welding and hammering) technique straightens the seam and the two panels while they are still hot and pliable, and the resultant seam when done by a good body man requires much less grinding or filling to make it ready for primer and paint.

The basic joint we have illustrated is a *butt* joint, where two pieces of metal are pushed together and welded along the seam where they meet. There are many kinds of joints, and it is helpful to try welding a few other types after you have practiced enough on butt welds on thick and thin materials. *Corner* welds, where the two edges meet at an angle can be either inside or outside corners **(see illustrations)**. The outside corner weld is the easier to perform because you can see the seam so clearly, and the pieces need not be beveled. Just placing them so that the edges form a groove or V will do it. On inside corner welds, depending on the angle involved, the action is harder to observe, being shrouded somewhat by the pieces. After you have practiced on these more difficult welds, try a lap weld. This is where the two pieces lay over each other (overlapping). You run a bead where the joint is, and depending upon the strength required for the application, you may want to weld the seam on the other side as well. In auto bodywork, sometimes panels have to be overlapped instead of butt-welded, but in such cases the backside seam is seldom welded.

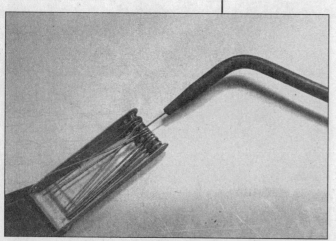

3.29 As you weld, it is inevitable that sparks and spatter will blow back onto your torch tip. If it plugs up, your bead will be spotty and your torch may go out entirely. Keep the tips clean with a set of fine-wire cleaners that come with your gas set.

A T-weld is where you join a piece of metal to another larger piece at right angles, forming a letter T in profile. This requires some additional practice to perform well, as part of the weld puddle is being made uphill, and the larger piece may take more heat than the smaller part. You have to play the torch back and forth over both pieces and get a feel for how much heat each requires.

Further practice sessions for you may involve trying to weld pieces of tubing and angle-iron together, both typical materials for home/shop projects. Try joining a flat plate to a tube, or making a corner between two pieces of angle-iron. Careful measurement and cutting will be required to make gapless corners for a good weld. Square or rectangular tubing is often used in projects such as shop equipment or a utility trailer, and you should practice making 90-degree corners from two pieces cut at 45-degree angles. The inside welds will be the tougher ones, and you'll find when you stop practicing and assemble a real-world project that you can't always turn the work around to make the seam area flat in front of you on your bench. Often you will be forced to weld in a vertical seam, or even weld upside down underneath something. The latter is difficult and dangerous, requiring the best in full-face eye protection (a helmet instead of goggles) and a leather apron over your arms and shoulders to protect you from falling sparks. Welding an exhaust system under a car, especially if you don't have access to a lift, can be extra challenging.

When these don't seem like a challenge anymore, you're doing very well, and you can try making nice-fitting joints between pieces of *round* tubing. To fit two pieces of round tubing together, such as in a roll-cage for a race car, requires a measure-twice, cut-once procedure and lots of patience in cutting and grinding round tubing to join them with full contact. Another procedure to try with round tubing is to make a slip-fit, with one piece of tubing sized to just fit over another. In such cases, you can weld around the joint, or, for high-strength applications, cut the outside tube in a "fish mouth," as if it were being joined at a 90-degree angle to another piece of round tubing. When this piece is welded onto the inner tube, the fish mouth makes for a much longer weld seam between the two and gives greater strength.

Other types of welds you may run across in your projects are spot-welds and rosette welds. The former is found often in auto sheet metal work, where you join two pieces of light-gauge material together without welding the seam entirely. The spot-weld is just a round welding spot, rather than a bead, and is made when one piece is on top of another and you just melt a puddle that fuses the two panels together, then move a distance away and make another spot-weld. Filler rod is often not used in such cases, especially where appearance is more important than strength. Most spot welds lie flat enough that little prep is required to make them ready for paint. Modern cars are welded with thousands of spot-welds, but these are accomplished by special electric welders, usually computer-controlled and robotic.

Where a little more strength than a simple spot-weld is required, a rosette or plug-weld can be made. This is where the panel on top has holes drilled or punched into it at intervals. You weld up the holes, puddling both upper and lower panels together, which joins them securely in that spot. Plug-welds often do require some filler rod.

Sometime in your gas-welding work, the torch will go out and you'll get a loud pop at the torch which will really get your attention because you don't expect it. When welding in tight quarters, you may tend to get the tip too close to the work, which will overheat the tip and cause a tiny explosion as the gasses POP inside the tip, which is called a backfire. This will alarm you greatly when it happens, but the answer is simply to not get so close. You may have been working close to get the pieces hot enough, but if that is the case, you really need a larger tip or more flow of oxygen and acetylene from the tank regulators to maintain the right heat level with your torch further away from the confinement of the weld corner. Welding too close to the work will also dirty your tips. So if you have a backfire, stop work, shut off the gas at the torch and remove the tip for a

FLASH ARRESTORS

TORCH-MOUNTED TYPE
UL-LISTED

STOP DANGEROUS FLASHBACKS

L-TEC

L-TEC
WELDING & CUTTING SYSTEMS

OXYGEN and FUEL GAS PAIR

- Fit on all torches with "B" size inlets
- Oxygen inlet pressures up to 150 psig
- Acetylene inlet pressures up to 15 psig
- LPG, MPS, Nat. Gas inlet pressures up to 50 psig
- Both models incorporate reverse flow check valves
- Delivery pressure must be increased to compensate for pressure drop — see instructions

P/N 20357

3.30 These prevent serious accidents from a flashback, indicated by a loud squealing noise. Flashbacks are caused by gasses burning *inside* the hose. For safety reasons, both hoses should be equipped with flash arrestors, which are reverse-flow check valves. Some readjustment of gauge pressures may be necessary when using check valves.

thorough cleaning. Your welding set will have come with a set of wire tip cleaners. Cool off the tip with a water-soaked rag.

Something akin to a torch backfire but much more dangerous is a "flashback." This is where combustion actually follows the gas trail back into the torch and even the hoses. At the least there is danger of damaging the regulators and hoses, but if the combustion reaches the tanks, there is a possibility of a serious explosion. In a flashback, the torch goes out and there is a loud squealing or hissing noise with black smoke coming out of the torch. If this happens, shut off the oxygen at the torch, then the acetylene at the torch, then the cylinder valves. Your welding supply center should have available "flashback flame arrestors" that install in your two gas lines where the hoses attach to the regulators **(see illustration)**. Acting like one-way valves, they are designed to prevent serious accidents caused by flashbacks, and they should be installed on any gas-welding setup, where the hoses attach to the regulators.

When making welds with filler rods, you will run across situations where the rod gets short enough for your left hand to get too close for comfort to the heat of the welding. Before making a bead, practice will have shown you how fast the welding rod gets used up and how long a rod you will need to complete the seam. Start with a rod long enough to do the whole seam. If the seam is longer and will take several rods to complete, you will have to stop welding and get a new filler rod. It will take some time and practice to get the hang of continuing a bead with a new rod where you left off before. The trick is to make the whole bead look like a continuous weld, without little piles of buildup where you stopped and restarted. When a rod gets short, many welders simply tack the short piece onto the end of a new rod and go right on welding. When you get good at it, the bead won't have a chance to cool off too much. In inside-corner welding, you may want to take the welding rod and put a bend into it, such that it puts your hand in a more comfortable position, further away from the heat of the action **(see illustration)**.

Checking your welds

Chances are, you won't be making nuclear-vessel welds in your home/shop, or other welds so critical that they require X-ray inspection to pass specifications, as is often done in commercial welding. However, you do want to learn how to make strong joints, and your practice time should include some testing as well. Looks are important, but a good-looking bead may not be a proper weld, especially if it doesn't have good penetration. Checking for good penetration requires looking closely at the backside of the welded joint, which is easy for you to do with your practice sample pieces. In real-world situations, it isn't always practical to get at the backside of something you have welded (like a joint between two rectangular or round tubes), so you should be familiar with the proper heat control and penetration before you consider yourself through with your practice phase.

In looking at the back of the weld, see if there is any buildup on the backside. A small amount of "dropthrough" is acceptable, but 100% penetration can be

SYMPTOM	CAUSE	REMEDY
FLAME FLUCTUATIONS	• Moisture in the gas, condensation in the hose. • Insufficient acetylene supply.	• Remove the moisture from the hose. • Adjust the acetylene pressure. • Have the tank refilled.
EXPLOSIVE SOUND WHILE LIGHTING THE TORCH	• Oxygen or acetylene pressure is incorrect. • Removal of mixed-in gases is incomplete. • The tip orifice is too large. • The tip orifice is dirty.	• Adjust the pressure. • Remove the air from inside the torch. • Replace the tip. • Clean the orifice in the tip.
FLAME CUT OFF	• Oxygen pressure is too high. • The flame outlet is clogged.	• Adjust the oxygen pressure. • Clean the tip.
POPPING NOISES DURING OPERATION	• The tip is overheated. • The tip is clogged. • The gas pressure adjustment is incorrect. • Metal deposited on the tip.	• Cool the flame outlet (while letting a little oxygen flow). • Clean the tip. • Adjust the gas pressure.
OXYGEN FLOW IS REVERSED Oxygen is flowing into the path of the acetylene.	• The tip is clogged. • Oxygen pressure is too high. • Torch is defective (the tip or valve is loose). • There is contact with the tip and the deposit metal.	• Clean the tip. • Adjust the oxygen pressure. • Repair or replace the torch. • Clean the orifice.
BACKFIRE There is a whistling noise and the torch handle grip gets hot. Flame is sucked into the torch.	• The tip is clogged or dirty. • Oxygen pressure is too low. • The tip is overheated. • The tip orifice is enlarged or deformed. • A spark from the base metal enters the torch causing an ignition of gas inside the torch. • Amount of acetylene flowing through the torch is too low.	• Clean the tip. • Adjust the oxygen pressure. • Cool the tip with water (letting a little oxygen flow). • Replace the tip. • Immediately shut off both torch valves. • Let torch cool down. Then re-light the torch. • Readjust the flow rate.

3.31 After you have gained some welding experience, and a good torch weldor isn't trained in one day, you will learn to read the welding conditions based on the flame from the torch. This troubleshooting chart indicates some of the causes and cures of torch flame problems.

achieved without extra material building up on the backside. Good penetration is particularly important in welding auto body panels, because the outside of the weld bead is probably going to be ground down with a body grinder in preparation for filling and painting. Thus the strength of the topside buildup or puddling will be gone and the joint's strength will rely totally on the fusion of the two pieces below the surface. In your tests of practice welds, it can be helpful to use a hacksaw to cut through the center of one of your welded joints to see just what the penetration is. You can't always tell by looking at the ends of the joints, because of how you may have ended the bead.

We're assuming that your home/shop has a good, sturdy bench vise. It can be useful in testing your welded joints. Your first practice welds may have been straight seams with two pieces butt-welded together. Take your best example and put it in your vise with the weld seam close to the jaws **(see illustration)**. Clamp a pair of vise-grip pliers on one edge of the upper piece and start hitting the upper piece with a hammer, while holding it with the pliers so it can't fly off. Hammer the upper piece until it's bent over all the way onto the vise (making a 90-degree angle in the welded pieces). Remove the sample from the vise and examine the weld. If the upper piece broke off during hammering, it obviously wasn't a strong enough weld.

Any of the various joints you may have practiced on can be tested by hammering. Whatever the joint, just secure the piece and hammer on one of the two joined pieces. Hammer from the backside area of the joint and toward the side that you welded on. If good penetration wasn't achieved, the backside will be weaker than the front and bending the metal this direction will really test the backside for good fusion. Even a weld with 100% penetration may not be strong enough if there was any "undercutting" on the top side. Undercutting is a groove along either or both sides of a bead, caused by applying too much heat or holding the torch at the wrong angle. In a stressed situation, the undercut area will be the weak point and the joint may fracture right along the undercut area.

3.32 Brazing with a gas torch has many uses, such as repairing castings and antique-car sheet metal. Here a flux-coated rod is being used. Brazing is not a fusion process, so it is used where higher, melting-point heat might damage the work, or surrounding materials.

Brazing

Brazing, or braze-welding, is not a true fusion process such as we have been discussing. The parent metal does not melt into a puddle. The parent metal is heated and the brazing rod melts into the joint securing the two pieces together. The brazing rod is made of brass (an alloy of copper and zinc) and is used in conjunction with a flux, which may come already on the rod, or in a can that you dip the rod into to coat it as you go. Brazed joints are as strong as welded joints when done properly and with an overlap of the pieces, but brazing is particularly helpful where the higher heat of fusion welding would harm the parent metal or adjacent materials, or where the pieces being joined are made of brass or copper.

The rod material melts at a much lower temperature than the parent metal, so the basic principle is to heat the parent metal just above the melting temperature of the filler rod, so that the parent metal, not the torch, melts the rod. Overheating the rod with the torch will boil the zinc out of the rod and cause poor adhesion in the joint. Brazing is most often done where there is an overlap of two pieces, or in building up a worn or broken area of a casting, that will be re-machined to original shape after brazing.

A joint to be brazed must be thoroughly *cleaned*, by grinding, filing, or sanding. When you have selected the proper rod for the material you are working on (copper/zinc for ferrous metals), you begin by heating the joint with your torch, using a lot less heat that you would for welding. You should pull the torch tip back 2-3 inches, which is much further back than with gas-welding. When the metal is dull red, apply the filler rod to the hot spot on the parent metal and see if it melts in. Heat next to that spot and apply some more fluxed rod, keeping this process going until you have completed your seam. When a long seam is contemplated with brazing, preheat the whole area. When the metal is the correct temperature, the brazing rod will flow nicely into the joint; if the metal is too cold, the braze material will ball up on the surface, and if it is too hot, it will spread out over a wide area. White smoke during the process usually indicates the area is overheated, and the smoke is the zinc boiling off. Not only does this affect the quality of the joint, but the fumes can make you sick if you breathe enough of them. Even if you don't overheat the rod, there are fumes given off during brazing.

Always braze with adequate ventilation, and a good respirator mask is also helpful insurance. Brazing is often used when joining pieces of galvanized metal because it will adhere better than standard gas-welding; however, this combination of brazing fumes and fumes from the plating or galvanizing should be avoided unless you are outdoors.

If you are familiar with basic soldering, you know that good adhesion is ensured by using *flux*, a compound that prepares the metal for a strong bond, and you may also be familiar with the term *tinning*. Tinning is a process (in soldering) of applying a thin coating of lead to the fluxed surface before the main solder is melted in. The procedure is similar in braze-welding, except that, when brazing thin materials, the tinning usually takes place as you are brazing, in one step rather than two. Brazing larger joints requires that a light coating of brass be flowed onto the surfaces, making it easier for the main brazing to stick to. The flux for brazing can be a part of the rod itself (pre-fluxed rods) which is convenient, or you may have a metal can of flux on your welding table. You simply heat the end of your brazing rod and stick it into the flux and withdraw it covered with flux **(see illustration)**. Once you have started the brazing process, the rod will always be hot enough to pick up flux as you need more. The pre-fluxed rods are convenient, but the coating is somewhat fragile and won't take rough handling. These rods must also be kept very dry.

When brazing thin sheet metal, the purchase area or overlap between the two panels is the key to the strength of the joint. When there is 3/4-inch or more of overlap for the brazing to adhere to, the joint will actually be stronger than the parent metal. Because the brazing rod melts at only about 1000° F instead of the steel's melting point of 2700° F, brazing will induce much less warpage in thin metal, which is why it has been used for years in many areas of traditional auto-body repair. The overlap in the brazed joint also makes the joint area much stiffer (two thicknesses of metal there), so a seam such as when installing a body patch panel will take less hammer-and-dolly work to prepare for painting **(see illustration)**. Brazing will not work on a butt-joint because there isn't enough "captured"

3.33 Most welders use dip-type powdered flux for convenience, since the pre-coated rods can flake if they are exposed to moisture. Plain brazing rod is heated with the torch, then dipped into can of flux and pulled out coated with enough flux for an inch or two of brazing travel.

3.34 Lap welds are best for brazing, such as when joining overlapping sheet metal panels where the brass has lots of contact area for adhesion. As with fusion welding, tack the ends before running the whole seam.

3.35 You should start with very clean metal when brazing, although the flux is designed to surface clean as you go, leaving some minor slag afterwards. You will have to keep the torch further away from the seam than with welding, to keep from overheating the brass.

3.36 End view of a brazed lap joint, showing how the brass flows in between the plates with capillary action, much as solder does when applied to a hot copper pipe. The base metal must be heated to the point where *it* melts the rod, not the torch.

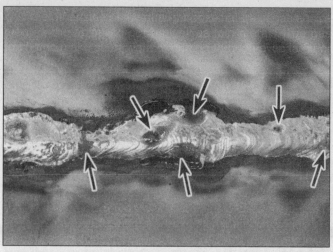

3.37 There is some silicon slag after brazing (arrows), which can be softened with water after the part cools enough so that water will not warp it, then the rest comes clean with wire-brushing.

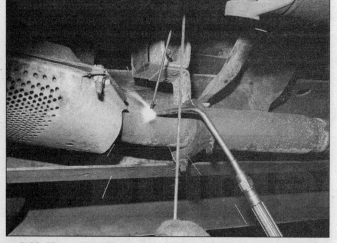

3.38 The versatility of gas welding equipment has always found favor in the exhaust system business. You must be careful not to cut or weld near fuel tanks, fuel lines, electrical components or brake lines, but the equipment is highly portable, and can cut as well as weld. Long welding rod can be bent to curve around exhaust pipes to weld in tight quarters.

area for the capillary action to flow the brass into each piece, although you can back up a butt-joint with a strip of similar material, which gives an overlap on both pieces and good bonding area for the brazing.

Although brazing is still a technique used by older body craftsmen in restoration of antique and collectible cars, it should not be used on new cars that are built of low-alloy, high-strength but lightweight steels. In fact, some car manufacturers specify that no torch work at all should be done on their body metal, that only MIG welding is acceptable because of the narrow heated area and faster welding-bread travel.

Other metals than steel can be brazed as well, such as stainless-steel, castings, brass, bronze and even aluminum when a special aluminum-brazing rod is used. If you have special project considerations or a question, ask your local welding supply for advice on choosing the best brazing rod for the job. One advantage of brazing is that dissimilar metals can be joined, which ordinarily can't be done with fusion welding. Also, where two pieces of different thickness are being joined, like a thin pipe to a thick flange, brazing is preferred. In ordinary gas welding, you have to be very good with the torch to play the right amount of heat onto the thicker piece while not burning up the thin piece. With brazing, neither piece needs to be heated beyond the melting point of the brazing rod.

After braze-welding a seam, you will see that the flux remains as a kind of crust on the parent metal. It should be removed with a wire brush, and can be softened with water first, which makes the wire-brushing work easier.

Oxy-acetylene cutting

The other side of the dual-purpose nature of gas equipment is the ability to *cut* as well as join metals. The gas torch can make short work of cutting through even large or

3.39 Muffler installers also find uses for welding rod to simulate the length and required bends for a pipe to be installed. Bent wire is taken over to the hydraulic tube bender where shape is duplicated in pipe.

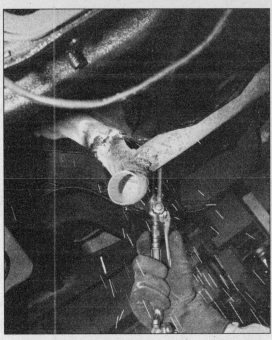

3.40 Sometimes, the oxy-acetylene cutting torch the fastest, easiest way to remove the old exhaust system.

thick pieces of steel. For sheet metal work you will probably continue to use shears and other hand tools to cut light-gauge material, but being faced with cutting through a half-inch steel plate with a hacksaw will easily convince you of the value of a cutting torch.

The only oxy-acetylene cutting component different from your basic welding setup is the torch itself. The cutting torch has one major difference from the welding torch: it has an extra oxygen supply, operated by a lever instead of a valve (see illustration). Actually, when you cut steel with a torch, it isn't the flame that is really doing the cutting; it is a strong flow of oxygen that hits a heated part and the oxidation of the metal happens so fast the affected area disintegrates into flying sparks. The basic principle of oxy-acetylene cutting is that the torch tip has several small holes surrounding a central larger hole. The smaller outside holes are where the basic oxy-acetylene flame comes out - actually several small flames. These flames are really used to preheat the metal to be cut. The weldor adjusts the gas and oxygen flow on the torch for the proper flames from the pre-heat holes and plays the

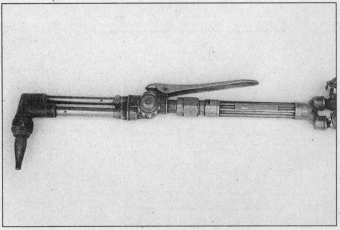

3.41 The cutting torch is adjusted for a good flame, then checked with the extra-oxygen supplied when the cutting lever is depressed. The flame should remain close to neutral. The excess oxygen is what is used to push the molten slag from the kerf as you cut.

torch on the end of the piece to be cut. When the end is heated to a cherry red color, the weldor presses down on the cutting lever, which activates a strong flow of pure oxygen through the large central hole in the tip. This is the oxygen that really cuts through the metal.

Because oxy-acetylene cutting involves a huge shower of sparks from the underside of the metal you're cutting, you must be prepared before cutting. Clear the area around your welding table, have the proper welding attire on (including leather welding gloves), and make sure the area under the test piece is clear of any obstructions. It's best to support your test piece on some firebrick, leaving the area under the cut line open. If there were any restriction to the flow of sparks under your test piece, molten shrapnel could blow back into the weldor's face.

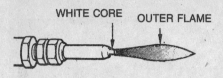

WHITE CORE   OUTER FLAME

Neutral Flame

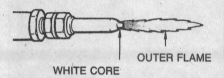

OUTER FLAME

WHITE CORE

3.42 As in welding, the flame of your cutting torch head should be adjusted to a neutral flame before cutting.

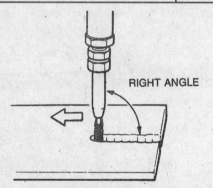

RIGHT ANGLE

Cutting Thick Panel

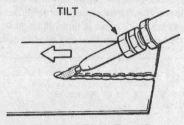

TILT

Cutting Thin Panel

3.43 The cutting torch should be held more nearly vertical to the work when cutting heavier metals, and angled back when cutting thinner material like exhaust pipe or sheet metal. Use scrap steel tubing or angle as a brace to guide the torch for steadier cutting.

Mark your cut line using a sharpened piece of soapstone and a straightedge. After marking the cut line, find a piece of tubing or angle-iron that you can clamp down onto the workpiece to act as a guide for the torch head (see illustration).

Before you begin cutting with your oxy-acetylene torch, you should reset the regulators. Adjust the acetylene gas to 2-3 psi, and the oxygen to 15-20 psi, since a much larger percentage of oxygen will be used in the process. Select a gas pressure and tip size that correlates to the thickness of the material you are cutting. Your setup's instructions will tell you the recommended sizes for that brand of equipment. Light your torch as you have learned to do in gas welding practice and watch for a neutral flame from the preheat holes in the tip. Watching the flame pattern, try cutting in the extra oxygen flow from the cutting handle. It shouldn't affect the quality of the preheat flames. Place the torch flame at the edge of the material you want to cut and hold it there a short distance from the material (1/16-inch or 1/8-inch away). When the metal is cherry red (about 1500° F), angle the torch tip back about 10 degrees (with the tip aiming in the direction of the cut) and cut in the oxygen. You'll find that oxy-acetylene cutting is much easier to learn than the welding process was; the main thing to learn here is the proper travel speed for the tip size, gas pressure and metal thickness you are working with.

When you cut through metal with the torch, the quality of the cut edges will tell you much about the process. At the bottom edges of the cut, slag may collect, leaving a rough edge that must be cleaned up with a grinder later. Also, remember when you are cutting that the torch takes out material as it goes; the part being removed is called the *kerf*. When you draw soapstone lines to cut out shapes, remember to cut *outside* your lines, or the part will wind up being too small. After your have experimented a little with the torch, you'll have an idea of how big the kerf will be with certain tips and certain materials.

If you try to advance the torch too fast, the bottom of the kerf may be irregular or not cut through all the way. When you look at the edge of the cut metal, you'll see vertical lines in the edge of the cut, in a good cut these lines are straight and smooth, in a rough cut the lines are almost like teeth on a saw blade. If you advance the torch too fast, the cutting lines will look curved back toward the direction you started the cut from, instead of straight up and down (see illustration). If you move too slowly with the torch, the top of the kerf will be rounded off, and the bottom edge may accumulate too much slag. If you have someone else in the shop with you, have them observe your cutting from a safe distance. When you are making good cuts, the shower of

3.44 Examine the cut edge of plates after you have used your cutting torch. The proper heat and travel speed is when there is the least amount of slag along the bottom of the cut. This hand-held cut was moved a little too fast, as evidenced by the angled cut lines.

sparks should come straight down to the floor. Your observer can tell you if the spark flow is going back toward the beginning of the cut, which indicates that the metal isn't being cut all the way until after the torch has moved on, the result is that the uncut area at the bottom directs the sparks back toward the beginning of the cut. Some of the sparks and blobs could also get blown back into your face or clothing, so learn to develop the right cutting speed for clean cuts.

You will find that the steadier you are with the cutting torch, the better the cuts will be, and half the problem of cutting is finding a comfortable position for your hands. Since only one hand is required to operate a cutting torch, you can use your other hand (gloved) to steady the torch and help advance it correctly along your cut line. Keeping the torch tip the same right distance from the work is also important, so find a piece of angle-iron or tubing in your shop sized such that, when you rest your torch neck on it, it puts the tip about the right distance away from a piece of steel the angle or tube is lying on **(see illustration)**. Mark and save this piece as your torch rest and it will be invaluable in making straight, clean cuts.

There are many methods for cutting steel for projects, like saws and abrasive discs, but the versatility of the cutting torch is that you can cut out a piece of one-inch plate in the shape of an elephant if you want to. Irregular shapes cut out just as easily as straight lines, as far as the torch part goes, though you will have to develop a rhythm of smooth hand movements with the torch to follow your soapstone lines accurately. As with any aspect of welding, this will take practice. You can also stack several pieces of plate together. Either clamp them together or tack-weld the edges, and when you cut (sizing the tip for the combined thickness) you can cut out as many as a dozen identical pieces. To keep them truly identical if necessary, these parts can later be tack-welded, clamped or bolted together for the final sanding or grinding of the edges, ensuring that they all match in dimensions.

Besides making straight cuts, which are easiest, you may find that some projects require certain shapes to be cut out more than once. Here is where various cutting aids can be used. If you can make the torch tip follow a pattern of some kind, you can cut out the same shape repeatedly. Perhaps you need four round discs of steel six inches in diameter. You can make a steel or wooden pattern that has a circle in it bigger than six inches. How much bigger than the six-inch measurement depends on the size of the kerf with the tip you are using. If you know that you need an extra 3/8-inch to allow for the kerf, make a template with a hole 3/8-inch bigger all around. When you use this as a cutting guide/rest for the torch, you can cut out as many circles as you want and they will all be round and the same size. You clamp the template over your workpiece and move the torch around your cut, always in contact with you template. The smoother your template and the steadier your hand movement, the nicer the cut will be. Watching a pro weldor some time will show you how perfect you can get with what seems like a relatively-crude method of making a part.

In fabrication shops, special equipment is used to make repeated cutout shapes where lots of parts are needed. One of the basic machines you would see in most street rod or race-car shops is a *"flame-cutter"* **(see illustration)**. This is basically a cutting table on which is

3.45 Clamp a piece of metal to your work that spaces the cutting torch head just the right distance to make your cut-line. The steadier your torch is held, the cleaner the cut. Travel at a very steady speed.

3.46 A tool you will see in most race car, hot rod and fabrication shops is a mechanized cutting torch, often called a flamecutter. It uses a motor-driven torch to travel around a template and cut out exact shapes. Templates can be temporary ones cut from heavy cardboard, to steel templates for frequent use.

3.47 This mechanized cutting setup from Daytona MIG uses a standard cutting torch, laid down and clamped in place.

3.48 The complete Daytona MIG shape-cutting table is shown here with the erasable porcelain layout table folded up to take up less space when not being used. This table can be used with a gas torch or plasma cutter.

mounted a framework that holds a special torch, with a straight cutting end instead of a 90-degree end like most hand torches **(see illustration)**. There is a series of arms that allow the torch to stay perfectly vertical and yet move to follow any shape on the table, and at the top is a small electric motor. There is a place at the top to mount a template, usually made of heavy-gauge sheet metal, and a magnetized, knurled tip on top of the torch assembly that follows the template exactly. The motor drives the knurled tip around the template at a steady speed (adjustable for the thickness of the material being cut), while below, the torch tip cuts out exactly the shape of the template. Removing the human element from the torch movement means that a flamecutter can make smoother, more repeatable parts. In most shops with a flamecutter, there is usually a large wall behind it on which hang a wide variety of templates for frequently used shapes, such as suspension brackets **(see illustration)**. In some shops, the flamecutting setup has a *pantograph* arrangement, which is a series of arms that make the torch cut out a shape dictated by the movement of a stylus around a template on a table next to the flamecutter. Some sophisticated machines have an electronic stylus that will follow the lines of a blueprint or even the lead of a pencil line drawn on paper.

3.49 Wherever you find a flamecutter, chances are you'll find a wall of metal templates nearby, used to easily and precisely duplicate commonly used shapes such as suspension mounting brackets. At lower left is a shape used to make a head for an engine stand.

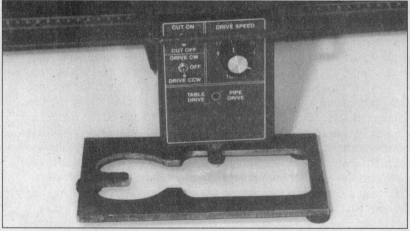

3.50 Most mechanized cutters have a drive head with a magnetized tip for following metal templates, inside or outside a pattern. The cutting speed is infinitely variable to suit the material.

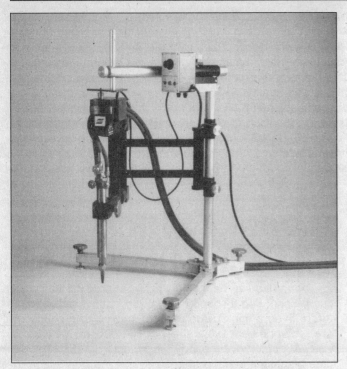

3.51 The ESAB Porta-Graph can be moved anywhere you have a source of electricity, and is useful for cutting shapes out of large steel plates that won't fit under a stationary cutting machine.

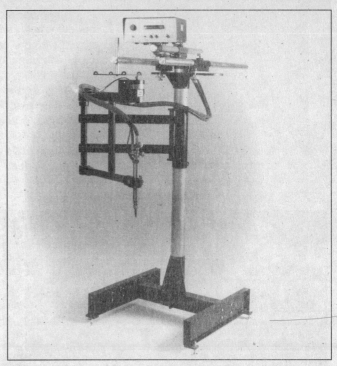

3.52 This flamecutter with swing arms can be mounted over a plate, or bolted to a table.

If you decide to cut out shapes with your oxy-acetylene torch, you will probably need to build a cutting table **(see illustration)**. On a straight cut, the end of the part can be laid over the edge of your bench; the work is supported and the cutoff piece just falls to the floor. But cutting out shapes larger than a few inches means you need a different surface to work on, or you'll soon be cutting into your bench! Look at the photos of some of the cutting tables pictured and you'll see how to construct one. A framework is made that holds long strips of 1/4-inch steel straps in an edge-up position, spaced an inch or two apart. The framework should be placed over some kind of fireproof container, like an old drum (sandblasted clean of any flammable residues first). This will capture the flying sparks and hot scrap pieces and keep the shop neater and safer. Another safety consideration to watch for is protection of your feet. Make sure when you are cutting out a heavy part that it isn't going to fall right on your feet. Either have a metal deflector under your cutting area, or keep your feet well away from where the very hot part is going to fall.

There will be times when you cannot start a cut at the outside edge of your workpiece, and you will have to cut from *inside* a pattern. This requires a little different technique to get the cut started. Adjust the torch to a neutral flame with the cutting lever depressed. With the lever *off*, start heating a spot on your workpiece along the cut-line. When the molten puddle starts to appear, pull the tip back about a half-inch (because this is a closed spot, there is a chance of molten metal and spark being driven back into the tip if it is too close) and slowly cut in the cutting lever. When the spot becomes a complete *hole*, you can proceed around the rest of your pattern or line.

3.53 Under a mechanized cutter, you need a grate like this to support the work while it is being cut. After some usage, the 1/4-inch by two-inch slats will be fairly cut up, but can be pulled out and swapped end for end, top for bottom or simple replaced.

Some parts cut with a torch need to have a beveled edge if they are going to be joined with another part by welding, such as when joining sections of heavy pipe. Cutting a beveled edge on a round pipe by hand is challenging, and in the pipe-fitting industry they often use a machine that clamps around the pipe. The fixture holds a cutting torch, and a motor drives the assembly around the pipe smoothly and evenly, and is adjustable for speed and the angle of the bevel. There's no place for such equipment anywhere but in the pipe business, but it's interesting to see the ways in which the human element of hand control of the torch can be eliminated with special equipment. When you do make beveled cuts in thicker metals with your torch, you should remember to size the torch tip to the measurement *across the bevel*, which is thicker than the straight thickness of the metal.

3.54 The rosebud tip will be useful for heating metal parts to be bent, freeing press-fitted parts, and for preheating castings before welding, such as here where a cast-aluminum mailbox post is preheated before TIG welding.

3.55 A great aid to cutting straight lines manually is this "compass" guide. It holds the torch tip firmly, but in a swivel arrangement that allows it to turn as you move along the line, and the torch stays the same distance from the work and much steadier. Here it is being demonstrated against another great tool, a magnetic steel guide that sticks strongly to the work and saves the hassles of setting up a bar or tube with some clamps.

Heating with oxy-acetylene

You will be surprised how easily a piece of heavy steel can be bent into a shape when it is properly heated with a torch. Even a thick piece of steel, heated to a cherry red color, can be bent like a sheet of soft copper. Your bench vise will come in very handy for projects like this. The old-time blacksmiths hand-shaped everything they made the same way, except that they had to heat the part in a coal or wood fire, while you can do the same thing in seconds with an oxy-acetylene torch.

Depending on the thickness of the metal and the area to be heated and bent, you can use a welding torch or cutting torch to heat up the workpiece. It shouldn't take too long to get the area cherry red; if it does, use a larger tip on the torch. There is another type of tip that can be used called a *rosebud*, that is expressly designed for heating. If your oxy-acetylene set was a deluxe model, such a tip may have been included, or you can easily get one at your welding supply center.

The rosebud tip has a much larger end that flows a huge amount of gas. You will have to crank your tank regulators up to perhaps 25 psi on oxygen and 10 psi for acetylene to feed this device (never exceed 15 psi on the acetylene regulator). The big, wide flame of the rosebud tip is ideal for spreading heat, and lots of it, more evenly around a part than with the tighter flame of a welding or cutting torch tip, although those can be used to heat small areas, especially if you are just freeing frozen, rusted fasteners.

The most common usage of the rosebud tip is for heating components that are press-fitted together. Heat expands metal, so logically, if you can heat up the exterior part while not heating the interior part, the heated part will expand and can be removed (with tongs). This is most commonly done in automotive or industrial situations where there is a gear pressed on a shaft, or an axle bearing must be removed. In some situations, however, you cannot simply blast the area with uncontrolled heat, or damage may occur to one of the components. You need to apply only as much heat as it will take to separate the parts, no more. Your welding supply shop should have a variety of paint-marking sticks or crayons that are designed to melt or change color at specific temperatures. One brand, called Thermomelt, is available in 87 different temperature ratings, from 100° F to 2200° F, and in a liquid, stick or pellet form. You use this product on the part you need to protect, and only heat the area until the product melts or changes color, then you work on separating the components without adding any unnecessary heat. These products are also useful when tempering or retempering tools that have been reground, which is a lengthy subject unto itself.

Deciding which type of welding equipment to buy is always a tough decision, but one that is made easiest by carefully defining your needs before buying any equipment. When you have read all the chapters in this book, you should have a good idea what the benefits and drawbacks of each system are, and what is best-suited for your work. Any weldor will tell you that the versatility of the gas-welding/cutting setup becomes valuable when you need it. Even when most of your work is done with some sort of electric-welding equipment, you'll find so many handy uses for oxyacetylene equipment that if your budget can handle it and you have enough work to utilize it, a great idea is to have the gas equipment and some form of electric welder, too.

3.56 The same tool can be used, with different attachments, to cut a perfect circle of any size from a few inches to two feet in diameter. Removing as much of the human element of hand control makes for better parts that require less grinding to finish.

Notes

4 Arc welding

One of the oldest forms of welding, arc or "stick" welding offers versatility, strength and the ability to handle big projects and thick materials. Also, introductory equipment can be purchased inexpensively. There are some rather expensive arc-welding machines, but the most common AC-current machines will do fine for the home/shop user doing standard projects and repairs.

If you have thoroughly read Chapter 2, you should have a good understanding of the various kinds of welding equipment and what each type is capable of. If you think the arc welder serves your needs, then this chapter will give you a basic introduction to the equipment and procedures involved. When shopping for a machine, you may see them referred to as SMAW welders, which is the technical description of the process and stands for Shielded Metal Arc Welding.

Basic-yet-rugged arc machines are available today in welding equipment stores, major nationwide stores such as Sears and Montgomery Ward (and their mail-order catalogs) and can sometimes be found at a good savings in large lumber/home supply centers that carry a lot of power tools. Most starter units are sold with a complete setup, including welding gloves, helmet, chipping hammer, sample electrodes, and a basic instruction book. Other than the consumable welding rods, there will be little else you will ever have to buy to continue arc-welding.

4.1 Arc welding will always be with us, as the best welding method for joining heavy plates for commercial, farm and industrial work. The weldor requires considerable protection from the spatter and radiation, usually wearing heavy leather protective gear.

4.2 For home and farm use, the Lincoln 225 is the classic AC buzz-box welder, having been in production relatively unchanged for decades. Most home/shop units are AC only, and require some rewiring to accommodate the required 220V input.

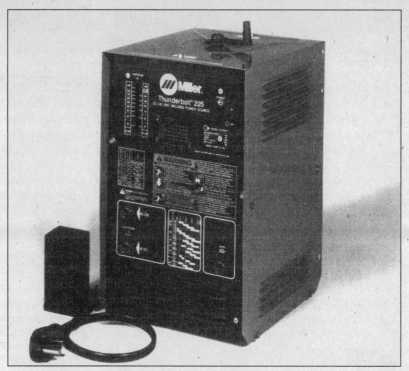

4.3 Another popular AC 220V welding machine for non-industrial use is this Miller Thunderbolt 225. The crank handle on top changes the output amperage, which is read on a scale at the top left of the front panel.

You can find arc machines priced from less than $200 to professional units costing several thousands, depending on the features, but most home/shop projects and farm repairs can be performed with machines at the lower-priced end of the spectrum. There are really no moving parts involved in the machinery, and most of the name-brand equipment is rugged enough to last for many years of service. The larger machines offer certain advantages for application in professional shop use only, such as higher amperage, AC/DC switching and higher duty-cycles.

The principle of arc-welding is to attach a ground cable to the workpiece, set the machine for the correct amperage based on the thickness of the material, fit a consumable electrode (welding rod) in the electrode holder, and with your helmet down strike the rod against the work to start a flow of current, the arc, that produces intense heat and light and welds your seam together. Welding thicker materials requires more heat in the form of higher amperage from the machine. The basic arc machines of interest to you generally have an amperage range of 40-225 amps. The arc process is best suited for thicker materials, but you will probably *never* use your machine at the higher settings. Even when welding on materials one-inch thick (which you will most likely never encounter in your home shop), or when repairing large castings, the seam isn't completed all in one big bead, it requires several passes on overlapping beads to totally join the parts.

At the same time, you will probably never use your AC welder at the lowest settings. For materials thinner than 1/8-inch, there are other welding processes more suitable, such as gas, heli-arc or MIG-welding. Most of the basic welding performed with AC arc-welding machines is done at 90-125 amps, on materials from 1/8-inch to 3/8-inch and sometimes 1/2-inch.

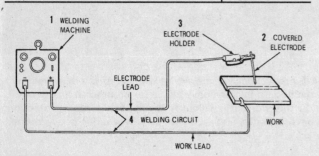

4.4 The layout of the arc-welding setup is simplicity itself. The rod (also called a stick, stinger or electrode) is both the source of the arc and the shielding gas, produced as the rod melts its flux coating.

Comparing duty cycles

What you will look for in an arc machine, therefore, is not the highest amperage it offers, but the *duty-cycle* at the 90-125-amp ranges you will use most often. We discussed the duty-cycle in chapter 2, but it bears repeating in brief. All electric welding machines have a duty-cycle rating, which refers to how long they can weld at a specific output without overheating. The duty cycle is described as a percentage. If a machine has a 100% duty cycle, it means that it can be operated virtually all day, except to stop when you change electrodes. The percentage is actually based on a ten-minute period as a test, meaning that if the duty-cycle was 50%, the machine could be used for five minutes out of ten. You could weld non-stop for five minutes and then "rest" the machine for five before starting again.

The duty-cycle rating confuses most first-time buyers, because different companies may take their published ratings from different amperage settings. The higher the amperage you weld at (for thicker material), the less the duty cycle will be. Obviously, the machine will overheat quicker at the higher amperages. On every machine's range of amperages, there is probably a point where the duty cycle is 100%. A specific machine may have a 50% duty cycle at its highest setting, yet have a 100% rating at the mid-range settings you will use most. It's important when shopping for a welder to find out what the ratings are for the high range *and* the mid-range. In the larger professional machines designed for welding shops and production-line work, the duty cycle must be close to 100% for any situation, and thus these machines have to be built with much more expensive components and reserve capacity.

Some of the duty-cycle rating comparisons may be academic for the average home/shop user. If the only long seams you weld are on thin materials at lower heat settings, most machines will be fine for your purposes, and there is no reason to spend many times more for the machine to get a higher duty rating. In a typical home/farm project, say where you are welding together steel tubing to make a utility trailer, the *setup* of the work takes half or more of your time anyway. Each welded joint between pieces of tubing may only take one or two minutes of actual welding, and then it may take you four minutes or more longer to set up clamps on the next joint or flip the work over before you're ready to make another weld. The point is that, in this example, a welding machine with a 40% duty-cycle at the amperage you were using would be perfectly adequate for the job. You wouldn't find yourself being slowed down on the job because you had to weld and then wait for the machine to "catch up." However, there is something to be said for having some duty-cycle "cushion," and if you were considering two machines in the same price range and featured similarly, you would take the one with a higher duty-cycle at the heat you would most often use it. Generally, the machine with the higher duty-cycle at a mid-point amperage will also have higher ratings at other settings.

4.5 Virtually any building over single-family-home size requires structural steel in its construction, and that requires arc welding. Here a large beam is being prepared for earthquake retrofit in a public school.

4.6 In industrial use, the arc welding is generally all DC, and you will see these venerable Lincoln welders performing their duties day in and day out for years. Most industrial machines have a 100% duty-cycle for production work. This one is housed outside in a steelyard, enclosed in a weatherproof box.

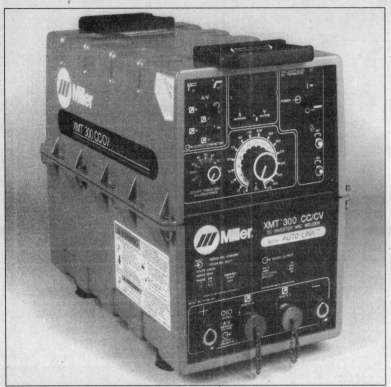

4.7 In larger welding shops, a more sophisticated power source is used, such as this 300-amp Miller DC machine, which has a few more "bells and whistles" than the home-type units.

AC, DC or both?

Most of the basic machines in stick welding are AC-powered. For those readers who may have taken electricity for granted since high-school physics classes, AC refers to *alternating current*, which is what we have in our houses, businesses, and power lines. The DC designation refers to *direct current*, for which the most common daily usage is in the 12-volt systems in our cars. When electricity was first being used in the 1890s, Thomas Edison, for all his genius in other scientific regards, was insistent on DC current being the standard for home lighting and any other usage. Unfortunately, DC current isn't practical to send any long distance through wires, and with DC every neighborhood would have to have their own power plant. The brilliant Nikola Tesla (the true inventor of the radio and many other breakthroughs) developed the alternating-current system and licensed it to Westinghouse, which became a giant corporation when AC was accepted as the world standard (AC could be sent hundreds of miles along power lines).

How AC "alternates" is by traveling in a wave, alternating in polarity up and down in a repeating cycle. Most electricity in the US alternates at a rate of 60 cycles-per-second. What all of this means to arc-welding is that the less-expensive arc-welding machines are AC-only. The AC welder is very good at producing less welding spatter, at welding heavy plates with large electrodes, requires less electricity to run and usually has less maintenance expense than bigger machines. They take the standard line current, which is high voltage but low in amperage and reduce it through a transformer to a low-voltage/high amperage current for welding. The only drawback to AC arc-welding is that the constant switching of polarity can make for tiny inconsistencies in the weld bead, imperfections you and I would never notice, but something that could be critical in an oil field pipe line, high-rise-building framework or a nuclear reactor. For this reason, most professional arc welders are DC, which produces a much smoother weld, a more stable arc and there is a wider selection of special electrodes (rods) for the DC-type professional arc welder. The AC-only machines are generally used strictly for joining ferrous metals, but the DC machines can also be used for stainless-steel and for hard-surfacing industrial parts. In addition to the two current-specific types of arc welders, there are also combination AC/DC machines, which usually have a rectifier added to a basic AC machine.

Another factor separating the larger professional machines in terms of flexibility is the choice of polarity, and the option of a TIG torch setup. In the DC mode of operation, the operator of some machines can choose between negative or positive polarity, depending on the type of metal he is welding and the rod he is using. Most DC welding is done with reverse polarity, meaning that the rod is positive, and the work clamp is negative. This method keeps the rod very hot and makes for smooth welds and improved out-of-position work (anything other than flat on your welding table). This is not of concern in using AC machines because the nature of the current is switching polarity 60 times a second anyway. Many of the professional machines are versatile power supplies that can perform arc welding, MIG-welding (with the addition of a motorized wire-feeding attachment), or TIG-welding with an optional torch and foot control **(see illustrations)**.

This is the kind of equipment you will find in professional welding/fabricating shops, but most shops today don't perform much arc welding, using their power supplies mostly for TIG welding, and using a separate machine for most wire-feed requirements. The arc-welding arena in professional welding is usually in industrial jobs or construction, pipelines, etc.

Not to confuse you any further about electricity, but the larger professional machines are often available for several types of input. The most basic machines, home or shop, require 220V, and industrial units may be set up for 440V or more, and there are different *phases* as well. The type of current we have in most homes is called single-phase. The larger professional arc welders are made in three-phase configuration, which simply means that there are three identical inputs spaced 120 electrical degrees apart. The waves in these inputs overlap, so that voltage never falls completely to zero, making for smoother welds. Many industrial shops have big motors on lathes, mills and other machinery that run on three-phase power, which is smoother and cheaper to operate on large equipment. We will not find three-phase power at home, and some expensive equipment is required to set up a building for industrial three-phase power.

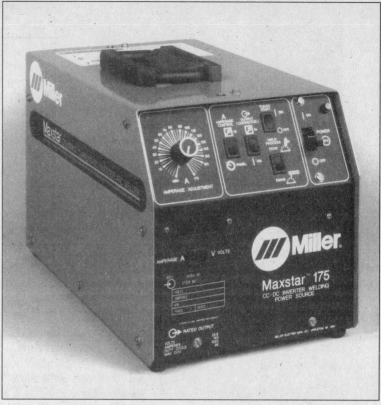

4.8 Many shops utilize a "power source" machine which not only powers arc welding work, but can be set up to take a TIG torch, and some can use an optional wire-drive to perform MIG welding.

Rewiring for an arc welder

Except for a few small, household-current machines capable of 100 amps or less, even the most basic AC arc welders require 220V input. Depending on the present wiring of your house, this may require an additional expense in rewiring to accommodate the welder, a factor to take into consideration when choosing the right system for you. Some homes already have a 220V outlet for hooking up an electric clothes dryer or stove (the most common household appliances to run on this voltage), but this outlet may not be where you need to weld. If your washer/dryer setup is in the garage, you're ahead of the game, and rewiring may not be necessary. Likewise, if you plan to do most of your welding in the kitchen, then your case is simplified.

If you have to run a new circuit in your house to put 220V where you need it for the arc welder, put it on it's own separate circuit with a 30-amp circuit-breaker. The kind of current you may be drawing when welding thick material may blow a standard 15 or 20-amp household breaker. Call a few electricians before you buy an arc welder. Tell them what size electrical box you have (how many amps), how many open spaces there are for new circuits, and how far a new 220V circuit would have to be run to get an outlet in your proposed welding area. They should be able to give you a rough estimate of the rewiring costs. It may cost as much or more than the welder itself, and may ultimately influence

4.9 Contractors often use an engine-driven arc welder mounted on a truck bed or a small trailer. Besides powering the welder, the gas engine also has a large generator to run power tools in a remote work site.

4.10 Even if you do have a 220V circuit in your shop for a clothes dryer, you'll find the outlet prongs are different on a 220V welder's plug. You either have to rewire your outlet box to accept a welding plug, put a household 220V plug on the welder's power cable, or use an adapter.

what kind of welding machine you finally purchase.

Even if you do have an existing 220V outlet you can use, you'll be rudely surprised when you find the welder can't be plugged in, at least not directly. The arrangement of prongs on the welder's power cable is slightly different than the layout of the typical 220V home appliance plug. You can make or purchase an adapter, or have the electrician install an outlet box in your welding area that matches the kind of plug on your arc welder **(see illustration)**. Before plugging a new stick welder into a household 220V outlet with an adapter, you should have the system checked to be sure the wire gauge and circuit-breaker are up to the task of handling a welding machine.

The arc process

All electrical-welding processes use the flow of electricity to create heat. The power flows from the torch or electrode to the work, which is grounded to the source at the machine. In arc welding, the consumable electrode or rod makes the connection that creates the arc to the piece being welded. The welding rod is a metal rod coated with a hard flux material. As the arc is created when the tip of the metal comes to the workpiece, the heat generated at the bead is 6000° F or more, which melts both the parent metal and the filler rod, while simultaneously vaporizing the flux coating to create a gas shield around the bead, protecting the solidifying weld from contamination by gasses in the air **(see illustrations)**. The flux actually re-solidifies on top of the bead as a hard coating of flux and slag, and when you look at a completed bead, you'll see a dome of ceramic-like material over the weld. At this point, the weld doesn't look very impressive, but when you remove the slag with a chipping hammer, a beautiful, clean bead is revealed **(see illustrations)**. Depending on the type of rod and amperage used, there may also be some spatter (tiny beads of metal) stuck alongside the bead. Most of these beads will come off with stiff application of a wire brush, and more stubborn ones can be removed with the

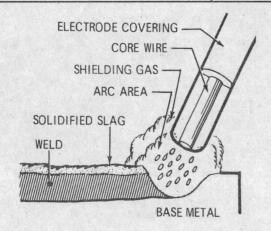

4.11 Arc-welding electrodes or rods are a metal wire, covered with a flux coating. The metal wire must make initial contact with the work to initiate the arc, then it is pulled back to a proper rod-to-work distance. the vaporizing flux makes a shielding gas, but also deposits a layer of slag over the weld as it forms, to further protect the weld from contamination.

4.12 This is what you will see through your helmet and welding lens. The arc is intensely bright, but the lens cuts this down to just a bright glow around the arc itself. here you can just about see where the shielding gas cloud forms around the arc.

4.13 The slag formed over the weld bead must be removed with a chipping hammer like this, and most spatter and slag residue can be cleaned up with a wire brush after chipping.

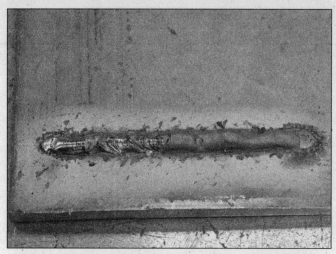

4.14 At right on this bead, you can see the dark gray slag coating covering the weld. The portion at the left has been chipped off to reveal a bright, shiny weld.

chipping hammer or a chisel.

Making your first passes with the AC stick welder will be relatively easy, although really good passes will require considerable practice. The instruction book that comes with your welder will specify the right rods to use for various materials, and the amperage to set for different thicknesses of ferrous metal. The rest of the technique is finding the most comfortable position for your electrode-holder hand, and maintaining the proper arc distance and travel speed to make good joints.

Safety considerations

With every method of welding, safety is of paramount consideration, but each type has precautions that apply to that type of equipment in particular. In all forms of electric welding, including arc welding, high-amperage electrical current is the primary hazard. All of your cables, plugs and leads should be inspected regularly for any signs of defects. Even dirt or paint overspray on connections can cause arcing and poor welds. Water, of course, is a good conductor of electricity, and therefore should be avoided in the work area. Your clothing, equipment and especially the floor must be kept dry to avoid the possibility of electrical shock. Rubber-soled shoes are recommended, but athletic shoes (non-leather) are not. Most experts will tell you not to wear metal jewelry such as watchbands, rings, bracelets, necklaces or belt buckles when welding. If electric-welder power comes into contact with metal articles you are wearing, they can become instantly hot to the point of melting, or can cause electric shock.

Of the electric welding methods, arc welding requires the most protection of your face and body during welding. The intensity of the arc produces strong UV and infrared radiation. Any skin exposed during the welding process can become burned, in severity ranging from mild sunburn to serious burns, with the symptoms not appearing until eight hours after the exposure. Leave the top button unbuttoned on your shift and you'll have a nasty V-shaped burn on your neck after only a short while arc-welding. Likewise, wear fire-resistant, long-sleeved shirts, and keep your sleeves rolled down at all times. Keep these shirts just for welding, and tear off the pockets if they have any, or keep them empty and buttoned. An experienced weldor friend of ours was recently burned painfully when welding overhead with just a shop shirt on — a hot bead of spatter went right into his shirt pocket and burned into his chest. Without the pockets, there's a chance the bead will roll off onto the floor rather than stay in one spot on your shirt. For this

4.15 The arc spatter and radiation are dangerous. Do not allow any bystanders to observe the arc while you are welding. Also, notice how much smoke is around the weldor's helmet here. The fumes are dangerous and you should have an electric fan of some kind to blow it away from you when you are welding in a corner like this.

same reason, your pants should be kept uncuffed, and never tucked into your boots.

If you are going to be doing arc-welding often, we'd recommend you invest in some leather safety clothing, like jackets, vests or pull-on sleeves that go over your regular shirt. Arc-welding is prone to more spattering than other types of welding, and these leather weldor's clothes are highly resistant to arc spatter.

Probably your most sensitive and fragile body parts exposed to welding dangers are your eyes. Even the tiniest bit of spatter in an unprotected eye can have truly long-lasting negative effects. Always wear a full-coverage safety helmet when welding, preferably with a leather flap at the bottom-front that protects your neck area. Especially when welding overhead, like underneath a vehicle, wear a cloth cap backwards (bill to back) to cover your hair and the back of your neck. Your helmet should be equipped with the proper safety lens for the type of welding you are doing, or your eyes could receive overexposure of UV and infrared rays in a very short time. Never observe *anyone else* doing arc-welding unless you are wearing proper eye protection, and make sure that when you are welding that there is no one observing you who could be hurt by watching, particularly children. Watching too much arc will not show immediate effects, but later the affected eyes will be sore, and with a sensation almost like having lots of sand in your eyes. If you do not yet have your own welder, but want to watch someone else work, get your own helmet to observe through. If you do have a welder, you may want to keep a spare helmet around in case someone wants to observe *your* welding prowess.

Your eyes can be permanently damaged by overexposure to arc rays, but they must also be protected when working around most shop equipment, such as grinders, mills, drills and sanders, all equipment that may be involved in your welding project. Keep several pair of good safety glasses around your shop, the kind that have protection all the way around the sides. After arc-welding, you will also want to wear these safety glasses when chipping slag from your welds. The little fragments that break off are like glass. Always keep a very complete first-aid kit accessible in your work area in case of accidents.

A particular hazard with arc welding is the presence of fumes. When the electrode is consumed, the flux is vaporized, creating the shielding gasses that protect the weld from contamination during formation. Depending on the metal being welded, other gasses may be released as the metal is melted. Most welding gasses are colorless, odorless, tasteless and inert, but this is not to imply that they are harmless. Any of the common welding gasses can displace oxygen, and when you are breathing in air that contains less than 18% oxygen, you may experience dizziness, or even lose consciousness. For this reason, arc welding, or any welding process, should be performed only where there is adequate ventilation. In the case of arc welding, there is less chance of the shielding gasses being blown away and causing a bad weld, so if you find yourself welding in one spot too long, or in a confined area, you can use a household fan somewhere in your work area to maintain air circulation.

Beginning arc welding

If you have already read the previous chapter on gas welding, what you will have learned in practicing that mode will help you greatly in learning all other forms of welding, including arc. Stick (arc) welding is easier in some ways than gas-torch welding, and more difficult in others. Practice and more practice will put you on the road to good welding in any mode.

What you will find different at first about arc welding is that you only need one hand. The electrode holder and its electrode or rod is *it*, other than the ground clamp, which should be clamped to your workpiece or your steel welding table. The rod is both the source of filler metal and the shielding gasses, which are generated when the flux covering is vaporized. Have some scrap steel handy and some 1/8-inch rods. There are a great many specialized rods, but one of the most common is an E-6011, which is one of the easier rods to start and maintain an arc with. Although the arc process only involves the one hand-held tool, you may find that the 14-inch-long rods put your hand a much further distance from the weld area than the other welding processes. One end of the rod is bare of any flux coating for about an inch, this is the end you put in the electrode holder.

It's a good idea to practice the arc "setup" *without* turning on the welding machine. Just situate yourself comfortably in relation to the work, and practice holding the electrode 1/4-inch away from your work joint or seam area, following the proposed seam while slightly weaving the electrode tip side to side as you travel along. This will give a feel for what is required in terms of coordination.

Now if you're ready, set the machine for the right amperage for the thickness of your scrap steel, say 1/4-inch steel plates, or perhaps slightly hotter than the instructions recommend to make it easier to learn the starting procedure. One drawback of the arc-welding process is getting the arc *started*. You can't just flip down your helmet or lens and stab the rod against the work.

The starting procedure has been described as similar to striking a match, in which you draw the rod tip across the area you plan to start the bead. At some point in your "scratch" the rod will momentarily contact the work and the arc will start, but the rod must continue moving. Arc welding is essentially a process of creating a short-circuit across the rod and the work, and it can only be started by a momentary contact of the two. Once started, this short-circuit heats the air around the weld and ionizes it to the point where the air conducts electricity and continues the arc without actual metal-to-metal contact. As soon as the arc starts, the rod tip must be pulled back to the suggested tip-to-work distance. All of this sounds tedious and difficult, but you *will* pick the technique up in the first half-hour of practice.

If you touch the rod to the surface for more than a split second, it may stick firmly, in which case the rod can get red-hot for its whole length in a very short span of time. As soon as you feel the rod stick to the surface, squeeze the clamp on your electrode holder to release the rod, which is the only way to stop the rod from melting. The hot rod will stay stuck to your work. You can take it off with some pliers, but when it is really hot, don't try snapping it off with your gloves, it may burn right through the leather. Let that rod cool off and start another rod until your have mastered the arc-starting process. When you are more experienced, you'll react quickly enough to a stuck rod that you can simply break the connection immediately by twisting the electrode holder and rod side to side.

Another method of arc starting favored by some weldors is a "tapping" style, in which you quickly tap the electrode tip to the work to start the arc, not in a "pressing" action, but in a short in-and-out jerk that makes contact at the bottom of the tip's travel toward the work.

Once you understand the starting process, the tip to work distance is next. When the arc starts, you must pull the rod back for a second to make a relatively-long arc (about twice the thickness of the electrode you are using) as a way of inducing some preheat into the metal, then immediately drop the rod closer, to about one rod-thickness away from the work. Keep the rod moving along the seam, and move the rod side-to-side slightly as you travel. Some weldors use a movement like a series of tiny, overlapping ovals, others a zigzag or even a "weaving" pattern. Stay in one place too long or with the rod tip too close to the work, and you'll melt a hole in your work; also, if you pull the rod back too far, you can lose the arc process and have to restart. On small seams in thin materials, you won't need to weave the rod much. When joining thick materials, the joint is usually Vee'd or beveled, and a straight pass is made along the bottom of the joint, followed by one or more passes where the oscillation or weaving of the tip spreads the bead circles out larger in the wider gap at the top of the bevel.

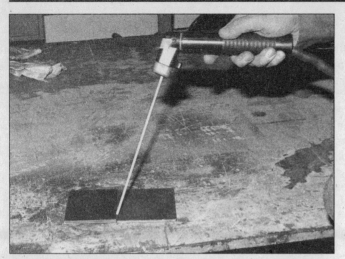

4.16 The electrode is usually held more or less perpendicular to the welding surface to start the arc, then laid back to continue the bead. Some weldors prefer a forehand technique, others a backhand direction, such as here.

The rod should be more or less vertical when the arc is struck initially, where it can really preheat the metal, but should be angled forward (in the direction of travel) 20-30 degrees as you make your pass, i.e. you hold the electrode holder somewhat ahead of the puddle, with the rod 20-30 degrees from vertical **(see illustration)**. Try making some straight passes along a flat, horizontal plate, until you get the hang of running a bead. Run a straight bead with the puddles being about twice the diameter of the rod you are using. While you are welding, it is important to remember not to watch the arc, but rather focus on the puddle you are leaving behind it. The shape, size and crown of the puddle are the keys to determine how you are doing.

When you have the travel speed, amperage and rod-to-work distance correct, you'll find out why they used to call an AC arc welder a "buzz box," because you'll get a very satisfying sound, which is a steady, crisp noise something like bacon frying. This sound your welder makes, and the way the bead looks will tell you much about your progress. If you have the arc gap too large, you'll have uneven puddling, a bead that is too wide, and the sound will be uneven. Such a weld will have more than normal spatter. On the other hand, if you have the rod tip too close, it may stick to the work, the bead will be high but not very wide and the sound will be softer.

One of the hard parts to learn here compared to gas welding is that the part you are holding, the electrode holder, must continually be brought closer to the work as the rod gets shorter, while in gas welding the torch stays the same distance from the welding. The hand-eye coordination you must learn involves keeping the tip the right distance from the work, the rod at the right angle, the correct speed of travel, and compensating for the shortening of the rod. Speaking of electrode length, when the rod gets fairly short, it's best to stop and then re-start with a new rod. When the electrodes are too short, a lot of extra heat travels to the electrode holder and your gloved hand.

The speed you travel is almost as important as the rod-to-work distance. If you travel too fast, the resulting bead will be too narrow, and you may not get 100% penetration. If you proceed too slowly, you'll wind up with a large bead,

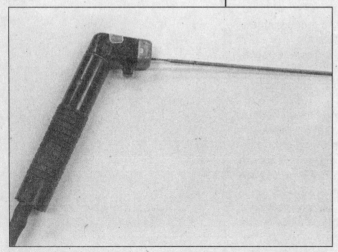

4.17 Arc-welding electrode holders are usually a clamp-like affair, with notches to allow the rod to be clamped at several different angles. Many arc weldors prefer this style, called a short-stub, in which the rod is inserted and the handle is twisted to lock the rod in place.

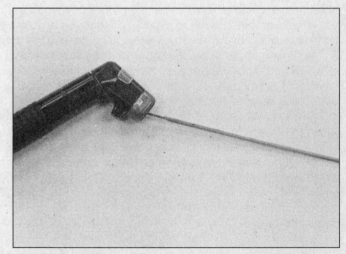

4.18 To achieve a different rod angle with a short-stub electrode-holder, just bend the rod near the holder to the desired angle. In some situation, where you have to reach down inside something to weld, the rod can be bent straight out.

and you may induce excessive heat into the workpiece. After you have practiced speed and arc-to-work distance, practice stopping and starting a bead. In real-world welding, you will encounter seams that take several sticks to complete, but you want the completed weld to look continuous even if it wasn't. To stop a bead, when you have to change electrodes for instance, just pull the rod back up quickly to break the arc. Any time you stop arc welding, you must chip the slag away from the place you last stopped, before continuing with a new rod. When you pick-up again with the new rod, start about 1/2-inch ahead of where the last puddle was and re-strike your arc and proceed. The arc will melt the original "last puddle" and continue the bead without any apparent interruption. This will take some practice. If you have seen professionally-welded seams, they look like they were applied by a continuously-operating machine, so integrated are the stops and starts, and that's what you are shooting for.

Types of joints

After you are experienced at making straight beads on plates lying flat in front of you, begin to practice on joints between two pieces. The simplest to learn on are butt joints. If the material is 1/4-inch or thicker, you should bevel the edges of both parts before welding. As with any parts to be welded, either ferrous or nonferrous, cleanliness of the work is very important to making a sound weld, so grind the pieces to be joined not just on the bevel, but at least 1/2-inch on either side of the joint, so that impurities don't contaminate the weld.

Most seams are started by tacking the parts together at either end and perhaps several places along the way, depending on how long the seam is. Because of the growth of the parts from the heat of welding, you may need to "build-in" a gap between them during the tacking phase. Some weldors place a small piece of bare copper wire between the two parts, tack one end, and then move the wire "spacer" to where the next tack will be, continuing so that the two parts are tacked slightly apart from each other with an even gap. As you weld up the seam, the parts will "grow" together. Whenever we mention tack-welding in conjunction with arc welding, remember that the slag must be chipped and wire-brushed away from the tacks before you "connect the dots" with continuous welds.

Depending on the thickness of the material you are working on, you may make a two-pass weld, one on the top and one on the bottom. This would only be feasible on plates, not on pipe or tubing, but makes for a very strong joint, and the opposing forces of distortion may keep the parts flatter than if you made only one large pass on one side. Looking at an end view of the plates, the first pass should go into the joint a little more than halfway, then the second weld on the other side should bite into that first bead for a completely-welded joint. Usually, such joints do not require as high an amperage setting on the welder as for making a single-pass weld.

One of the common uses of arc-welding equipment is in farming and ranching, where the equipment being repaired is usually too large to bring into the shop. That means that most welding that requires a bottle of shielding gas may be too susceptible to wind to be effective, and the arc-welding

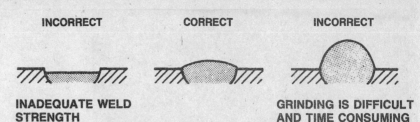

INCORRECT   **CORRECT**   **INCORRECT**

INADEQUATE WELD STRENGTH   **GRINDING IS DIFFICULT AND TIME CONSUMING**

4.19 Too much amperage and the bead will sink too far into the work and leave cratering or undercutting on the top. If your welding speed is too slow, the bead can build up unnecessarily on top.

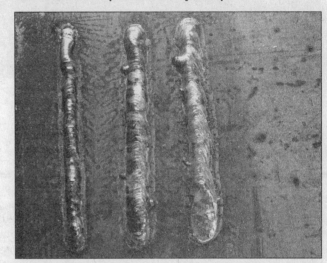

4.20 In these three practice arc-welding beads, the left-hand bead was too "cold", meaning not enough amperage. The center weld is OK, and the right has too much amperage, with increased spatter and too wide a bead for the thickness of the material.

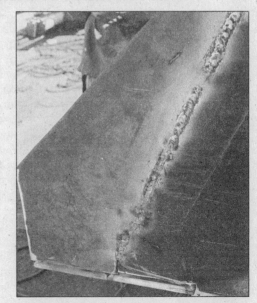

4.21 Welding large plates, such as here where new metal is being added to a John Deere dirt scoop, requires either multi-pass welding, or using a large rod at high amperages. This seam was done with a single pass with 1/4-inch electrodes.

4.22 Here half-inch plate on the sides was welded with one pass, but a gap was left where the one-inch, beveled lower plates join. The bigger plate will be welded with several passes and strength is improved if the joint starts all the way at the ends.

4.23 An outside corner weld on 5/16-inch plates is made with one pass with a wide weaving pattern, spread equal heat on both parts.

process is advantageous here. Also, most farm equipment is rather heavy, with large components, and arc welding's ability to fill large breaks, weld castings, and deposit large quantities of filler metal if needed makes arc a good choice. The visual beauty of the welds is seldom a factor in agricultural repairs: it's getting the equipment back into service that counts. Building up of worn agricultural parts is a common task in which the weldor makes repeated beads right next to each other to literally build a new and higher surface on the part. The work is tedious, but necessary.

Generally, you make the first pass in normal welding mode, then make succeeding passes with the electrode held at a slight side angle to the work. Remember than when arc welding, the hot filler metal is virtually sprayed off the end of the rod like a spray gun, and where you aim the rod is where the metal will be deposited. The slight side angle allows the succeeding passes to bite slightly into the previous bead. Alternate the direction of the beads and overlap them about one-third of the bead width. There are even special rods made that deposit a hard-facing on metal. These can be used to renew or create a hard cutting edge on a part, which can be later ground or filed to an edge that will stay sharper longer than the parent metal. When making any kind of 'buildup' welds, each bead must be chipped clean before you begin the next pass, or slag and impurities could be trapped by the next bead. Also, when you are building up a part, rather than fusing a seam as in regular welding, you can run the bead much wider than we have suggested so far. The idea here is not to fuse two parts but to deposit as much metal as possible onto the surface. In these cases, you can "weave" the rod tip back and forth in a zigzag or other pattern to make a wider bead.

You will find that "out-of-position" welds, welds that are not made with the parts lying flat in front of you on the welding table, are the toughest to learn. Corner joints, vertical seams and overhead seams offer increasing levels of challenge. Corner joints are commonly found when joining two plates where one plate is perpendicular to the other, like a T. The electrode should be at a 45° angle between the two parts, so that equal heat and filler metal is directed onto both pieces. In some cases, you may find you have to place the arc such that it puts more heat on the bottom plate (which is dissipating more heat from the joint) while aiming the electrode "spray" more at the upper plate to avoid "undercutting". which is when you see a slight crevice along one or both edges of a welded joint after you chip the slag away.

4.24 This sample weld shows how large plates are joined by multiple passes with large rods. Compare this front view (right) where the weld passes began, to the cutaway photo (left) which illustrates how integrated and free of contaminants even such a large weld can be.

If you are joining heavy plates, the fillet weld may take three passes, in which case the first bead is put right into the corner, then a second pass is made alongside that one with the electrode aimed to "spray" slightly more toward the side between this bead and the corner's edge, and the third pass is aimed to the opposite side of the center **(see illustrations)**. If, on the other hand, you are welding a thick plate to a thinner one, then favor the angle of the electrode towards the heavier plate to give it more heat. In practicing such welds, it may be advantageous to use plates that are only an inch or two by six inches. This will make for less work when cutting a cross-section through them afterwards to examine your weld for penetration and lack of voids or impurities, especially if you have to hand-hacksaw through them.

While basic, flat butt joints are most common in typical home/shop projects, the Tee or fillet joint and the lap joint make up the majority of welds in industry and construction. The lap joint, where one plate lays on top of another, is approached much like the Tee joint, with the electrode angle at about 45°, aimed at the inside corner where the two plates meet. If they are different thicknesses, then the electrode may need to be aimed to give more heat to the heavier piece. Another difference between industry and home projects is that you will seldom encounter any joint that requires more than one pass to complete in a home/shop project. The use of really thick plates just isn't that common in automotive, arts and crafts or making shop equipment, with the possible exception of building an engine stand, which might have a half-inch plate welded to a tube for the part the engine-holding arms attach to. This is one reason that arc-welding isn't that common anymore as a home/shop tool. Other methods seem better suited to the thinner materials encountered in hobby projects, though farm equipment repair does sometimes require the large-scale abilities of an arc welder.

Choosing electrodes

Your home AC arc-welder will probably come with an assortment of basic welding rods to practice with. After that you'll have to shop at your local welding supply or order from a catalog, and you should have a good idea by then of what type and thicknesses of metals you'll be working on, and thus what size and type of rods to use. Your local supplier should be able to give you good advice on what best suits your purposes. As you read or talk with other people about arc-welding, you may hear the rods termed any of the following: stinger, rod, elec-

4.25 Some arc rods melt the wire at a faster rate than the flux, leaving the wire recessed inside. During the welding, this makes a more concentrated arc spray. When re-striking an arc with such a rod, the extra flux around the tip must be broken off with your gloved fingers or pliers (with the rod cooled off) to expose the metal for re-striking the arc.

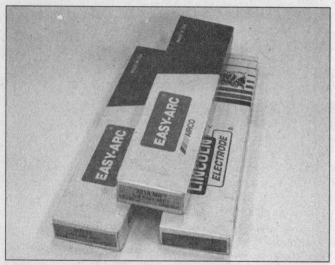

4.26 You'll find a wide variety of electrodes at your welding supply store, but there are only a few rods you will use in normal home/shop projects on mild steel. Don't buy much more than you will need for the next project.

trode or stick. They all mean the same thing.

While there is a confusing array of arc-welding electrodes on the market, the bulk of them are specifically designed for industrial and other specialty usage, and you will never have a call for them. There are perhaps only a half dozen rods that would cover your needs. Rods differ in the type and diameter the central metal wire is made of, and in the thickness and composition of the coating of flux as well. In actual use, the flux burns away at a slower rate than the rod inside, which makes for a sort of "collar" around the tip of the rod, further shielding the weld process and helping concentrate and direct the "spray" of metal coming off the wire **(see illustration)**.

Many of the hundreds of special-purpose arc rods are designed strictly for the professional DC welder, so you won't have to worry about those if you're using a typical 220V home AC welder. For your needs, there are perhaps three types you will use the most. Of these, E-6011 is the designation for what is the most commonly-used electrode. It is one of the easiest for a beginner to master, can be used on AC or DC, in virtually all positions of welding, and can be used in situations where the parent metal hasn't been prepared spotlessly. It's main drawback is that it produces a lot of spatter. Where the *appearance* of the weld is less important than the ability to make a strong joint on rough or dirty materials, such as in farm equipment repairs, this is a good choice. After practicing with this one, you may want to move on to more "sophisticated" electrodes. The E-6013 rod works great in many situations, and, although it requires better surface preparation and cleaning than the 6011 rod, it will produce much better looking welds, is suitable for a variety of positions and handles metals up to 3/16-inch thickness with most home-type buzz-boxes. It can be used for lots of projects like building shop equipment, and there are even variations on this rod from different manufacturers that are specifically for sheet-metal work, in sizes down to 1/16-inch. When the size of a welding rod is mentioned, it refers only to the diameter of the wire *inside*. Obviously, the flux coating makes the rod appear much thicker, and if you need to check a rod, measure the bare end meant to go into the electrode holder.

There has been a variety of methods used in the past to identify welding rods, including numbers and color codes, but most rods you find today have both a number and code from the manufacturer, as well as a standard A.W.S. number, such as E-6013 **(see illustration)**. These standard designations come from the American Welding Society and should be easy to find somewhere on the boxes of rod you buy. The E stands for electrode (for arc welding), the 60 part is multiplied by 1000 to give you the tensile strength of the wire (in this case, 60,000 psi), the next digit is a code for the type of position the rod is recommended for, and the last digit refers to the type and polarity of the current required. The 1 in our example in the "position" spot indicates the rod is good in all positions, a 2 would mean flat position. The last number indicates that this rod can be used with AC or DC, and on DC can be used with straight or reverse polarity, though straight polarity is seldom used.

Another good rod for starting out is E-7014, which is higher in strength and produces good-looking beads. It and the E-6013 mentioned earlier require a little different arc procedure than what we have described so far. These are called "contact rods" because, instead of maintaining a basic 1/8-inch gap as you go along, you keep the tip just in contact with the parent metal, in a sense dragging the rod lightly along the seam.

A special-purpose rod used in repairing cast-iron, such as automotive blocks, cracked heads, transmission cases, and various farm equipment, is EST, although there are several brand names in the trade just for cast-iron rod. Most rods for this purpose have a high nickel content. Although these rods are available, it doesn't mean that cast-iron welding is easy. Any cast part should be thoroughly preheated to 400° F or better to prevent cracking after the localized heat of welding is induced into the part. Parts, depending on their size, can be heated in an oven or with a rosebud tip on an oxy-acetylene torch, using temperature indicating paints to tell when you have it evenly heated to the proper temperature. Even then, there can be cracking problems. It can be very difficult to get a cracked cast-iron part thoroughly cleaned before welding, usually requiring a deep Vee to make a good repair. Better success on cast iron may be had by welding in short strips 1/2 to 3/4-inch long, with the part cleaned and allowed to cool off in between. In automotive use, broken cast-iron exhaust manifolds are a common repair item, and the high-nickel rods can be used successfully, but a well-used exhaust manifold needs to be sandblasted inside and out beforehand to get rid of as much of the carbon baked into the pores of the casting as possible. Usually, a brand-new casting will take a much-longer-lasting weld, such as when modifying manifolds to accept turbocharger flanges. Most small cast-iron repairs are better made with brazing by an oxy-acetylene torch, where much less heat is introduced, although the part should still be preheated.

Arc-welding electrodes are also marked with color codes. Usually, the flux coating itself is a different color to indicate a type, as well as markings or dabs of colors near the tip. The E-6011 has a white flux coating and a blue spot color, E-6013 is a dark tan with a brown spot, etc.

Proper storage of electrodes is critical to their performance (see illustration). They are very susceptible to moisture, and must be stored in a perfectly dry environment. Once they absorb moisture, the flux coating tends to loosen and flake off, and the rod is useless. In large production operations where critical welding is done, the rods are stored in a special oven that keeps them at a constant 100° F or more to ensure that they are dry, and only enough rod that will be used in a few hours is removed at one time from the oven.

In a home/shop situation, buy only as much rod as you think you need to keep around for unexpected projects, a few pounds of each type you normally use. Keep these in either sealable metal cans or plastic bags with desiccant inside. Desiccant is a moisture-absorbing compound, the stuff we always find packed in little "teabags" with electronic components and camera equipment. You can save up these bags whenever you get a new electronic goodie. The bags can be dried out in the oven for a short while, then put into the container holding your welding rods. If you have a bigger project in mind, buy what you need for that project only, fresh from the welding supply, and don't keep any large quantities around. We have seen a variety of methods used by weldors to keep electrodes dry, including racks of custom-built metal tubes with screwcaps.

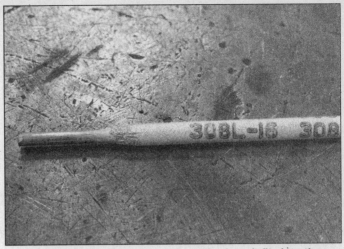

4.27 This is the bare end of the rod, where it fits into the electrode holder. You can judge the size of a rod from this bare end - don't measure the flux coating. Rods are marked as to their type and color-coded.

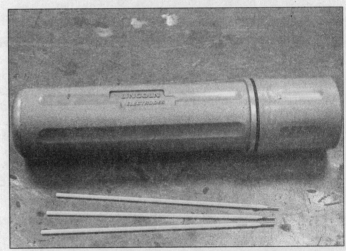

4.28 Rods must be kept dry for the flux coatings to work properly. Keep only as much rod as you need, and store them in a tight container such as this Lincoln plastic rod box with gasketed screw cap.

4.29 These L-TEC portable arc power sources are lightweight, and offer up to 90 amps on the STW 90i (right) and 130 amps on the STW 140i. Unlike most small arc welders, these are DC, and can even be set up with a torch and power adapter to run a TIG torch. They are available for 110V or 220V input.

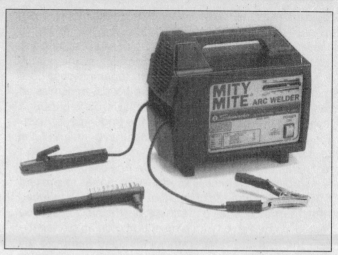

4.30 The Eastwood Company markets a lot of equipment and supplies for auto restoration, and this is their small 110V arc welder. At its maximum of 70 amps, it delivers a 10% duty-cycle, so you won't be welding any bridges together, but it only weighs 26 pounds, so it's extremely portable and welds up to 3/16-inch.

If you have reviewed the above introduction to arc-welding, you should have a good idea by now of whether it will suit your particular welding needs. It can be both easy-to-learn and challenging, simple and complicated, and can produce results from "farm-grade" (where strength is primary) to automotive-quality to atomic-reactor quality. It has the advantage of simple operation, low maintenance, low initial cost (not considering the cost of rewiring for 220V if necessary), and the unmatched ability to weld outdoors without being affected by wind, making it suitable for structural-steel construction, pipelines, iron-fence work, and farm repairs, as well as being the best choice for welding and repairing thick materials.

4.31 Auto manufacturers build cars with spot-welding machines, and with Eastwood Company's spot-welder gun, you can repair one the same way. The replaceable electrodes last for 60-100 welds.

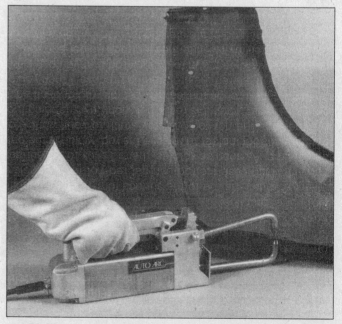

4.32 The spot welder is a self-contained mini-arc-welder, designed for joining sheet-metal panels on auto body work.

5 MIG welding

Welding books written as recently as ten years ago may have recommended oxy-acetylene and arc-welding equipment as the basic tools for home/shop welding. At that time, MIG, or *wire-feed*, welding equipment was considered too expensive for amateur use, despite its advantages. The MIG equipment was recommended, and indeed was originally designed, for high-production shop work only. Much has changed in the intervening years, and the introduction of lower-cost MIG units and the competitiveness of the marketplace has brought wire-feed welding into an affordable range for the home/shop weldor.

An outgrowth of arc welding, the MIG process was conceived as a way to speed up production in industrial applications. The basic difference with MIG, which stands for Metal Inert Gas welding (sometimes also referred to by its technical description as Gas Metal Arc Welding, or GMAW), is that the welding filler rod is automatically fed through the gun whenever welding takes place. The weldor doesn't need to stop to change arc electrodes. The Airco company developed the MIG process

5.1 The use of wire-feed MIG welding has expanded greatly in the last ten years to encompass body shops, muffler shops, race-car builders and home hobbyists as well as the industrial production work it was designed for. It has advantages of speed, simplicity, cleanliness, and the ability to work well on thick and thin materials.

5.2 Among the compact MIG welders in the 110V field is the L-TEC MIG 130, which features 100% duty-cycle at its 30 amp setting for thin material, and has a 25% duty-cycle at 130 amps. It's designed for body shops, hobbyists and light maintenance use.

5.3 For the larger-scale shop, the heavy-duty 220V machines like this Migmaster 250 offer more amperage, more amp settings, higher duty cycles, and various extra features for timing various weld functions.

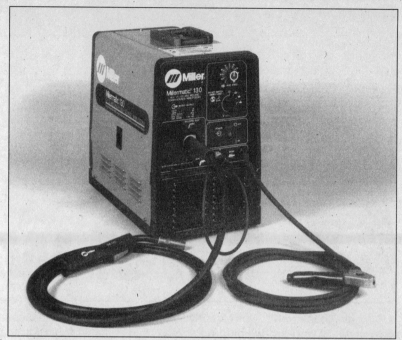

5.4 The Miller Electric Co. makes a variety of larger professional welding machines, but they also offer this Millermatic 130, which has a 20% duty cycle at its maximum 130 amps, putting it right in the midst of the 110V home/shop MIGs.

right after W.W.II, and it has been refined continuously ever since.

The many advantages of the MIG process, besides the basic one of not having to stop to change electrodes, include: being able to weld in all positions; there is no slag removal and the welds are much cleaner and with very little spatter compared to arc welding; the welding can proceed a lot faster than with other methods because the wire-feed rate is automatic and adjustable, which also makes for less distortion of the workpiece because less heat is concentrated on the seam; the process works well on joints that are irregular or have gaps; and the amperage, wire size and wire-feed speed can be tuned down to do ideal, almost distortionless welds on thin sheet metal. There are more advantages that relate to how the weldor uses the equipment, and we'll see these points as we continue.

There are technically three different processes of metal transfer with MIG welding equipment, but the one we are concerned with is called the *short-arc* or short-circuit process. The other types are used in larger industrial welding processes where high amperages and large-diameter welding wire is used. Most of the MIG machines suitable for home/shop use are designed for short-arc process, where the molten end of the welding wire touches the weld puddle and creates a short-circuit, and the wire diameters are from .023-inch to .045-inch. Amperages in these machines are seldom higher than 225 amps yet can handle materials from the thinnest auto-body sheet metal to plates as thick as 1/2-inch, a range that certainly covers everything the home/shop weldor, metal sculptor, body man, farmer or ornamental iron worker will have a call for.

In the short-arc process, the basic components of the MIG equipment consist of the welding machine, which contains an AC-to-DC rectifier with constant voltage potential and a wire-feeding mechanism that holds a large roll of wire, a bottle of shielding gas (in most models), a welding cable that routes wire, power and gas to the torch, a simple trigger-operated torch or gun and a ground or work cable. In operation, the weldor brings the torch down to the work until the bare wire electrode, which sticks out of the gun 1/2 to 3/4-inch, is touching the

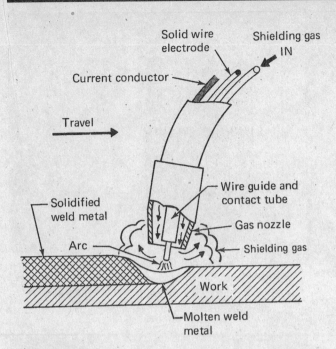

5.6 There are very few user controls on the panel of a basic MIG welder, just a switch for the different amperage settings, and a variable knob for controlling the wire-feed speed.

5.5 The cable leading to the MIG torch has to carry several different materials, from the electrical current, to the wire electrode and the shielding gas. The torch itself is rather simple, feeding the wire out to maintain a short-circuit arc against the work, while keeping the weld under an envelope of shielding gas.

work where the seam is to be; he then flips his helmet or lens down and pulls the trigger. The trigger immediately puts power to the wire, which arcs against the work to create very localized heat while shielding gas is simultaneously released that puts a shielding "envelope" over the forming weld, preventing contamination (see illustration). The short-arc process actually is alternately melting and not melting the electrode wire about 90 times a second. Each time the wire touches the work it melts and creates a gap between itself and the work, which is when a drop of molten wire attaches to the work and blends in. The constant arc-on-arc-off is what gives the MIG process its characteristic "sizzling" sound when you weld with the correct wire speed, amperage and travel speed. The current used is DC with reverse polarity (like most of the professional arc-welding machines), which provides for deep penetration. Only a few applications and machines have the straight polarity option, and this is only for shallow-penetration work where the coverage or speed of deposition is most important.

The weldor has few controls to worry about in setting up a MIG machine. There is a voltage knob or switch to control the current, and a wire-speed knob that determines how fast the welding wire comes out of the gun (see illustration). Selecting the amperage is based mostly on the thickness of the material to be welded. A rule of thumb from the Miller Electric Company is "one ampere for every .001-inch of plate thickness." For example, an 1/8-inch (.125-inch) plate would require 125 amps. Of course, this doesn't mean that a 1/2-inch plate would take 500 amps, because large plates are generally beveled before welding and joined with a root pass in the bottom and several more passes on top. There are, however, industrial machines that routinely weld large plates, such as on ship decks, with very large wire diameter and high amperages. This is just a general rule, and other factors, such as the wire speed and welding travel speed affect the current requirement. In the smaller home-type MIG machines, the amperage settings are fixed, with perhaps four different positions on the current knob, but the wire-speed knob is infinitely variable on all MIG machines. The

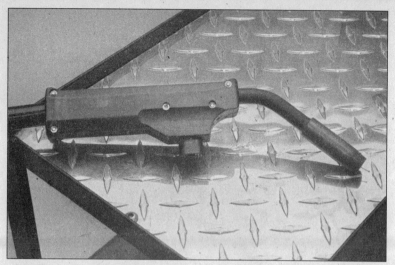

5.7 The basic MIG torch is quite simple. Inside is a guide tube that the wire comes through, a switch that turns on the power and the shielding-gas flow. The curved neck, called a "swan neck", holds the contact tube and the nozzle.

5.8 The wire must fit the contact tube closely, as this is where power is transmitted to the electrode wire. Note that the contact tube is recessed inside the nozzle, and the wire sticks out 1/2-3/4-inch from the nozzle.

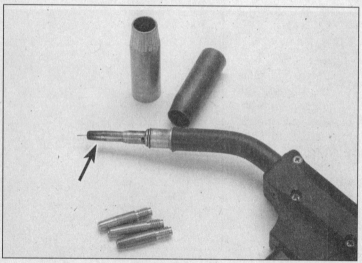

5.9 Most MIG nozzles just twist off past a snap ring, exposing the contact tube (arrow). You should keep an extra nozzle as a spare, and several spares of the sizes of contact tubes (below) that you use most. Eventually, you will weld the wire to the contact tube, and have to unscrew it to get it off, then clip off the wire and install a new tube, also called a contact *tip*.

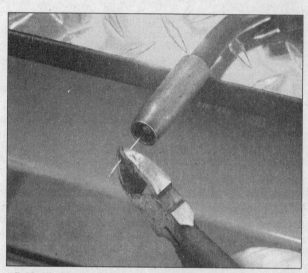

5.10 It's important to keep a pair of side-cutter pliers handy at all times to your MIG welder. Not only do you need it to maintain the correct protrusion of the wire from the nozzle, but when the wire develops a ball on the end, the arc is easier to start if you snip the ball off.

more expensive, more professional MIG machines have variable-current output, or at least more positions on the switch, and may have other optional controls for timing weld events.

The torch cooling on almost all MIG machines, certainly the ones we are considering for home/shop use, is by air, although there are some industrial applications which have a water-cooled torch because of the heavy wire and high amperage being used. Looking inside the MIG torch, the main body of the handle contains the switch or trigger, a wire conduit with a metal or plastic-tubing liner, and the curved "swan neck" that comes out holding both a contact or wire guide tube and a nozzle. The contact tube is so called because it actually puts the power to the wire. Usually made of copper, the contact tube also keeps the wire output centered in the gas cup or nozzle **(see illustration)**. Since this is where

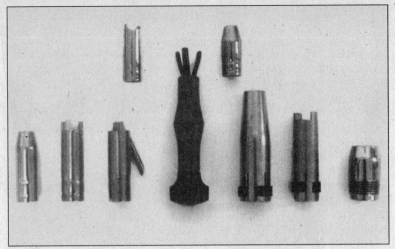

5.11 For some MIGs, there is a variety of different-size nozzles, some with special purposes like spot-welding. At the center here is a tool for scraping debris from inside a nozzle.

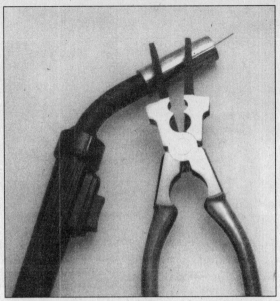

5.12 Eastwood Company makes these multi-function MIG pliers, which can be used to clean nozzles, snip wires, and hold contact tips to unscrew them.

the power is transferred to the wire, the contact tube must have a specific size related to the size of the electrode wire being used. Because of the unavoidable wear in the contact tube, and occasional arcing that ruins a contact tube, these are considered consumables in MIG welding, and you should have several spares of any of the sizes you normally use.

The nozzle's main function is to contain the shielding gas in an envelope around the arcing wire. Most MIG machines have only one size nozzle, but in production applications smaller nozzles are used on smaller-amperage work and larger nozzles on bigger jobs **(see illustration)**. The nozzle takes some punishment in MIG welding, with spatter and weld debris constantly building up inside. Special tools are available that scrape out the buildup, and most MIG weldors use an anti-spatter or "nozzle-shield" gel or spray to keep down the buildup and allow easy removal of the gook when necessary **(see illustration)**. Obviously, if too much debris builds up inside the nozzle, it will affect the gas flow to the weld area and thus cause deterioration and unevenness in the bead. The sprays can be directed inside the nozzle after cleaning, to prevent future buildup, while the gel comes in a jar that is left uncapped while welding. Every so often, you take the hot MIG gun and stick the nozzle directly into the gel, which leaves a coating inside the hot nozzle and on the contact tube.

Shopping for a MIG welder

The array of available MIG machines aimed at the consumer and small shop market has greatly increased in the past decade. Many automotive body workers and fabricators in small shops used to dream of having a MIG welder to round out their capabilities, but the machines available at that time were either very expensive self-contained MIG machines or wire-feeding attachments for already-expensive, large-size arc/TIG power supplies found only in welding shops. The hobbyist, auto body man or muffler shop couldn't justify the expense.

That changed when imported MIG machines started making their appearance in the US, aimed at the hobbyist market specifically. The companies advertised in hobbyist publications, attended auto enthusiast shows, and made a presence in the business community. At first, the big domestic welding-equipment manufacturers took little notice, but after a few years they realized there was a gap in their marketing and price structure and began to produce similar equipment to gain back this emerging hobbyist/small shop interest in MIG weld-

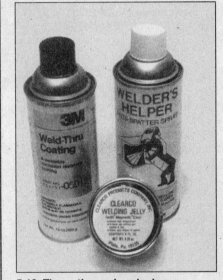

5.13 These three chemicals are helpful in performing clean welds and maintaining your MIG torch in good condition. The anti-spatter spray and gel are used on the nozzle to make removal of debris easier, and the weld-through coating by 3M is used when welding high-strength steel in late-model cars. Unlike the other sprays, it is applied to the area to be welded, providing extra corrosion protection after the weld.

5.14 The bigger and better the machine, the more expensive the internal components. Sometimes you can get an idea of the relative complexity inside a MIG machine by comparing shipping weights when shopping for a welder. The more expensive ones are generally much heavier. This is the inside of a MIG 200 from HTP.

ing. Today there is a wide variety of machines offered from both domestic and imported sources that run the gamut from very small, very portable units that can be powered from a 3000-watt generator if necessary, to larger shop units with all the "bells and whistles."

When the domestic manufacturers started competing with the imports for the lower-price end of the MIG market, there was considerable talk at the local welding supply level about how the imports weren't as good as the domestic machines and that anyone who bought the cheaper imports would have trouble later on finding replacement parts. In the beginning of this marketing struggle, there was some truth to this, but the competition of today's marketplace has pretty much sorted these problems out. There are some very reputable companies selling imported MIG and Plasma machines, and most of them have a full line of consumables and other replacement parts on hand.

As with automobiles, there will always be some debate on import vs. domestic, but today such distinctions are harder to draw than they used to be. Like our cars, some domestic welding machines use components made overseas, and some imported machines use American-made parts. As you shop for a MIG machine or plasma cutter, you may still find resistance to imported equipment at your local welding shop. The answer is to listen to everyone, including especially anyone you know who has purchased and used the equipment you are contemplating. Find out if they have ever needed parts or service for their equipment, and did they have any problems with equipment under warranty. Be sure to compare the usage they put the equipment to, because there is a big difference between what is required in hours of welding on a daily basis in a shop, and your needs of welding a project or two a few times a year.

We have discussed duty-cycle comparisons in the previous chapter. Most manufacturers give you a duty-cycle rating at the highest amperage and the lowest amperage, and you may never have to use either one. If you contemplate a machine with say 140-amp capacity, it may have a duty-cycle rating of 95% at 30 amps and a 30% duty-cycle at its peak of 140 amps. The cycle relates to how many minutes out of a ten-minute period you can weld continuously without overheating the machine. At a 100% rating, you don't need to stop for anything, even if you are welding long seams together. In most home/shop situations however, you are not on a production schedule or a time-clock, and most of your joints will not be long seams. Also, you will probably weld a seam, such as a corner joint on a tubular framework for a utility trailer, that will take you only a minute or less to weld up (doing one side at a time), then you will move to another part of the project, perhaps set up some clamps or fixturing to ready the next joint for welding, and all this time the machine is cooling off so you may never exceed the duty-cycle even at higher amperages. This is where the big difference in cost in MIG machines is. The heavier-duty, shop-type machines have more expensive electrical components inside to handle a higher duty-cycle **(see illustration).** You should buy as much duty-cycle as you can afford to, but don't be too concerned that in your garage you'll spend all your time sitting around waiting for the machine to cool off. You'll find you will not often weld at the highest amperage output anyway, and when you do, even a 30% duty-cycle is livable.

There are two basic types of smaller MIG machines you'll be looking at, the gas-shielded type that uses bare electrode wire and a bottle of compressed gas, and the flux-core type that uses no shielding-gas bottle but has a special wire with a fluxed core inside that produces the shielding gasses as you weld, much like the vaporizing coating on arc-welding rods. There are advantages and disadvantages to each type, and your choice depends on the kind of work you will be doing. Most of the machines on the market are for use with bottled shielding-gas, and there are some units that can be equipped for either type of wire, in case you have need for both. These machines cost a little more than single-use MIG machines because they have to have a switching device inside to change from reverse polarity (with the torch being positive and the work negative) which is required for the solid wire and straight polarity (with the torch negative) for the flux-cored wires.

The flux-cored wire machines do not make as pretty a weld, if that is a concern to you, and there is some slag to be removed afterward, though it is easier to remove than the slag from arc-welding. With some kinds of flux-cored wire, the slag will peel off the seam in strips. In body shop work, the extra thickness of the flux-cored wire may make them too hot for light-gauge sheet-metal work. Some experts say

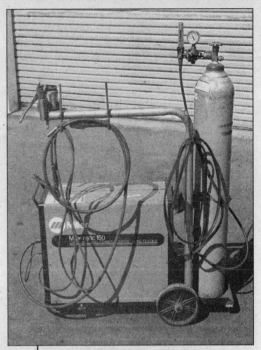

5.15 Sometimes a medium-size machine is all that is called for in a particular shop, like this Miller 150 used in a muffler shop, but the weldor uses a large-sized shielding gas bottle for extra weld time. Note how this weldor has added a tubing arm to the cart, to organize the cables and hold pliers and and-spatter gel.

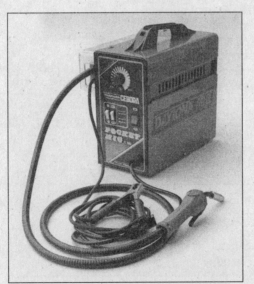

5.16 A popular entry-level MIG machine is this 110-V Pocket-MIG from Daytona MIG. Though it weighs only 42 pounds, it has an amp range from 30-110 amps, capable of welding up to 1/4-inch steel. Very portable, it's ideal for home/shop use, especially on sheet metal.

5.17 A 110-V, 130-amp MIG is made by several companies for the home/shop market, this one is by Daytona MIG and welds up to 5/16-inch steel. It features a cooling fan and a 30% duty-cycle at maximum amperage, 95% at 30 amps.

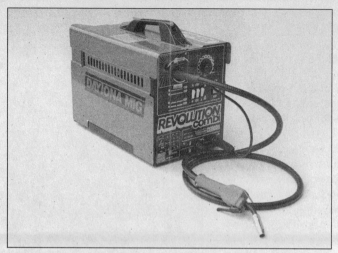

5.18 If you need the flexibility of welding indoors and out, a combination MIG that uses either gas-shielding or flux-cored wire fills the bill. This Combi 888 runs on 110V power, with 130-amp capacity.

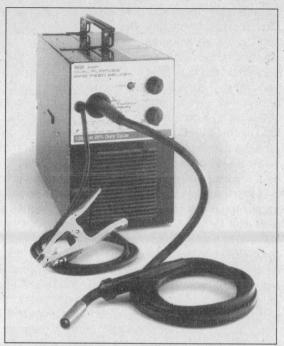

5.19 There are small MIG machines that come equipped for use with flux-cored wire, but have an optional kit that can be attached to work with shielding gas and solid wire. Eastwood Company's wire-feeder uses 110V current, and has a 20% duty-cycle at its maximum amperage of 85. It's fan-cooled and adequate for light-gauge welding.

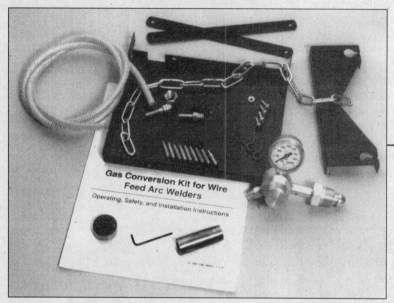

5.20 Eastwood's gas conversion kit for their MIG welder contains the regulator, nozzle, tips and other parts to adapt a shielding-gas bottle to their 85-amp welder.

that flux-core MIG welding is best suited for 18-gauge or thicker metals, and most cars today are using 22- to 24-gauge steel, except for 20-gauge in areas like floor pans. Even replacement steel patch panels for cars are seldom thicker than 20-gauge. Virtually all of the newer cars are using lighter-gauge metal of higher-rated alloy to reduce the overall weight of vehicles to meet tougher fuel economy and emissions standards. The main advantage of the flux-cored machines are in outdoor or drafty situations where wind can blow away the shielding gas from a "bottle-fed" machine, ruining the weld consistency. The flux-cored wire works well for fencing repairs, farm equipment too big to be moved indoors, outsized sculptures and similar projects. These machines also have the advantage of not needing periodic refilling of gas bottles. As long as you have electricity and a spare roll of wire, there's nothing for you to run out of halfway through a project on a Sunday afternoon when you can't get your gas bottle refilled or exchanged.

The advantages of the bottle-fed machines are numerous, the primary benefit being the higher quality of weld and the ability to work on very thin materials without burning through. With shielding gas, there is very little spatter, no slag, and you can even weld body panels that are painted or rusty, though a cleaner parent metal will always make a better weld and produce less hazard from fumes. We have seen a big-rig repairman MIG-welding a new and painted fan guard to a rusty truck radiator-support framework. The budget for the job didn't allow for the time that would be spent in grinding and sanding all of the edges clean - the truck had to be back on the road making money. The result wasn't

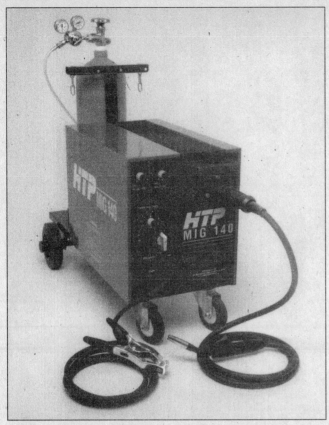

5.21 At the upper end of the 110V MIG scale are 140-amp units like this one from HTP America. It weighs 135 pounds, welds up to 1/4-inch steel, and has timing features such as stitch-welding and spot-welding.

5.22 Above the 140-ampere range, you are into the 220V category of MIG welders, with more features and higher duty capacities. This is HTP's MIG 160, which can weld up to 5/16-inch steel, has eight heat settings, and is suitable for street rod shops, muffler shops, or farm use.

pretty, but it was more than strong enough for the application and a testament to what can be done.

As far as running out of gas is concerned, this is an issue, but most home/shop users handle this by just buying a bottle that is twice as big as they think they need. There is, of course, a pair of gauges on the tank that indicate the gas-flow going to the welder and the total pressure left in the bottle, so you should know before any big project just how much welding time you have left. Bigger shops just keep a spare bottle of gas on hand and switch if they run out, then send the empty back to the gas supply company for refilling to become the next spare.

Input current is the next consideration in shopping for a MIG machine. There's a number of home-type machines that can be operated on standard household 110V current, which negates the need for any rewiring of your shop area and also makes them more portable in the sense that you can use one anywhere there is a source of standard power. However, any circuit used for a welding machine should be at least a 20-amp circuit, and, in the case of the bigger 110V machines, a 30-amp circuit is recommended. The 110V (it's confusing, but household current is also referred to as 115-volt at times, but 110V and 115V are the same) machines are available in power abilities with a range of 30 to 110 amps on the smallest home MIGs and a 30- to 140-amp range on the largest. Most of these machines handle wire diameters from .023-inch to .035-inch, though some of the imports are set up for metric wire sizes, which are close enough to US sizes that you can always find replacement wire to suit them.

Above the 140-amp range in maximum power brings you into the bigger shop-type machines that require 220V current input. Most of these machines

5.23 This 220V unit, the 181C from Daytona MIG, offers settings from 20 amps for light sheet metal to 180 amps for heavier work, and has a spot-timer and quick-disconnect torch. This is suitable for light fabrication shops.

5.24 For welding up to 3/8-inch steel, a MIG like HTP's MIG 200 will do the job. It has 24 heat settings, up to 200 amps, and is suitable for farm or ranch work, commercial fabrication, or repeated automotive projects like building trailers or engine stands.

5.25 This close-up of a commercially made street rod part has a thick steel ring MIG-welded in two places to a heavy bracket for suspension mounting. This is a large bead from a good-sized machine. Note how smooth and clean the weld is, the bead looks almost like one piece, rather than overlapping puddles, and look at the backside of the part (at right) to see the indications of penetration. A MIG is easy to learn, but it will takes lots of practice to make welds like this.

have an upper limit of 250 amps, which is a *lot*, and they offer a 50% duty-cycle even at this high amperage. These larger machines also offer more "bells and whistles" such as larger wire spools, the ability to handle more different wire sizes, wheels on the bottom of the machine as standard equipment and the capacity and bracketry to hold larger bottles of shielding gas. Designed as they are for bigger jobs, these medium-size machines can handle wire diameters from .023-inch to .0625-inch (1/16-inch), which is bigger than virtually any requirement you will have need for in your home shop unless you take up amateur bridge building. You will see these 250-amp MIG machines hard at work in many shops today, from muffler businesses to street rod shops, race-car shops and general steel fabricators.

Other options you may find on these mid-size machines are controls for timing various weld functions. If you were regularly spot-welding long seams in sheet metal, you could set one of these machines up with a special spot-welding nozzle which has a flat front face with cutouts on each side. You bring such a nozzle directly in contact with the metal and pull the trigger. An adjustable timer on the machine sets the weld time for a perfect spot-weld with little or no crown or buildup to grind off later. Also, you can set one up to do stitch-welding as well, where you join work with a series of spot welds that overlap. The welding machine has a stitch timer that turns the arc on, pauses, arcs, pauses, arcs, etc. This stitch mode isn't used very often but is helpful in joining very thin materials where there is a chance of burring through with continuous welding. In the stitch mode (in which the pause time is variable at the machine), the pause time allows the first puddle to solidify before the next puddle is made, reducing the overall heat.

Mid-size MIG machines also offer more range of heat settings than the entry-level MIGs. While the smaller machines may have four settings from their lowest to their highest amperage, their bigger brothers may also have a "fine-power" adjustment knob, which essentially gives four more positions for each of the four basic settings on the main amperage knob. So instead of four settings, you now have a possible sixteen.

Adapters and special attachments offered on some machines include a metal shrinker and a stud-welding attachment. The metal shrinker works to reduce high spots in sheet metal, much as you would do with an oxy-acetylene torch, but without the flames and with very controlled heat. The basic principle is to heat the center of the high spot (such as from having hammered out a dent from the backside) to cherry-red, then quenching it with a wet rag, which "shrinks" down the high spot of stretched metal. The MIG shrinker attachment screws on in place of your contact tube, the wire is pulled back inside the torch (the wire isn't used) and the wire drive and gas flow are disconnected. The shrinking tip is placed in contact with the metal and the trigger pulled briefly, heating the high spot.

The stud-welding attachment is another body-working tool that allows you to "spot-weld" small studs onto a dented panel. These studs fit a special slide-hammer that pulls on the studs to work the dent out without having to drill holes in the body and use a screw-type puller as has been traditional. The studs can be clipped and ground off easily after the pulling is done. There is also a separate stud-welding tool that operates on 110V current without the need for the welding machine (see the Safety and Shop Equipment chapter). Another stud-welding attachment is made to use a threaded stud as an "electrode" and fuse it in place of a worn-out stud in automotive work **(see illustrations)**.

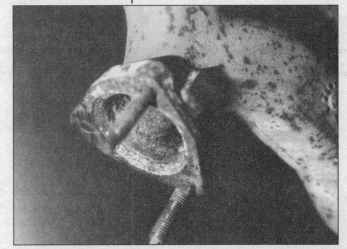

5.26 In exhaust system work, muffler shops deal with broken and rusted-away manifold studs all the time. HTP has a special feature to their MIG 160 that repairs such problems. First the old stud is cut off flush.

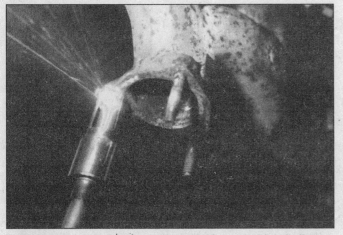

5.27 A special attachment to the MIG gun holds a hollow replacement stud. When the arc is turned on for about four seconds the wire feeds through the stud and welds it to the old stub.

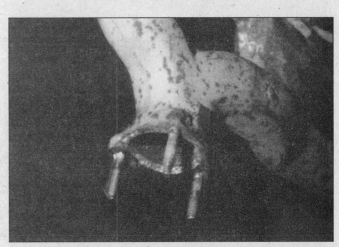

5.28 The new stud is now welded in place, with strength said to be up to 85% as good as original. This feature is a real time-saver for busy muffler businesses.

5.29 Spot-welding of sheet-metal panels is easy with a MIG, even a small one. For large panels, welds may be made through holes in the top panel. Here a new door jamb has been added to a 1932 Ford with a series of small spot welds. So little weld is above the surface that no strength is lost when the area is ground for painting.

To go to the top level in MIG machinery, you are now talking about very expensive professional welding machines with large, multi-purpose power supplies. As mentioned in Chapter 2, the bigger welding machines designed strictly for professional shops are often multi-purpose power supplies capable of high amperages which can be set up for Arc welding, TIG and MIG, with any polarity required. The amateur user will never need the high amperages or high duty-cycles of these top-level machines. To use the big machines for MIG welding usually requires that a separate wire-feeding accessory drive be set up, and, with the lower prices of today's MIG market, the big shops prefer to just buy a separate MIG welder for those needs, using the large power supply just for TIG welding.

Choosing shielding gas

By now, you should have an idea of what level of MIG machine will suit your purposes. If you are like most home/shop users who aren't going to be welding every day, your needs may be best served by a typical, entry-level 140-amp, 110V MIG machine using shielding gas. You now have to choose a shielding-gas bottle (not included with most MIG machines), some wire (a small sample roll may be included with your machine), and the type of shielding gas you want to use. This sounds like a lot of choices, but the field is narrowed down by what kind of work you want to do and how often you need to do it. In all cases, the choice of shielding gas and wire type must be matched to the kind of material you will be welding.

Capacity of the gas bottle is important, and most first-time weldors make the mistake of buying less capacity because the bottles are cheaper, only to find themselves someday working on a project over a weekend (when there is little

5.30 various size shielding-gas bottles are available for MIG setups. Check with your welding supply store on how long each size might last. Most home/shop users buy relatively small bottles because they want portability in a small garage area.

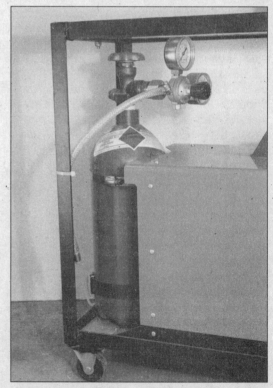

5.31 The smallest bottles are 20 cubic-foot capacity, and easily fit into even a small welding cart like this. The bottle and regulator are totally protected here. This is a good size if you only use the welder infrequently, or on small projects.

5.32 Gas-shielded MIGs are not made for outdoor work, but as long as you can keep the wind currents away, they work fine. On this driveway utility-trailer project, pieces of plywood are used as wind shields while welding.

5.33 Most of your welding with shielding gas can be done best with a 75% argon/25% CO_2 mixture, which is excellent for cleanliness and penetration, and can be used on cast-iron and stainless-steel as well.

chance of getting a bottle refilled) and they are out of gas. Gas bottles are available in sizes from 20 cubic feet to 40, 60, 80 and 125 cubic feet of gas. This roughly translates into welding time of from four hours for the 20 cu.ft. bottles to 14-16 hours for the 125 cu.ft. when used on a small machine like the 140-amp unit in our example. There's a number of factors involved in how long a particular bottle may last under different welding conditions, so these are just rough guidelines. Every time you use your MIG machine, you should look at your tank gauge to see how much more gas is left. You may even want to just lease a small cylinder of gas when your first get your machine just to see how long such a tank would last you, and then buy a bigger one if you think you need it.

The small bottles fit nicely under a small welding cart, making for a very portable arrangement for occasional home use **(see illustration).** The larger bottles are heavy and bulky, so you'll have to build a welding cart (most first-time weldors' first project) that can accommodate one. Of course, bottles of compressed gas are dangerous, even if the gas is non-flammable, due to the pressures involved, and any welding gas bottle must be securely mounted with chains or sturdy clamps. It's important to note that welding bottles for electric welding machines should be ideally mounted in an insulated manner, such as with rubber underneath and rubber hose over any restraining chains. This prevents the remote possibility of arcing against the cylinder, which could damage it.

Next there is the choice of shielding gas to use. One of the widely used shielding gasses for MIG work is plain carbon-dioxide, or CO_2. While it is in the bottle, CO_2 is really an inert gas, but technically it turns into carbon monoxide and oxygen under the intense heat of the arc process. The oxygen can combine with other elements in the air and in the parent metal to form undesirable oxides. Thus, plain CO_2 will not usually result in as clean a weld as with other gasses, but it is used often because it is the least expensive shielding gas for welding steel. It will weld very fast, with good penetration, but you should use a welding wire that contains deoxidizing elements to counteract the effect of pure CO_2.

Argon is a versatile inert shielding gas that is often used by itself, or in combination with other gasses to produce certain weld characteristics. For instance, welding of non-ferrous materials like aluminum is usually done with pure argon. It makes for good penetration patterns and a concentrated arc.

To weld ferrous materials, like the mild steel we will use for most home/shop projects, argon is usually mixed with another gas, or sometimes two other gasses, to provide special characteristics. While there are some esoteric mixtures of gasses in different percentages for specific purposes, a mixture of 75% argon and 25% CO_2 has become pretty much the standard for welding mild steel with short-arc MIG machines with wire diameters of .035-inch or less (see illustration). This mixture, often abbreviated as C-25, is more expensive than the plain CO_2 but produces much less spatter and consistently better looking welds, even on materials that exhibit minor rust or scale. It is what we would recommend for most of your welding needs. If you were doing a lot of thicker materials, overhead or other out-of-position welding and pipe welding, you might use a 50-50 mix of argon and CO_2 which offers good wetting and bead shape without the excessive fluidity that causes a bead to droop or fall when doing out-of-position welding.

If you are working in a body shop, you might be interested in a mixture that Airco calls Argoshield LG®, which stands for light gauge. It consists of mostly argon with small additions of CO_2 and oxygen. The combination is designed for metals down to 20-gauge, and produces good penetration, but with a smaller weld bead than normal for less sheet-metal finishing, less spatter and smoke and good arc starting. It is specifically formulated to work well on the thin, low-alloy steels now used on auto sheet metal.

For welding of non-ferrous materials, either straight argon or mixtures of argon and helium are used in various combinations which provide higher heat to a MIG arc. Usually, the thicker the material to be welded, the higher the percentage of helium that is included in the mix, and the HE-75 gas, which is 25% argon and 75% helium is typically used in industry to weld thick aluminum.

If you were interested in welding stainless-steel, you can actually use the C-25 gas we recommended above for mild steel, but a mixture of 90% helium, 7.5% argon and 2.5% CO_2 is widely used in stainless-steel MIG welding because it offers a higher heat for the normally sluggish weld puddle on stainless, as well as offering good stability, penetration and resistance to corrosion.

If you have to pick just one type of gas, the C-25 works great on steel, can be used on stainless-steel and is also useable on cast iron.

Choosing wire

The bare steel wires used in a bottled-shielding-gas MIG machine are all variations of the same basic metal, with varying amounts of deoxidizers added for different applications and shielding gasses. The most common deoxidizer is silicon. Others added may be manganese, aluminum, titanium, or zirconium, with nickel, chromium or molybdenum added to improve mechanical or corrosion-resistance properties. The welding wires with higher levels of deoxidizers generally are better able to weld on rusty or unclean steel surfaces.

Most of the steel wires for MIG welding fall under a designation from the American Welding Society (AWS) of E70S-something, with the last digit being the particular variation. For instance, one of the most common wire specifications is E70S-2, which is deoxidized, and makes a good weld with C-25 gas, even on rusty steel. Its main drawback is that it lacks fluidity; the puddle doesn't want to flow out width-wise and may not stick well in heavy materials.

The E70S-3 wire is one of the most common and least-expensive MIG wires available, with more deoxidizers and a more fluid puddle that makes a wider bead. It has been used successfully for years on cars, farm equipment and appliances.

Next up in terms of deoxidizer content is E70S-4, which is a medium-priced wire suitable for almost all steel welding. It offers good fluidity and better arc characteristics than E70S-3, but has slightly more spatter, and is used on structural steel, ships, piping and boiler vessels.

Probably the high-performance and higher-cost wire available is the E70S-6, which has the highest level of silicon and manganese as deoxidizers. It is suitable for welding almost all steels, from thin mild steel to 1/2-inch plate (in the appro-

5.34 Inside the wire-drive portion of a typical small MIG machine. this machine comes with a small wire roll such as at lower right, but comes with an adapter to handle the larger rolls such as in the machine. The small wire rolls are inconvenient unless you do only small projects.

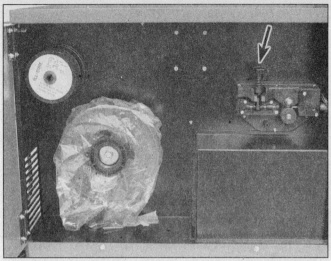

5.35 This is the drive section of a Daytona MIG wire-feed, which has a place inside to store an extra small roll of wire, good for keeping the spare clean if you occasionally switch to another type of wire for specific needs. Arrow indicates the knob for adjusting the wire roller tension.

priate wire diameter) and works with the most popular gas mixtures, offering good puddle fluidity, too (see illustration). It is one of the few MIG wires that is completely compatible with today's thin, low-alloy, high-strength body metal in unibody cars.

L-Tec markets a wire meeting the AWS classification for ER70S-2, 3,4 and 6 that they call Easy Grind, which is designed specifically for auto body work. It is said to require less skill to weld thin materials, and to have a reduced carbon content that means easier grinding to prepare for filler and painting. Besides automobiles, it is also used in welding ductwork, metal cabinets, lawn furniture, and is designed to be on metal as thin as 26-gauge with smaller MIG machines.

Non-ferrous metals, of course, require different wires. The basic rule of welding electrode selection is to choose a wire or electrode whose content is much the same as the parent metal you are welding. In the case of stainless-steel, it can be welded with the steel wire we have recommended above, but for better corrosion resistance (the main reason for making something from stainless-steel in the first place) stainless-steel wire should be used. There are various alloys of stainless-steel, but one of the more common varieties is type 304, and the best wire for MIG welding type 304 is called ER308, with variations of increasing silicone content in ER308L and ER308LS.

For aluminum welding, you need aluminum wire. Again, there are many alloy variations of aluminum, and several metal blends in aluminum wire, but perhaps the best MIG wire for aluminum is called ER5356, which has a chemical content proven to work in most situations. Aluminum welding is more difficult than steel in many ways, and often the exact alloy of the parent metal is impossible to determine, unless you have bought a large enough piece at a metal yard that is still factory marked as to its alloy and heat-treat. There are even some aluminum alloys which are considered unweldable, like high-strength aluminum such as 7075-T6.

5.36 Your welding supply store will have a variety of MIG electrode wires to choose from. The E70S-6 wire at left is one of the most popular. At right is L-TECs Easy-Grind for body work.

5.37 When starting in a new roll of wire, keep a pair of pliers on the end you take off the reel, or the wire can unroll everywhere. Feed the wire through the guide and over the drive roller.

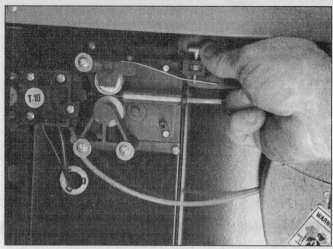

5.38 The wire tension is adjusted with a knob, and proper tension avoids wire-twisting problems inside the gun. The wire should be able to slip when it needs to. Most machines have a feature that allows you to retain the tension setting, once set, by swinging the tension arm away when changing wires.

Learning MIG welding

One of the attractions of MIG welding that has brought these machines into the home/shop market is how easy they are to learn. With a little instruction, virtually anyone can be MIG welding with an hour's practice time. As with anything else, the more you practice, the easier it will be and the better your welds, but before you get overconfident about your MIG welds, try cutting apart a seam you have made to check the penetration, and make the other tests (bending two butt-welded sample plates in a vise) we have previously described to see if the welds you're making are as strong as they are good-looking.

To set up your MIG machine, the first step would be to read all the directions and cautions in the instruction book that came with it. One of the few adjustments you will have to make initially is to put a roll of wire into the machine and set the drive-roller tension. The wire unrolls from the reel through a guide and over a motorized roller, which feeds the wire through another guide and into the cable going to your torch. Lay your torch and cable out on the floor as straight as possible. Mount the wire spool into the machine as per your directions, but be careful when cutting the end of the wire which is usually bent over to lock it into a hole in the side of the reel. There is winding tension on the wire and if the cut end of the wire gets away from you, it can start unraveling all over the place. Don't cut the end loose until you are ready to feed it.

Hold the cut end with some pliers or vise-grips and carefully file or sand the cut end until it is smooth. A sharply-cut end may snag as it travels through the cable or torch. Insert the end into the guide, loosen and swing away the wire-tension adjuster, and feed the wire over the groove in the drive roller and on into the next guide, still holding the wire firmly **(see illustration)**. Most machines are set up to handle several sizes of wire, but you must be certain that you use the drive-roller groove that is the right size for the wire you are using. Most rollers have two sizes on them and can be turned around on their shaft to put the other size in line with the wire. There will probably be an extra roller with other sizes on it that comes with your machine.

When six inches or more of wire have been fed into the welding cable, put the wire-tension adjuster back in place over the wire, keeping the wire centered in the groove. Turn on the welder and put the wire-feed speed about one-quarter

5.39 There are three choices in regulators for MIG shielding gas. The unit at right is a single-gauge, economy unit which indicates only the line flow, not the total tank pressure, at left is a dual-gauge unit that shows both, and in the center is the more professional model that has a floating-ball flow meter easy to read from a distance.

of the way and pull the trigger. At this point, adjust the pressure on the wire tensioner until the rollers are feeding the wire, and then turn it 1/4-turn more. With the nozzle and contact tube unscrewed from the end of your torch, keep the torch cable straight and run the machine until the wire comes out of the torch. Slip the correct-size contact tube over the wire, screw it in and attach the nozzle.

The final check on wire tension is to make sure the wire can "slip" if necessary. Eventually in your MIG practice, you will virtually weld the wire to the contact tube. When this happens, and you are still pulling the trigger, the machine tries to feed more wire but it can't come out of the gun, so it jams up inside in what is called a "birds nest." To prevent this, bend the wire to the side of your torch and put the nozzle right against the shop floor, simulating a stuck wire. While watching the drive mechanism inside the machine, pull the trigger. The drive rollers should have just enough tension to always pull the wire through, but not enough to prevent slippage in case of a jam. If your rollers *do* slip in this test, you're set.

If yours is a flux-cored-wire machine, you are ready to weld, but for the shielding-gas machines, you have to set up the bottle. With the bottle mounted firmly on your cart, attach the regulator to the bottle and attach the reinforced hose (should come with your machine) to the regulator with a hose clamp, connecting the gas to the machine. On some machines, a special adapter connects the reinforced hose to a small plastic hose going into the machine. Keep the two regulator gauges protected from impact, and always keep the gas valve turned off when you are not using the machine. Some cylinder valves only seal well when the valve is either fully off or fully on, so when your machine is on, turn the cylinder valve all the way, not just a few turns. You can check any of your gas connections for leaks using some soapy water solution. Bubbles indicate leaks. Adjust your gas regulator to the proper flow rate (cubic-feet-per-hour rate, according to your instructions) for the material and wire you are working on. **Note:** *One gauge tells you the flow rate and the other tells you how much pressure is still in the bottle. You can't read either one unless the cylinder valve is turned on, so don't look at your bottle one day and notice that the tank gauge looks empty - turn on the valve to really see what's left.*

Now you're ready to practice. Select some 1/8-inch steel, set your amperage according to the suggestions in your instructions, and set your wire speed a little

5.40 The basic MIG units have only a few power settings. Your instruction sheet will tell you the recommended thickness of metal for each setting, and a chart on the front of the machine usually tells you the amperage and duty-cycle of the settings. After some practice on different materials, you will learn instinctively which settings work best for your work.

5.41 The wire speed has a lot to do with the heat and quality of the weld. Generally when you have it right, the MIG machine makes a very satisfying steady "sizzle" sound. Practice by adjusting the feed high and gradually lowering it until the sound and results are satisfactory. If you do repetitive projects, write down the amperage and wire speed settings that have worked for you.

REVERSE ANGLE

WELDING DIRECTION

REVERSE METHOD

FORWARD ANGLE

WELDING DIRECTION

FORWARD METHOD

Gun tip inclination and the direction of the weld can be changed to match different welding conditions

5.42 Of the two methods of gun travel with MIG welding, beginners often like to use the reverse or backhand method because they can watch the puddling action much better.

higher than what's recommended. The wire speed is key to getting a good weld with proper heat and penetration, and tuning the speed is easy. Listen to the sound the welder is making as you make a straight bead. If the speed is too fast, most of the wire coming out will be red-hot and there will be a loud crackling noise. gradually adjust the speed down until you get a steady sizzling sound. The wire should be melting right at the weld. Practice tuning in the wire speed at different power settings and metal thicknesses.

There are two torch-holding techniques for MIG welding, forehand and backhand **(see illustration)**. The first is when the torch is angled and moved such that the weld is taking place ahead of the torch's direction of travel, and the backhand is when the weld takes place behind the torch **(see illustrations)**. Most beginner find the backhand (also called "dragging" the weld) technique works best on most steel-welding projects, giving the weldor a better view of the puddling action. In either style, the torch is angled about 35 degrees to the work. If you find yourself doing a vertical seam, you can travel either up or down, but use the forehand technique (sometimes called "pushing" the weld) only when going up, and the backhand technique going down, keeping the arc on the puddle's leading edge at all times for good penetration.

After making good straight beads on top of the plate, try joining two plates. If you are working with materials under 1/8-inch thick, most steels can be MIG-welded without beveling the edges, but you should tack the parts together with a slight gap between them before finishing off the seam with a full weld. This assures good penetration. On 1/8-inch and thicker metals, the edges should be beveled before tacking them. If you find that you are consistently burning through the material, the heat setting is too high, or you are moving too slowly. If it is "cold" appearing and not penetrating, the amperage may be too low, or you may be traveling too fast. You will adjust your travel speed with the torch by watching how the puddle develops, moving the torch along at a slow, *steady* rate. One of the great advantages of the MIG process is that your torch is right down close to the work, and there is much less intense light, heat and spatter as with arc-welding; you can get your head closer to the work to really see the puddle progress. Keep a pair of sharp wire-cutting pliers on your welder at all times. You will use it when you start each time to maintain about 1/2 inch of wire sticking out of the

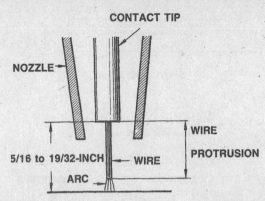

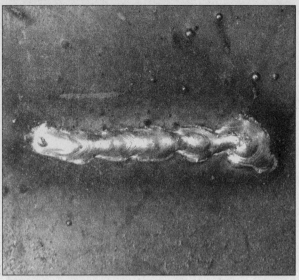

5.43 The tip-to-work distance is very important in maintaining the short-circuit arc. When practicing, watch the arc closely. The white-hot, melting end of the wire should stay about the same short distance from the puddle. Wire speed and welding travel speed control this.

5.44 This is what some of your practice welds will look like. The heat setting was too hot here, and the weldor wasn't very steady with the gun. Use both hands and find a very comfortable position to hold it steady. Note the amount of spatter from making and breaking the arc.

5.45 This production weld by a professional shows how clean and perfect MIG welds should look. The heat-affected area on either side is small, the weld has good penetration, and there is minimal spatter. Heat was evenly played on both pieces of tubing.

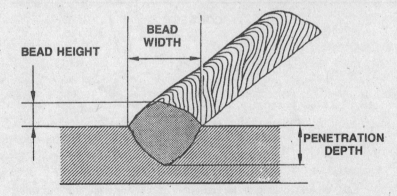

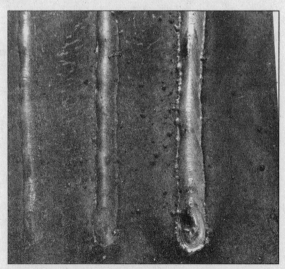

5.46 Welding current affects the penetration of the weld and the size of the bead. Ideally, you are looking for good penetration without a too-tall or too-wide bead.

5.47 At left here is a MIG bead that was too low in amperage for the thickness of the material. Penetration is shallow and the bead sticks up too high. At center, the correct amperage was used, and at right, the amps were too high. The right-hand bead may look OK here, but penetration was too deep (dropthrough on the backside) and there was some undercutting on either side of the bead.

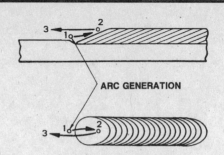

ARC GENERATION

OVERLAPPING BEADS

5.48 After you have practiced sufficiently, you'll develop a natural rhythm for the torch movements to create a good bead of overlapping oval puddles.

INCORRECT	CORRECT	INCORRECT

Insufficient penetration. Weld strength is poor and the panel could separate when it is finished with a grinder.

Good penetration and easy to grind.

There is good penetration but finish grinding will be both difficult and time consuming.

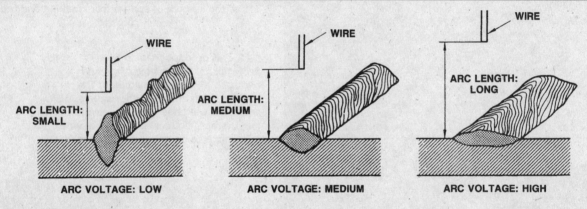

ARC LENGTH: SMALL

ARC LENGTH: MEDIUM

ARC LENGTH: LONG

WIRE

ARC VOLTAGE: LOW

ARC VOLTAGE: MEDIUM

ARC VOLTAGE: HIGH

5.49 Arc voltage and length affect the shape of the bead's profile and its penetration. Cut a few of your practice welds in half to examine the beads. The shape of the overlapping puddles should have rounded ends exposed, not sharp, triangle ends.

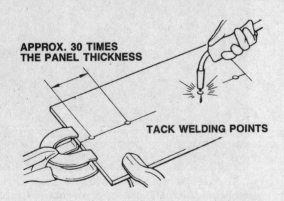

APPROX. 30 TIMES THE PANEL THICKNESS

TACK WELDING POINTS

5.50 The thickness of the panel you are working on determines how far apart your initial tack-welds should be to firmly align your parts. On thin materials, you need a lot more tacks.

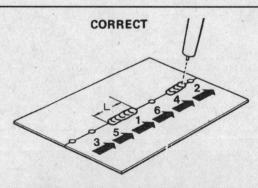

CORRECT

5.51 When working on large panels of thin material, such as when doing body work like welding on a new quarter-panel, warpage is a problem unless you keep the heat down by making lots of tack welds, then switching back and forth to the coolest section to add a short weld, then move to another section, and switch back and forth until the whole seam is done. A continuous weld might put too much heat in, and warp the new panel, requiring lots of hammer-work to straighten.

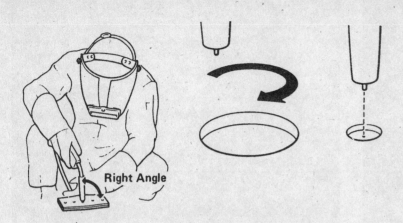

5.52 Instead of a straight butt-weld, panels of thin material are often joined with spot welds, in which the top panel is punched with small holes. You MIG-weld around the hole, joining the top panel to the bottom.

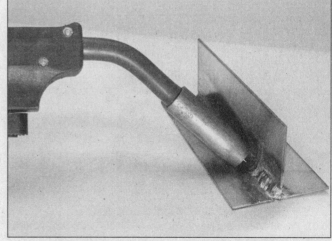

5.53 Door-handle and lock holes have been filled in on this street rod door, using small circles of sheet metal the same thickness as the original metal. In order to avoid warping, the circles were filled by tacking the filler pieces in a few places, waiting for the part to cool off, then adding a few more tacks, until the whole circle was made of tack welds.

gun. If you are welding thicker materials, or two edges that have irregular gaps, you can weave the arc back and forth from side to side as you travel, bridging the distance between the two edges.

Sometimes a start-and-stop technique works well for bridging gaps or filling holes. You watch the arc and weave from one side to the other, then pause (let go of the trigger) for a second with the torch in the same spot, allowing the puddle to solidify, then pull the trigger again, building a new puddle onto the last one. To fill a hole, just keep making tack-welds around the edge of the hole until you have made it smaller **(see illustration)**. Let the metal cool, then add an inner row of tacks inside the first "ring" until you close up the hole with filler metal. This is often done in filling sheet-metal holes in body work, but any hole larger than a dime should be filled by welding in a circle of new metal of the same thickness.

The beauty of the MIG process is that the torch is a one-hand operation, which allows you to use your other hand to steady your primary hand and draw a smooth bead. Also the torch stays the same distance from the weld at all times, unlike arc welding where the rod is always getting shorter. MIG welding doesn't require stopping to change electrodes either, so you can concentrate nicely on what you are doing. The one-handedness of MIG welding tempts some weldors to operate the torch with one hand while they actually hold something on the work with their other hand. This is OK for tack-welding, where you have a body panel you need to hold in alignment while you tack, but better seams are made when you hold the torch with both hands. Some users get used to the lower brightness and spatter of the MIG process, and are tempted to tack parts together without using a helmet. Body men in particular are prone to hold two panels in alignment, put the torch where it needs to be, close their eyes and make a tack weld for a second. Although MIG welding does produce less intense light and spatter than arc welding, you are still subject to both radiation burns and some spatter. Don't ever take a chance with your eyesight. One blob of spatter onto your bare eyelid could be really dangerous! A much better procedure (and the only one we recommend) would be to use some clamps or other devices (see the Safety and Shop Equipment chap-

5.54 When welding a corner joint such as a T-section, angle the gun at about a 45-degree angle to aim equal heat and filler on both pieces.

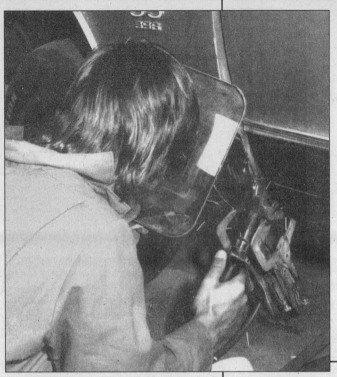

5.56 The best argon flow meters for professional use are the type with a floating ball inside a glass tube. Every time you pull the trigger, the ball floats up on the scale to indicate the gas flow to the machine. At a normal working distance from the machine, the weldor can more easily read this than a dial gauge. It makes it easy to see at a glance if you forgot to turn on the gas at all.

5.55 Don' be tempted by the low spatter of MIG welding to just shut your eyes when tacking body panels. If you need speed and convenience while tacking, use a hand-held safety-shield with lens as shown here. Weldor here has long sleeves, but should have gloves on and a turned-around hat to protect his hair from hot spatter.

ter) to hold your panels in alignment, and use a helmet. If you don't like the bother of flipping a big helmet up and down to just make a series of quick tack-welds, then use a hand-held face shield with lens **(see illustration)**. It's very easy to hold the shield in your left hand while tacking with your right, and it goes instantly from shielded to an unshielded view of the work.

If you are welding along and all of a sudden the bead goes bad, there are several things to consider. If you have been steady with your arc distance and travel speed, then perhaps a draft temporarily blew the shielding gas away from the weld. If it's not a draft, look to your main torch cable. If there are any bends or kinks in it, in the position in which you hold it when welding, the flow of gas can be restricted easily. Watch your gas bottle gauges while you pull the trigger for a second to see if the flow rate has changed or if the gas bottle is running low. The better equipped MIG machines in most shops have a type of regulator with a flow meter to indicate the flow rate **(see illustration)**. It consists of a glass tube with a colored ball inside that floats during gas flow. The numbered line it floats to indicates the flow rate. The advantage of these more expensive regulator/meter setups is that the weldor can see the gas flow from where he is *at the work*. He doesn't have to go back to the machine to read a gauge dial.

Aluminum welding will be more of a challenge than steel, regardless of the welding method used. Aluminum really soaks up heat, and you have to use thicker wire, and more heat, wire and gas flow to weld it. Equipping your machine to weld aluminum means: setting the gas flow almost twice as high as for steel, using aluminum wire, using the right gas mix, replacing the wire liner in the torch with a Teflon liner and using a contact tip that is one wire-size bigger than the aluminum wire. The reason for all this is that the aluminum wire tends to grow more with heat than the steel wire. The wire tension needs to be fairly light, because bird-nesting is more commonplace with the less stiff aluminum wire. In fact, there are special MIG guns made for

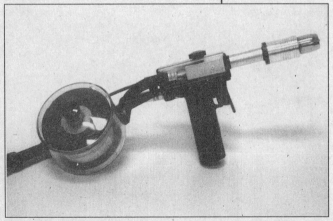

5.57 When MIG-welding aluminum, especially thin aluminum, the aluminum wire itself is fairly flexible, which can cause feeding problems inside the machine, because the drive rollers are *pushing* the soft wire a long distance. This is a spool gun, which holds a small roll of aluminum wire right at the gun for easy feeding.

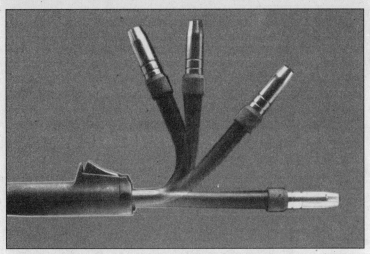

5.58 For tight quarters such as muffler work and other round-tubing situations, HTP makes this MIG gun with a flexible swan neck. It can even be used straight ahead, to reach into a spot where you can't get your hands.

5.59 Muffler shops are finding that the MIG machine is faster and safer to operate under a car than the traditional oxy-acetylene torch equipment. There is no constant re-lighting and adjusting of the flame to worry about when initially tack-welding various pipe sections together.

5.60 A handy welding cart for your MIG machine will probably be one of your first home/shop projects. This one is simply-built from one-inch angle-iron, fitted with a steel bottom shelf to hold the welder, bottle and accessories, and the top was made from a piece of polished-aluminum diamond plate purchased from a remnant pile at a scrap yard. Caster wheels were added quickly by welding their mounts to the bottom.

5.61 You'll find many uses for your welder once you get used to using it. This example of a typical home project is a plywood-covered rear bumper extension for a truck. It's used for carrying extra camping gear, and used as a tailgate for working or cooking when camping. Its also a wide step when stepping out of a camper shell on the truck.

production work with thin aluminum wire that hold a spool of wire right at the gun. Called spool guns, they eliminate the wire-feeding problems of trying to push a soft aluminum wire all the way through a cable to your torch **(see illustration)**.

The wire speed should be faster than for an equivalent sized steel wire, and the forehand technique is recommend because it puts more preheat ahead of the puddle. There are two extra steps in welding aluminum. The metal must be scrupulously clean and preheated to 350° F to get a good weld. You should keep

5.62 The camper-step was MIG-welded from one-inch steel tubing and braced to a 2x2-inch tube that fits into the truck's hitch receiver.

5.63 Street rod shops, customizers and restoration shops are using a MIG welder more and more, for its convenience and ability to handle delicate thin materials. This 1932 Ford door has had a new skin MIG-welded along the bottom where the original door was rotted away.

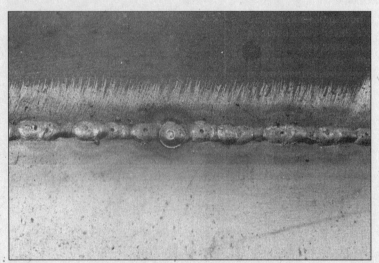

5.64 The door bottom was welded on with a series of very short welds, alternating from one area to another to keep from putting too much heat at one time into an area. Eventually, the whole seam is welded. L-TEC Easy-Grind deoxidized MIG wire is perfect for these kinds of jobs, because it grinds off easier, without inducing too much heat in preparing the seam for finishing and paint.

5.65 Customizers and restorers are fond of achieving a perfect gap around body panels on first-class vehicles. Often this involves grinding material off an edge or, as here, adding a sliver of metal along the door edge (at right) to close up a gap. Welding these thin strips is the perfect province of small MIG machines.

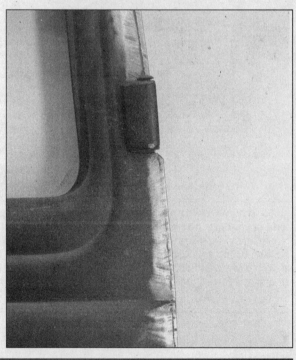

a stainless-steel wire brush handy that is strictly used for cleaning aluminum. Don't use it for brushing steel or it will later on contaminate your next aluminum weld.

Start welding aluminum with the torch further out than you would for steel, say one inch. Always start an aluminum weld with the end of the wire cut off fresh with snippers. As soon as the arc starts, move the torch closer, down 3/8 to 1/2-

inch from the work. Instead of the torch angle we recommended for steel, hold the gun almost square to the material and inclined only 5 to 15 degrees in the direction of travel.

The puddling will seem much different in aluminum than in steel. The puddle freezes very fast, and the only change you notice is that the molten area is the only place that is shiny. Aluminum has a narrow range of melting before it vaporizes and is highly susceptible to tiny amounts of foreign material. If you see black specks appearing as you go along on a seam, they represent impurities coming to the surface. The short-circuit type of MIG machines we have been discussing are best when the aluminum being welded is relatively thin. Thicker parts are better welded with TIG equipment or the spray-arc-pattern found on larger industrial MIG machines.

There will be a little more maintenance on the nozzle and contact tube when welding aluminum, due to increased spatter. The use of an anti-spatter spray inside the nozzle, or dipping the hot gun tip in nozzle gel, won't produce any less gunk inside the gun, but it will make its removal much easier, as it does with steel welding. If you use an anti-spatter chemical, it can act as a contaminant to the aluminum weld, so, after applying the anti-spatter, briefly use the torch on a piece of scrap aluminum to "burn-in" the chemical so it won't drip off onto your "good" weld.

One of the most common aluminum welding jobs in automotive work is repairing cracked cylinder heads, bellhousings and other large aluminum castings. The cracks should be well ground out to virgin metal and Vee'd before welding. These parts can really soak up heat so they should be thoroughly preheated, either in an oven or with an oxy-acetylene torch fitted with a rosebud tip. The old-timer's method of measuring the preheat was to coat the part with black soot from a overly-rich gas torch. Then with a torch set *properly*, the part was heated until the soot burned off, and that was considered enough preheat. Obviously, too much preheat could require complete re-machining of the part after the welding to correct warpage. Modern weldors use temperature marking sticks to get an exact preheat.

Maintenance on your MIG equipment is simple, but should be performed regularly to keep everything operating smoothly. The most often-maintained items are the gun components. The contact tubes wear out from frequent use as well as become burned such as when you hose kinks and the gas stops during a weld. Sometimes the hot wire welds itself to the contact tip. Often the problem can be fixed by filing on the end of the tip to free the wire's bond, or by pushing the wire to the side with your cutting pliers. If not, you can remove the nozzle, unscrew the contact tip and cut off the wire. Then feed the wire through a new contact tip and screw the tip in place and replace the nozzle. Use anti-spatter agents often, and clean out the nozzle and contact tip before starting a project, during the project, and after the project. When you replace the roll of wire, use a blow-gun on your air compressor hose to blow any dust out from inside the cabinet, and blow off the roll of wire before you install it. Keep the drive rollers clean with mineral spirits and lint-free cloth. Often professional weldors will tape piece of lint-free cloth inside their MIG welder such that it drags across the wire as it comes off the roll. The cloth helps to snatch any lint or dirt from the wire before it can collect in your cable or torch.

That's about all there is to MIG maintenance. This is a welding system that has really become the prominent method for the home/shop user in the last decade, and if you have read all of the above, you can see why it has many advantages. Once you start using one, you'll really appreciate it. The lack of paraphernalia, the ease of starting and maintaining the arc, the cleanliness of the welds, reduced shop fire hazards and the ability to weld various materials, including thin sheet metal, have combined to take the MIG process out of the exclusive hands of production weldors and give hobbyists, artists, farmers and restoration technicians a very practical, easy-to-learn welding system.

DEFECT	DEFECT CONDITION	MAIN CAUSE
PORES/PITS		• There is rust or dirt on the base metal. • There is rust or moisture adhering to the wire. • Improper shielding action. (The nozzle is blocked, wind or the gas flow volume is low.) • Weld is cooling off too fast. • Arc length is too long.
UNDERCUT		• Arc length is too long. • Gun angle is improper. • Welding speed is too fast.
OVERLAP		• Welding speed is too slow. • Arc length is too short.
INSUFFICIENT PENETRATION		• Welding current is too low. • Arc length is too long. • The end of the wire is not aligned with the butted portion of the panels.
EXCESS WELD SPATTER		• Arc length is too long. • Rust on the base metal. • Gun angle is too severe.
BEAD NOT UNIFORM		• The contact tip hole is worn or deformed and the wire is oscillating as it comes out of the tip. • The gun is not steady during welding.
BURN THROUGH		• The welding current is too high. • The gap between the metal is too wide. • The speed of the gun is too slow. • The gun to base metal distance is too short.

5.66 It will take some practice to become competent with any welding equipment, but MIG is the easiest to learn and the most forgiving in most automotive and home/shop applications. Test your practice welds for strength and cut them apart now and again to compare with the illustrations shown in this MIG-welding troubleshooting chart.

6 TIG welding

When those who are interested in welding talk about fusion techniques, the subject of TIG welding is held in a certain reverence. Its reputation in this regard partly stems from its place in history as the method used for construction of a great many famous aircraft. Although developed initially in the 1920s, TIG (Tungsten Inert Gas welding) wasn't used much because the helium shielding gas was too expensive. The intensified research atmosphere of W.W.II spurred further development as aircraft were being made lighter and lighter and TIG became the preeminent method of joining such non-ferrous materials as aluminum and magnesium. The Linde Corporation (now L-TEC) was the first company to capitalize on the technique, and after the war their trademark name "Heli-Arc" became the de facto generic name for TIG welding. Many weldors today still use the term heli-arc more often than TIG as a description of this type of welding, even though a number of other companies have been making TIG equipment for many years.

Besides the romantic beginnings, the TIG process has been considered quite special for other reasons. It does take considerable practice to be good at it, and, because the equipment has always been rather expensive, a weldor who had one and was good with it developed a reputation, particularly in the field of esoteric materials and exotic construction in aircraft and race cars. Basically an outgrowth of

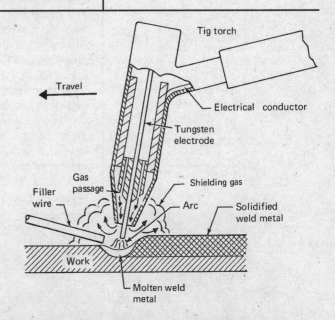

6.1 The TIG process is considered the most precise, most controllable and cleanest method of welding. The arc is made between the work and the central tungsten electrode in the torch, while a flow of shielding gas comes in from the nozzle. Note the low angle of filler rod addition. TIG or heli-arc welding is also one of the most observable welding process, with no spatter and little smoke.

6.2 Where the TIG process is unequaled is on non-ferrous materials or on thin materials. Here a custom bicycle frame was heli-arc-welded from very light, very thin-wall 4130 chrome-moly tubing for strength without a weight penalty. For the same reasons, this kind of material and welding process is use in race cars and aircraft.

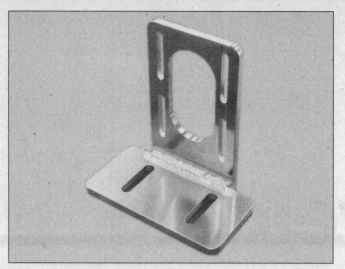

6.3 Where welds on aluminum have to be as pretty as they are strong, TIG is again the top choice. The weld on these two machined and polished parts can easily be wire-brushed to look as good as the polished parts.

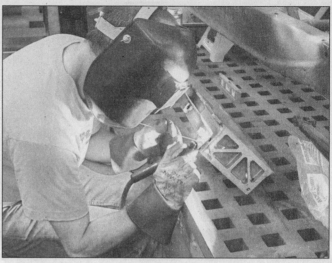

6.4 Unlike arc-welding or MIG-welding, the weldor can get very close to his work with heli-arc equipment. Even when welding on this cast-aluminum dry-sump oil pan, smoke is minimal and the arc not nearly as intense.

6.5 Where precision welds are involved, especially in tight quarters such as on this stainless-steel race-car header, TIG welding's wide range of operator control is seen as an advantage.

arc welding, the TIG process is done with a lightweight torch that uses a tungsten electrode to draw an intense, concentrated arc, shielded by an inert gas. The gas comes out of the torch, all around the electrode and displaces the air from the weld zone to exclude oxygen and nitrogen from contaminating the weld. Although helium was the original gas used, today argon is the most common shielding gas for TIG welding. The tungsten electrode is not considered a "consumable" in the usual sense, since filler metal is supplied by separate, hand-held rods, much like in oxy-acetylene welding. In many ways, heli-arc welding is like a high-tech version of the old-fashioned gas torch.

The concentrated nature of the TIG arc is one of its strong points. Welds of great strength and quality can be made on thin materials, light materials, dissimilar materials, in fact most available metals, and all with minimal distortion or corruption of the adjoining base metal. The process does not generate sparks or spatter, and the welds are as clean as can be, which is why it is the method of choice in aircraft, race-car construction, and stainless and aluminum products made for the medical, dental or food-handling services. There is no slag involved, and, because there is very little smoke generated, the weldor has a good view of the process, allowing him to make very precise joints.

The weldor has greater control with TIG than most other welding methods. The amperage control is infinite because, besides the settings on the power source, the weldor has a foot control he operates as he welds. We recently asked a veteran weldor to make some sample TIG welds to photograph for this book. There was to be one good bead and several bad ones. Even when we set the amperage way too high and way too low, he instinctively tried to produce a good bead, adjusting his torch speed and foot control to compensate. He couldn't make himself do a bad weld, and once the arc was started he tried his best and made fairly good welds even with the machine parameters way off.

With good torch manipulation, a TIG weldor can weld thin materials to thick ones, steel to stainless steel, steel to cast iron, and enough other oddball situations that a good TIG weldor begins to be regarded as some kind of magi-

6.6 When thick-wall mild steel tubing is used in a race-car chassis, welding is usually done with MIG equipment, because of its speed. However, this chassis of lightweight, thinwall 4130 chrome-moly tubing was TIG welded. There are a lot of man-hours represented here in precisely-fit joints and welding time.

6.7 Most shop-type TIG welders are heavy, bulky power sources that require three-phase input power and water connections, making them less portable than other welding machines. This is a Miller Synchrowave 250, a popular unit in many fabrication and race-car shops.

cian. In the time that we were in our friend's fabrication shop, he did a production job heli-arc welding some aluminum brackets, some prototype motorcycle seat frames, repaired a Lamborghini aluminum water-pump casting, welded up a fancy cast-aluminum mailbox post that had been run over, and finally a gunsmith brought in a trigger and barrel from an antique cavalry carbine to be repaired with TIG-welding. He handled them all with equal aplomb, and it was obvious that people from all around brought the tough jobs to him knowing he could handle it.

We've discussed many types of welding systems to this point, and each has been shown to have its advantages and disadvantages. With TIG welding there are only few disadvantages. There are very few jobs a TIG welder can't do, but there are some jobs other techniques are better suited to for practical reasons, not because of a difference in quality or strength of weld. For big jobs, like welding up a car trailer or a big metals rack made from steel tubing, the heli-arc is just too slow - an arc welder or MIG would be much faster. However, there are applications in aircraft and race-car chassis work where a large project may be tediously done with a heli-arc, simply because a lightweight, high-strength material like thinwall 4130 chrome-moly tubing is used where TIG would be the preferred method **(see illustration)**. For outdoor work, again an arc welder or flux-core-wire MIG are the best choices because they aren't as affected by air currents.

The cost and complexity of the TIG system has kept it out of the hands of most small shops until the last few years. Most large TIG setups are heavy, some weigh up to 800 pounds and have to be moved with a crane or hydraulic pallet-jack, and most professional units have a water-cooled torch assembly which often involves some plumbing connections in the shop beside the normal electrical hookups **(see illustration)**. So the big shop-type TIG machines have always been about the most expensive welding machines available, which has increased their mystique but not widened their market. In the last few years, however, manufacturers have built smaller and lighter, solid-state-electronic TIG machines to make them more attractive to the small fabrication shop, race-car shops and street rod builders. Many of these machines are now air cooled, and, at about one-third the cost of the traditional TIG machines, they are being seen out in the field more and more. As one street rod builder told us, "There isn't a thing on a car that would require me to have a 600-amp welder, and when you design and build a car two brackets at a time, the torch never gets that hot."

That is the main difference between the usage of the large, industrial TIG

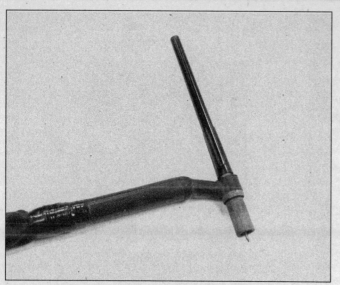

6.8 The basic TIG torch is very light, easy to hold comfortably, and quite durable. The only "consumable" is the filler rods, if used, and to some extent the tungstens.

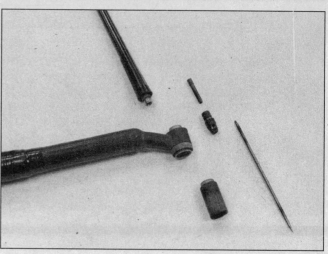

6.9 The exploded view of the typical TIG torch shows the tungsten (right) and from top to bottom: the back cap, collet, collet-chuck, torch body, and ceramic cup or nozzle. To assemble, the collet-chuck is screwed into the torch body on the bottom, the nozzle is screwed in on the bottom, the collet slides in from the top, and then the tungsten is slid in and retained by the back cap.

welding machines and the "economy" TIGs on the market today. The big boys can weld all day long at any amperage they need and never overheat the torch or the electronics. the air-cooled smaller TIGs are fine for anything but long seams or welding big aluminum castings.

The equipment

The basic components of the TIG setup include the power supply, foot control, water circulation system and the torch. The latter differs from the other types of electric-welding torches by being smaller and lighter and holding a central rod of tungsten as the electrode for the arc (see illustration). Taking the torch apart, there is a ceramic shield at the business end (called the ceramic, the gas cup or the nozzle), then the collet, which retains the tungsten in the collet body, and the back cap (see illustration). There is customization of the torch, depending on the work to be done, in that there are different-sized tungstens, different gas cups with shapes for specific kinds of jobs and different back cap lengths depending on how tight the quarters are where the weld has to be made. For instance, you could use a short tungsten and short back cap to fit into a tight corner better. The shape of the gas cup can create a different shape and size envelope of shielding gas over the weld area. From the larger welding-machine companies, there's a variety of different-size torch bodies with different amperage capacities as well as some special models made for tight confines, including one in which the tungsten and ceramic nozzle come straight out of the handle rather than at an angle like most TIG or MIG torches.

When it comes to the basic power supply, you will not find as great a range of choices as with say, MIG welders. The marketplace for TIG equipment is still pretty much a professional arena, and the newer, less-expensive air-cooled TIGs are at one end, and the big, shop units are at the other, with few choices in the middle. A TIG setup is still not a home/shop type welding process, though there are certainly some small specialty fabrication businesses run out of a home garage that could utilize a TIG machine, particularly if the work involved aluminum, stainless steel or other non-ferrous parts, and high-quality, squeaky-clean welds were important to the products' strength or appearance. If you had a

6.10 There are only a few small, more-portable TIG units, like this 100-amp "pulse-TIG" from Daytona MIG. It is a 220V, DC-only machine, but is said to be suitable for steel, stainless-steel and chrome-moly up to 3/16-inch thick.

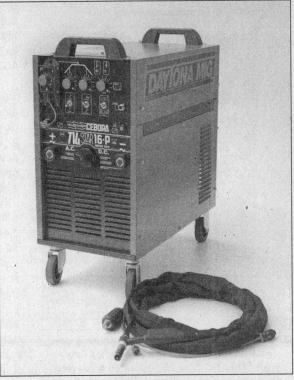

6.11 Mid-size TIG machines are in the 160-250 amp range, though this fairly-portable Daytona MIG unit is 130-amp, 220V. Mid-range machines offer options like slope control and post-flow. This one has square-wave technology, and AC/DC operation.

small business making stainless-steel rope clips or other items for rock climbers, for instance, you might weigh the cost of an air-cooled TIG versus sending all your parts out to be welded in a shop. If you had the volume of work to justify the one-time costs and the learning process, it could be a good move to do your own. However, it would be a wise move to take some TIG classes and get yourself certified first.

Input voltage on TIG machines begins in the 220V range of single-phase power, and the bigger professional boxes are for 460V three-phase. The professional units range in amperage capacity from 250 amps to 300, 400, 500, and 650, though the larger ones are multi-technique machines on which the high amperages are probably used only on the arc-welding process. It would be pretty rare to use more than 300 amps on a TIG weld, unless you had to weld really thick aluminum plates or castings. When welding at 300 amps or more, tiny bits of the tungsten electrode can come off and become included in the weld, which would weaken the joint. The three-phase current models are definitely for shop use only, where the amount of shop equipment and power used every month makes the expense of transformers and rewiring the building economical over the long run in utility bills. Home shops generally do not have three-phase power.

On the small-shop scale, there are very few TIG-capable units in the 115V range. One we have seen is the Hobart Ultra-Weld 130, which is an arc-welder with TIG capability, but with a limited range for either. In its 115V version, it offers 75 amp capacity with a 40% duty-cycle, and the 220V model offers 130 amps at 60% duty-cycle. It does not include the TIG torch, and its TIG range of material thicknesses would be limited. We expect that as the home TIG market expands, there may be some interesting, smaller 115V and 220V units to come. A few imported TIG units are built with DC-only capability to keep the price down to a starter level, and they are fine for steel (only) up to 3/16-inch **(see illustration)**.

Of the medium-range TIG units, there are several of the domestic and imported brands offered in the 160-250-amp category that can handle virtually anything in the small shop environment **(see illustration)**. Most of these are 220V or more in input current requirement, but most are single-phase, which means you could easily wire your shop to accommodate them. Be advised though, that even the 160 amp units can draw 36 amps of input power at their highest settings, and

6.12 When you go up in welding machine size, you get more amperage and higher duty cycles. This TIG-Star 250 operates on several single-phase input currents, and has a 60% duty-cycle at 200 amps, with 100% duty-cycle at 140 amps.

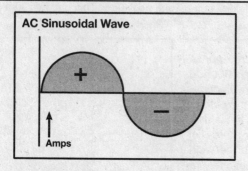

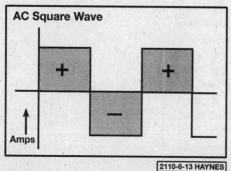

2110-6-13 HAYNES

6.13 As a standard "sinusoidal" wave of AC current flows, it is constantly reversing its polarity and its output is always fluctuating as the wave flows. With the new square-wave technology, electrodes can be used at higher currents and have good arc staring and stability, but without the radio interference of traditional high-frequency superimposition. The square-wave design inverts the current much faster, for better welds on non-ferrous materials.

the 250-amp machines can draw 60 amps or better on full load. This means that your household 30-amp 220V circuit would blow at any of the higher settings. You would really need a separate circuit and box for the welder, with a 50-amp breaker for the smaller mid-range machines and 100-amp breaker for the bigger ones.

The mid-range machines offer several special features, such as *slope control* **(see illustration)**. This refers to how the wave of current cycles when the machine is welding. Picture the wave as a curved line that goes up, down, crosses the baseline and then curves back up and over again in repeated fashion many times a second. This is called a sinusoidal wave in alternating current. TIG machines use both AC and DC current, with the AC used for non-ferrous metals like aluminum or magnesium. One half of the AC wave is actually straight polarity, and the other half is reverse polarity. The straight-polarity portion of the wave builds the heat in the arc, while the reverse current has the effect of cleaning the oxides from the aluminum being welded. So the TIG torch on AC is constantly cycling between a hot arc and a cleaning cycle, but at lower amperages the arc can be obstructed at the changeover point or actually go out. Most of the TIG machines have a special circuit inside that produces a high-frequency, low-power extra current that keeps the process going at all times. The high-frequency control makes the TIG arc easy to start without touching the tungsten to the work, and makes a more stable arc while welding. On many machines the high-frequency system can be set on the front panel of the welder to arc starting, off, or continuous use. On ferrous metal welding, the high frequency is used mainly for arc starting.

The slope control is a feature in which the weldor can adjust the parameters of the wave on the up side or the down side to get the perfect combination of penetration and cleaning action on aluminum. Even a clean piece of aluminum contains some aluminum oxides in the base material, and the slope adjustments allow a good weld to be made without these oxides being included in the bead. Most of today's TIG machines offer *square-wave* AC. The traditional sinusoidal wave with high-frequency over it creates a lot of radio interference as well as some problems on welding aluminum **(see illustration)**. The new machines are all solid-state electronics, with features that make a wave made of up and down squares, rather than half-circles. This means the high-frequency control intervenes less often, and the same-sized electrode can be used at higher currents. This discussion of the current waves may be more than the home/shop user needs to know, but at least you may better understand the language used by manufacturers to describe their equipment. Suffice it to say that the modern square-wave technology and solid-state electronics are desirable features in a full-on TIG machine.

Another feature you may see mentioned is post-flow. When you are making a bead and get to the end of your seam it's a good idea to allow gas to flow over the end of the weld as it cools, to keep out contaminants. On most professional machines, there is an adjustable timer that allows gas to flow for so many seconds after you have stepped off the foot control to quit the arc. You keep the torch in place just where you stopped, and gas keeps flowing for the specified time. This is

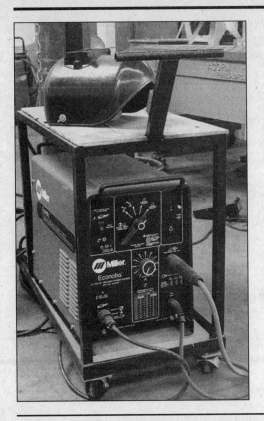

6.14 Less expensive, air-cooled-torch TIG machines have been available now for some time and are making inroads into shops where TIG was previously considered too expensive. This Miller "Econo-TIG" is being used in a street-rod shop on a home-built cart to make it as portable as any MIG machine.

6.15 Today's state-of-the-art in TIG machines is represented by this 300-amp Heli-arc 306 by L-TEC (the new name for Linde Corporation, the original trademark-holders of the name heli-arc). All solid-state with square-wave technology, it provides high performance and high reliability. The bells and whistles include: slope control, spot-weld control, wave balance control, post-flow, and an "arc force" fine-tuning adjustment.

helpful on steel, but is essential on aluminum, magnesium and brittle, high-strength steels like the 4130 used in aircraft and race-car construction. It's called post-flow because it is post-welding gas flow. The post-flow of water and gas to the TIG torch also helps to cool the tungsten electrode down to the point where it can't oxidize when regular shop air flows around it after the welding stops.

Most shop-type TIG machines feature a water-cooled torch, but some are air cooled, with the water-cooling system as an option **(see illustration)**. Obviously, the extra equipment for a water-cooled torch adds to the total price of the package. In some shops, the water-cooling system consist of a unit added on to the basic power supply, containing 1-5 gallons of water, a water-circulating pump and a small radiator and fan. It's like a miniature automotive cooling system. In shops where the amperages used can be quite high, or where long welds are made, the torch may be hooked to a source of regular cold tap water, and the heated return water flows back into the shop's drain. This system uses more water, but keeps the torch cooler than recirculated water systems **(see illustration)**.

The shielding-gas system for TIG welding isn't much different than for MIG welding, as discussed in the last chapter, except that you will use helium, argon or a mixture of the two in your bottle. Most TIG setups use as large a bottle as possible because portability isn't usually a concern in TIG welding **(see illustration)**. Shops that do TIG welding usually have the machine set up right near their welding table and don't move them around, although the newer air-cooled units can be wheeled around a shop without too much trouble.

Unlike oxy-acetylene bottles or most MIG-welding gas bottles that use two-gauge regulators, TIG setups have a single round-faced gauge on their tank and a flow meter instead of the other gauge for the line flow. The flow meter has a vertical glass tube with numbered increments marked on it and a colored ball inside. When the gas is

6.16 Argon bottles are available in a number of sizes, depending on whether you are trying to make your TIG setup portable or not, and how much welding time you need. Shown here, from left, the sizes are: 20, 55, 80, 125, 154 and 248 cubic foot.

6.18 Argon is versatile enough to be used as the shielding gas for almost all TIG work, simplifying the storage of bottles. Often one large bottle mounted on a welding cart is all that's needed in most smaller shops.

6.17 Flow-meters for argon bottles in TIG use are generally used in place of twin-gauge setups. Inside the glass tube on top is a colored ball that floats along a measured scale to indicate gas flow, but without requiring the weldor to step away from his work.

turned on and you click your foot-control on, the ball will float up inside the tube, indicating the level of gas flow in cubic feet of gas per hour (see illustration). Professional weldors like the flow meter better than a gauge because that colored ball can be seen floating in the tube from as far away as their welding table - they don't have to get up and look at the face of a gauge on the tank. They can just step on the pedal to start gas flow and see if the flow meter is set right. They can also tell if they have forgotten to turn on the gas bottle before starting.

The correct gas flow is very important in maintaining the integrity of the weld by keeping out contaminants. For most basic steels, a flow rate of 8-10 cubic feet per hour with argon is sufficient up to 1/8-inch material, but the gas flow requirements go up with the amperage used and the thickness of the metal being welded. Stainless-steel requires only a little more gas flow than for plain steel, but if you were welding aluminum, the gas flow recommendation would go up to 15-20 CFH for the same thicknesses, and a larger-diameter tungsten may be required.

Argon is certainly the basic, all-around shielding gas for the TIG process today, and is useable on virtually all metals (see illustration). Straight helium is seldom used, but often in production work a mixture of argon and helium is used to get the best properties of both gasses. Argon has the qualities of good arc-starting, cleaning action and best puddle control, while helium makes for a hotter weld for greater penetration and a faster welding speed, such as when welding thicker materials. An argon-helium mix is often used to allow welding of non-ferrous metals at higher speeds. The helium in the mix helps make more heat for aluminum welding in a way that one weldor described as like "adding on a turbocharger."

The process in action

Basically, TIG welding is enough like oxy-acetylene welding that if you have already learned well how to weld with a gas torch, the learning curve for TIG welding will be much shorter than for most other weldors who have never learned

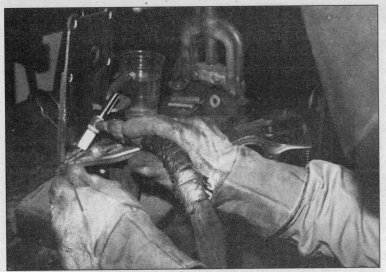

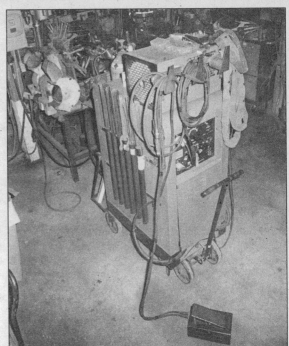

6.19 Finding a comfortable position for your torch hand is more than half the battle in achieving steadiness with TIG welding. Practice making a bead on your proposed setup *without* turning on the arc, just to find a comfortable position. Note the low angle and position of the filler rod in the weldor's left hand.

6.20 This is a TIG welder of some years back. Today's current crop of TIGs are half this size. The water-cooling unit here is mounted on top, and at left is a rack of metal tubing holding various welding rods. The foot-pedal amperage control is in front.

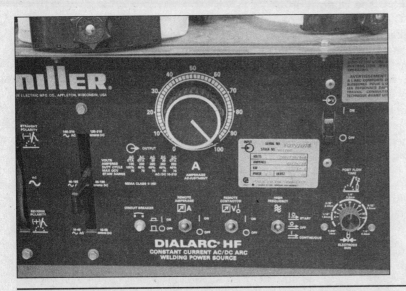

6.21 Layout of this front panel is typical of most TIG power sources, with controls for coarse and fine amperage, current type, high-frequency control and post-timing.

with a torch. It can be as challenging as it is rewarding. Like gas welding, the operator must use both hands, one for the torch and one for the filler rod, each of which must be moved along the weld seam at the same, steady rate **(see illustration)**. In addition, the TIG weldor has to operate a foot-pedal-controlled or hand-controlled amperage device (usually clamped directly to the torch body) that is remote from the welding machine **(see illustration)**. Using the remote control is one of the operator privileges of the TIG process, allowing the weldor to start an arc, infinitely vary the welding current *as he is welding*, and end the arc without moving the torch. Being able to vary the amperage while making a weld is what makes TIG welding so versatile in handling different thicknesses of metals and the joining of dissimilar metals. Just the right amount of heat can be aimed at each side of a joint, and this also helps make TIG a technique that can work for all positions of welding, too.

TIG machines produce either AC output with high-frequency over it (HFAC) or DC with the high-frequency for arc starting only **(see illustration)**. Most TIG machines have a control on the front panel that switches between the types of

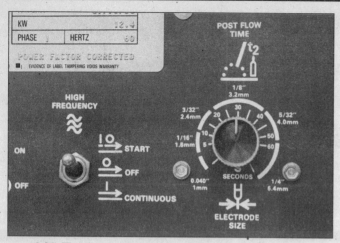

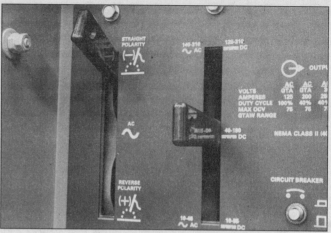

6.22 The three-position switch at left is for the high-frequency, and at right is the post-flow timing as related to various sizes of tungstens. The bigger the tungsten, the more post-flow timing to cool it off.

6.23 The lever at left on this Miller TIG sets the polarity, while the right lever is the coarse amperage, with a bottom setting of 10-55 amps, a medium range of 40-190, and a top range of 125-310 amps. Within each range, the fine-amperage knob sets the upper limit for the pedal.

current, a control to select the basic amp range and controls for high-frequency and post-flow (see illustration).

The AC is used on non-ferrous metals and usually has the high frequency on during welding, except for the newer square-wave machines that don't require high frequency all the time. The DC current can be either straight polarity or reverse polarity. The straight polarity (DCSP) is used for steel, stainless-steel, silver, silicon copper, brass alloys, cast iron, deoxidized copper and titanium, with the AC mainly for aluminum and magnesium.

Set your Machine to DCSP (sometimes marked DC-), the high-frequency to the start-only position, and set the amperage for the material you are working on. Experienced TIG weldors usually set the three-position amperage lever as a coarse adjustment, then dial in the fine amperage control with a knob (see illustration). Often weldors will set the fine control all the way up, using their pedal as the ultimate control. That way, if during the welding the weldor needs a little more heat, he just puts the pedal down further. Whatever you set as the limit on the fine-amperage knob, that's as much as you can get from the pedal (see illustration).

There should be a chart with your machine that tells you the correct size tungsten electrode to use with various amperages and material thicknesses. You will probably use a 1/16-inch, 3/32-inch or 1/8-inch for almost everything you do. There are two basic kinds of tungsten materials, pure tungsten or thoriated tungsten. The pure tungsten works under all conditions and metals, but is *required* for AC TIG, while the thoriated tungstens for DCSP welding are used often because they make slightly better starts and penetration.

Tungstens are somewhat expensive, but can be made to last a long time (see illustration). The sharpness of the tip is important to good arc starting and penetration on steels, so TIG weldors keep a small supply of sharpened electrodes handy to slip into the torch (see illustration). Most weldors will sharpen both ends of a tungsten, so that if they need a new point right away they just loosen the back cap on the torch, slide the tungsten out and reinsert it with the new point down. Good weldors can do this in a

6.24 The pedal is the final weldor control of the amperage in TIG welding. Until you are experienced, you may want to set the amperage knob at the highest you need for a particular job, and know that when you are welding, the pedal can go all the way. It takes some experience to know *how much* pedal to give, if the knob is set to the max for the amp range on the coarse adjustment.

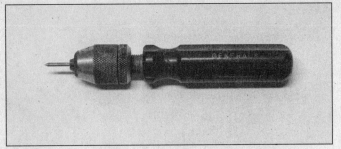

6.25 Make the most of expensive tungsten electrodes by using them until they are too short to fit the torch. Shorter tungstens can be safely sharpened without burning your fingers, using a tungsten-holder like this.

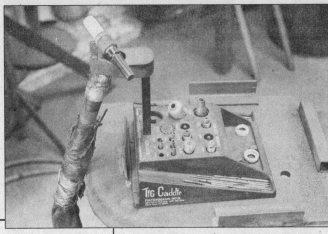

6.26 Spare, sharpened tungstens should be kept handy. This is a TIG caddy, which holds extra tungstens as well as spares for all your torch parts and different size collets and nozzles. The caddy is magnetic, and features a convenient torch rest.

blink of an eye. A belt sander or grinder is usually used for sharpening tungstens, but it should be a dedicated sharpening source **(see illustration)**. A grinder used for smoothing steel or aluminum will have deposits on it that can contaminate the tungsten. Sharpen the tip (like sharpening a pencil) only by grinding *lengthwise* on the electrode, grinding from the tip back to the main body. Grinding it held sideways to the grinder will leave a pattern of marks on the tip that may contribute to arc scattering. Electrode tips for use on aluminum with HFAC should be sharpened to be clean but with a much duller point than used for steel **(see illustration)**. Theoretically, you should have separate ceramic cups for aluminum work too, but many weldors do use the same cup for both steel and aluminum TIG welding. When tightening the electrode in the torch, push the whole torch straight down against a solid surface (with the welder off) to see if the tungsten will slide in. If it slides, the tungsten wasn't tightened enough **(see illustration).**

At some point, your tungsten tip *will* contact the puddle, this isn't desirable, but it happens to everyone. Pull the pedal back all the way to break the arc, and keep the tungsten in the gas flow for a few seconds until it cools off a little. You cannot continue to weld with this tungsten after it has touched either the filler rod or the puddle because it will

6.27 It's important to sharpen tungstens lengthwise on the tip, so as not to leave any radial grinding marks that could cause arc scatter. Grind points for steel like a pencil, like a crayon for welding aluminum.

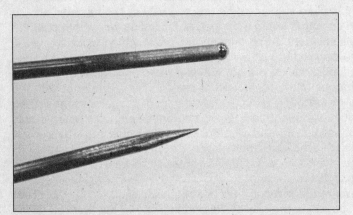

6.28 The tungsten at bottom has been sharpened for use on steel, while the top one is for aluminum, with a small ball-shape on the end. In theory, you could create a ball-end like this by striking an arc on a piece of copper before using the tungsten on aluminum, but a suitably-dull point will turn into a ball like this with a few seconds use on HFAC for aluminum.

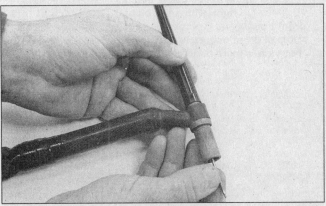

6.29 The sharpened tungsten is inserted into the torch body, and when the tip is sticking out the right distance, you tighten the back cap to hold it in place.

6.30 Although you can crank up the gas flow and extend the tungsten tip out further for reaching into a tight corner, the normal extension of the tip should be 1/8-inch to 3/16-inch from the end of the nozzle.

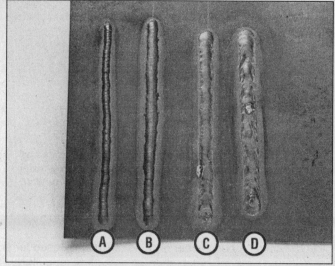

6.31 You'll make a lot of practice beads while learning to TIG weld. Here at left we have: A, a bead with too low an amperage, the bead sits up proud, B, the current control seems about right., C, the amperage is set a little too hot even though the bead seems OK on top, and D. way too hot, with the bead too wide and sunken.

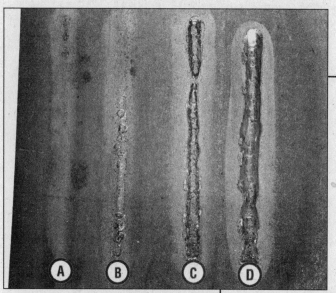

6.32 This is the backside of the same plate as the previous welds. Note how A has only a slight discoloration, B is close to being right, with a tiny bit of dropthrough, and C is too hot, with lots of dropthrough, while D is so hot there's more bead underneath than on top.

be contaminated, and the arc won't be clean and steady. The blackened and pitted section of the tungsten will have to be broken off with a pair of pliers, and the tip will need to be re-sharpened. Although tungstens are not considered consumable in the normal sense of the welding term, they do get shorter every time you break off a piece and every time you re-sharpen them, so eventually they become too short to use. When welding in tight corners, a short back cap can be used with a stubby tungsten, but otherwise use a long cap to protect you from contact with either a sharpened tip (when you have sharpened both ends) sticking out or a hot tungsten. The long back cap covers even a full-length new tungsten.

Turn on your gas and set the flow to 10 CFH, attach the work-lead to a sample plate and run some practice beads. The tungsten should be held in the torch such that 1/8 to 3/16-inch of tungsten extends out past the ceramic cup **(see illustration)**. At no time should the tungsten touch the work. When you bring the electrode to within about 1/8-inch of the work and hit the foot pedal, the arc should start and there will be a red-orange glow at the tip of the tungsten. As you move the tip around in small circle in one spot with the torch perpendicular to the work, bring the pedal control down for more amperage. When the puddle is a bright fluid, move the torch along your seam slowly and evenly. The torch should now be tilted back to a 75-degree angle for the rest of the bead. To stop the process for any reason, just back off the foot control all the way to break the arc, but keep the torch over the same spot to cool the weld and tungsten with gas flow.

When adding filler rod as in most joints of any thickness other than thin sheet metal, move the electrode to the rear of the puddle and dip the filler rod to the forward edge of the puddle. Then bring the torch to the front again and make a new puddle, move back, add filler, move again. This may sound like too much work, but really it is very similar to gas-torch welding and the movements become instinctive after enough practice. The filler rod should not touch the electrode, and it should be kept near the forward edge of the seam to keep it hot between "dips." When it is brought to the molten leading edge of the puddle, a drop of molten steel will come off the rod into the puddle and be blended in when the torch advances over it. The filler rod is usually aligned with the direction of weld travel and held down to a shallow angle with the work.

The rate at which you travel will depend on the thickness of the material you are working on, the amperage and the desired height and width of the bead. If you are too cold with the amperage or travel too fast, the bead will tend to stand up more, and even if it looks smooth and uniform, the weld won't pass a bending test because of lack of penetration **(see illustrations)**. If you are too hot or moving too slowly, the bead will settle into the parent metal and leave a long crater or at least some undercut on either side. On metals thicker than 1/8-inch, the edges of the parts should be beveled, and you will probably make more than one pass. The bottom pass or *root* pass ties the pieces together, and subsequent passes can be made at a higher amperage. TIG welding is not a process that quickly fills in large gaps or beveled seams on thick plates. MIG or arc welding is better for that.

The filler rods used for TIG welding may look exactly like those for gas welding, but they aren't. The TIG rods for steel welding have deoxidizers added, in fact one brand calls theirs "triple-deoxidized," and if you accidentally use a gas welding rod, you can make a bead but the weld will exhibit porosity. The proper TIG rods are very helpful when welding low-quality steels, which may be the "hot-rolled" steel you find at the salvage pile at your local metal supply. There are a variety of filler rods, including special blends used for the low-alloy, high-strength sheet metals now used in automobiles.

After welding, your tungsten tips should be silvery and relatively clean. If they show signs of contamination, or are rough to touch, it usually indicates that air is leaking in somewhere in the torch or that shielding gas is leaking out somewhere. Check the cables and the fit of the collet and ceramic cup. If the electrode looks like it has a ball on the end like a miniature flagpole, then the amperage may be too high for that diameter of electrode. The tungsten shouldn't have a ball on the end bigger than 1.5 times the diameter of the electrode itself. If the tungsten tip is black or blue, check the timing of the post-flow on your machine. If the tip is black, it means the tungsten is cooling off in atmosphere instead of shielding gas and you need a little more time on the post-flow setting.

Look at the inside of your ceramic cup after welding and check it for contamination. A cup that is too small for the work will show deterioration and even cracking. Cups are usually sized in 1/16-inch increments. A #4 nozzle is four-sixteenths or 1/4-inch, a #8 is 1/2-inch. The general rule is for the size of the cup to measure 4-6 times the size of the electrode being used.

Your practice time before obtaining suitable beads will vary with your skill and previous welding experience. As we have said, the similarities between TIG welding and oxy-acetylene gas welding are such that you can pick-up TIG welding much faster if you are already an accomplished gas weldor. When you have practiced straight beads and flat, butt welds and have those down fairly well, then try some corner or Tee welds, and then vertical seams. When you are comfortable on these more difficult welds and the pieces you have done pass simple bending tests and cutaways to examine the penetration, you may be ready to do some actual projects with a TIG welder, but don't start right away with something critical like an automotive suspension or steering part, or anything that goes on an airplane.

TIG-welding aluminum

Perhaps a little more difficult to learn than welding steel, precision joints in aluminum or magnesium are among the primary reasons for having a TIG welder, so this should be your next area of practice.

You need a well lighted area to do TIG welding because the arc is not as bright as with other electric arc techniques, and on aluminum you really need to see how the puddle is developing. Set your machine to HFAC, with the high-frequency on continuous, or use the square-wave feature if you have it, and adjust the post-flow for 1/8-inch electrodes. Use a clean 1/8-inch electrode (pure tungsten) with the tip shaped for aluminum (not a needle-sharp point), and adjust the flow meter for the argon to 17-20 cubic feet per hour. Set an 1/8-inch-thick aluminum plate that has been cleaned thoroughly down on the welding table. Aluminum tends to age-harden when it is exposed to air, and aluminum oxides will constantly build up on the surface; such oxides are not always visible. Parts to be welded need to be cleaned just before welding to provide the freshest surface. Do not use chemical cleaners for preparing aluminum, unless it is something you have purchased at a legitimate welding supply store. Household or automotive cleaners may contain chemicals that will vaporize during welding and create toxic fumes. Use a stainless-steel wire brush (not steel wool) only, and never use this stainless-steel brush for cleaning plain steel. Since most sandpapers are made from aluminum oxide, and this is exactly the material we are trying to eliminate when cleaning aluminum for heli-arc welding, don't use ordinary sandpapers to pre-clean.

Use an aluminum welding rod, and clean the welding rods before starting, using alcohol and a lint-free cloth to wipe them down. The aluminum part you are welding should be well grounded to your table. If it is lightweight plate, put a heavy weight on part of it to keep it in contact with your grounded table, or attach the work clamp directly to the part. Otherwise, you may find that the bottom of an aluminum part you have welded on your table will have arc burns from intermittent contact with the table. Draw a bead on the aluminum for a short distance, then immediately cut off the arc. Examine this weld and you will probably see that where you stopped there's a small depression at the end of the bead. To avoid this at the end of every weld, don't back off suddenly, but rather ease out of it while slowly moving the tip back over the end puddle, and it should keep from sinking.

Try to maintain a puddle of molten aluminum about 3/8-inch wide. Going too fast will keep it narrower, and vice-versa. You won't see any real changes in the aluminum in the way you are used to seeing steel alter during welding. The only clue that an area has become molten is that it gets very shiny in that spot. You'll have to watch for this change in reflectivity when making a series of puddles that make up a bead, because aluminum melts at 1250°F, much lower than steel and can be overheated easily with the intensity of an arc. When welding steel, you have a whole range of colors that the metal turns at different temperatures. These colors make it easier to tell when you have the metal molten and when it is just starting to cool off. You won't have this advantage with aluminum, and you'll probably burn through a number of samples before you learn temperature control on this metal **(see illustration)**.

After the weld is completed and cooled, you'll see your bead is nice and shiny because all of the bead material has been melted and it looks as good as virgin aluminum just out of the foundry, but along each side of the bead you'll see a light-colored band that is contrastingly dull. This is an area where aluminum oxides have been vaporized from the weld bead by the high frequency in the arc and deposited next to the weld. If the aluminum plate you have been practicing on was not entirely clean, you may see some black spots, black "smoke" residue, or a wide dull area on either side of the weld bead, indicating too much aluminum oxide was present. Inspect your welds for uniformity, appearance and cleanliness, and check the backside of your welds for evidence of sufficient penetration.

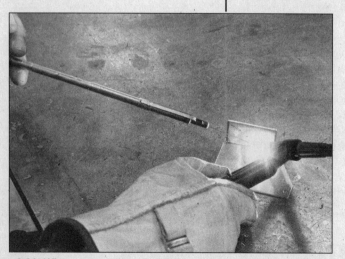

6.33 When you are learning TIG welding on aluminum, keep your torch angle so that you can get a good, close look at how the puddle develops and the molten area becomes shiny. You need enough heat to form the puddle, but not much more or the aluminum vaporizes.

6.34 When welding thick aluminum materials, or aluminum castings like this fancy mailbox post, the edges must be thoroughly cleaned and beveled before welding.

6.35 The rosebud tip on an oxy-acetylene torch is the easiest method for preheating thick and cast aluminum before heli-arc welding. In order not to warp cast-aluminum heads, manifolds and blocks, use heat-markers on the metal while preheating.

When TIG welding any aluminum thicker than 1/8-inch, it is desirable to preheat the aluminum to 350°F before welding (see illustration). This is also particularly important when welding aluminum castings such as repairing cylinder heads, water pumps, aluminum engine blocks, bellhousings and other automotive castings. If the casting isn't preheated before welding, it will probably crack again later on, due to the welding section being expanded more than the adjacent metal, and then shrinking. Aluminum castings soak up a lot of heat, so the initial welding is made easier if the part is preheated because the part doesn't draw off the heat you're putting in to make the seam melt (see illustration). Preheating on automotive castings also helps bake out any dirt or oils that may be present, although any aluminum castings should be thoroughly cleaned before even attempting to weld them. Even starting with a clean casting and a Veed-out crack, impurities in the casting may keep coming out while you weld.

Ideally, aluminum parts should be evenly heated in a temperature-controlled oven, but some parts won't fit in a regular oven, and perhaps the boss of the kitchen may not allow it anyway. The alternative is to use temperature-sensitive paint sticks from the welding supply. Use one made for 350°F and dab some on various parts of the casting. Heat the whole part with a rosebud tip on an oxy-acetylene torch just until all the temperature indicators have melted (see illustration).

TIG-welding stainless steel should prove to be very similar to your practice on mild steel. What makes stainless steel different from ordinary steel is its content of both chromium and nickel, part of the reason for its much higher expense. You will find some characteristics that are different, such as the heat staying in the bead area longer than in plain steel because stainless steel is only about half as conductive of heat as regular steel. Once stainless steel does take on heat, it expands some 50% more than mild steel, which can cause problems of warpage in thinner materials if the pieces aren't clamped or jigged securely during the welding process. In critical welding in industry, jigs may be made of copper because its conductivity helps to carry heat out of the stainless parts quicker.

In terms of setup, stainless steel can be TIG welded with the argon flow set only slightly more than for steel, from 11-13 CFH for thicknesses

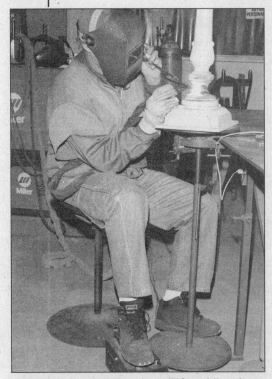

6.36 Weldor Bill Maguire is TIG-welding the heated mailbox post, using his rotating welding stand he invented. At the bottom is a round disc you can spin with your foot, leaving your hands free to continue welding, especially where you have to go *around* something. These should be available for sale at the time of printing.

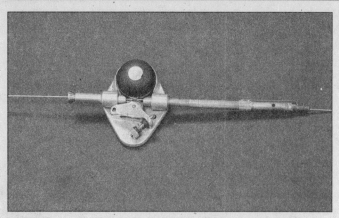

6.37 No one knows better what a weldor would need than a weldor. Another invention of Bill Maguire's is this "Pocket-Feeder", which is patented and for sale through major suppliers. It hand-feeds a welding wire, from .020-in. to 3/32-in., to your weld, while your hand stays the *same*, comfortable distance from the work. Your thumb on the wheel determines the feed speed.

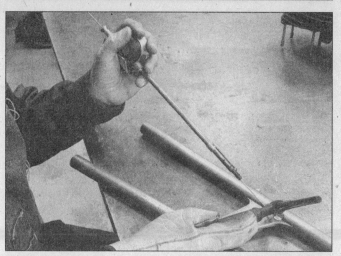

6.38 In use, the Pocket-Feeder can be used with either left or right hands, and you can reload new wire with one hand. Sensitivity on the thumbwheel is good, even with a light glove on.

up to 1/4-inch. Set your current controls for DCSP as you would for steel, with high-frequency for starting only, unless you are working on very thin pieces, in which case you might use HFAC instead because of its lower heat input and lesser tendency to burn through thin material. When using DCSP, the 2%-thoriated tungstens work best, with the pure tungstens good for HFAC on thin material. Of course the welding rods must be stainless steel. Practice on some stainless scraps until you get the hang of handling the different heat-transfer capabilities of stainless. Your puddling and rod-dipping action will be at a different pace than for mild steel.

In industry, critical welds on stainless steel are often made with a setup on the backside of the part to exclude air from the weld area. Of course, the shielding gas on top from the torch takes care there, but on the backside the weld can be contaminated. The pros form a box or shield around the back of the weld area and plumb some extra argon shielding gas in one end and out the other end into a tube to carry it away from the weldor. This will purge any air from the backside of the weld where it could cause any molten stainless-steel to crystallize. This technique is also used in protecting the back of titanium when TIG welding. When they weld critical tubing and can't get at the inside with a shield, they plug each end of the tube or pipe with tape and cardboard and fill the pipe with shielding gas. This is particularly true when welding stainless-steel tubing meant to carry medical ingredients or anything else that must be kept from contamination or oxidation.

Although you will likely never encounter other metals in your home/shop use, there are a variety of special alloys and rarely-used metals that are used often in specialized industries, and for which TIG is the primary or only method found to do the job properly. For instance, in the food-service and canning/bottling industry, there are numerous products that are transported through tubing or pipe. Besides stainless steel, nickel is often used in these applications, for its resistance to alkalines and acids. For the same reasons, it is used extensively in the chemical industry. But nickel-alloy pipe used in these situations cannot tolerate the possibility of a particle of slag, such as from stick welding or MIG welding, becoming included in the weld bead. It would become a weak point when faced with continued chemical attack if high temperatures are involved, until surrounding material is affected and the joint is weakened. For this reason, nickel work must be thoroughly cleaned before welding without using chemical cleaners, or a black nickel oxide coating can form.

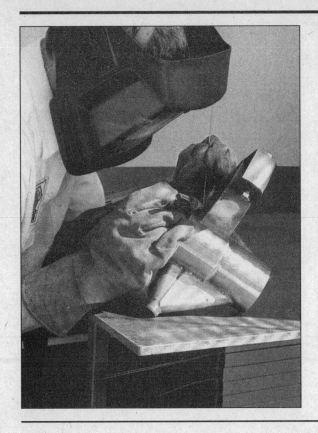

6.39 TIG welding is especially helpful in situations like this race-car suspension upright, where you have thin chrome-moly plate and tubing, and need total heat control. If you burn through on a job like this, the whole part may have to be scrapped.

6.40 Beautiful, precise welds on this race-car exhaust system typify experienced, professional TIG welding.

For metals like nickel, copper, titanium, and others, TIG welding has proven itself to be the most adaptable method, especially in critical applications. Since there is no flux of any kind used in TIG welding, there is no chance of even minute slag particles being included in the weld bead. Industry is also capitalizing on the fine-grain structure of TIG welded seams (and the heat-affected areas nearest the weld). Helium is most often used as a shielding gas on nickel for its hotter arc, which allows for a higher welding speed, with a gas flow of 8-30 CFH, depending on work thickness. Polarity is usually set at DCSP (except for thin work where HFAC can be used to prevent burn-through), and the high frequency control set for *start-only*, using thoriated tungstens. Filler rods must be nickel or nickel alloy. Oxidation can be kept to a minimum by keeping the filler rod at a low angle to the work and keeping the rod tip in the shielding-gas envelope.

It isn't done often, but TIG welding can be used to repair cast iron. Your welding supply store will have some special rods that are cast of gray iron, called "three-in-one," and these should work for either gas or TIG welding although the same preheating instruction apply as above when we discussed welding cast aluminum parts.

Heli-arc or TIG welding is likely to remain as mostly a shop-only process due to the expense of the equipment and the length of the learning curve, but don't discount it as something you can't try. If you know someone in a shop with TIG equipment, ask them if you can spend a few hours closely observing them (with a suitable spare helmet on, of course) performing TIG welds. The lack of spatter and smoke from TIG welding means you can observe this process better than most other welding methods, and this will tell you much more about how the process works than a chapter in a book. If you feel you have observed enough to get a good idea, see if they will let you try it out, but first offer to pay for any tungstens you ruin in your practice. You may find you have a hidden aptitude in hand-eye coordination, and TIG may be a process that appeals to you.

Notes

7 Plasma cutting/welding

Just as the emergence of lower-cost, higher-efficiency MIG machines has made something of a revolution in small shop and home/shop welding in the last ten years, so has plasma technology changed the face of metal *cutting*. While the technology has been around for a while, it has been seen by most weldors as a high-technology setup that seemed complicated or hard to use. Plasma technology's biggest usage had been in plasma arc welding, or PAW, and it is still used in this form in many industrial applications.

The simpler plasma-arc *cutting* (or PAC) technology got very little play at the time, and it has taken some years for the equipment to filter down to the general welding/cutting marketplace. As with the MIG welders, what was originally considered to be a professionals-only setup has entered the province of the small shop and the amateur fabricator, due mainly to the introduction of less-expensive imported equipment that really opened up new markets with hobbyists. The domestic welding manufacturers suddenly became aware of these newer markets for smaller versions of equipment they had been selling to industry all along and brought increasing competition to the fray. Today there's a wide selection of plasma machines to choose from, from small 110V AC portables to large shop equipment for materials up to one inch thick.

7.1 Plasma cutting can be done outdoors, being very little bothered by wind, makes very clean cuts on ferrous and non-ferrous materials, and produces no smoke and very little sparks. It has become the modern way to cut metal. The operator here should be wearing gloves and a long-sleeved shirt.

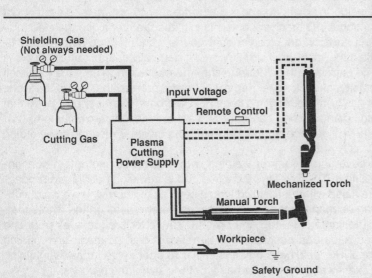

7.2 This illustration shows the basic components of the plasma-arc layout. The two bottles of shielding gas are really only required on the large industrial machines, not the home/shop portables which run on compressed air. The medium and larger sized plasma cutters can be used with a straight (mechanized) torch body for trace cutting.

Usage today is increasingly with the cutting side of plasma technology. With an incredibly easy learning curve and not a lot of special installation costs, the benefits of plasma-arc cutting, usually just called plasma cutting, are being reaped today by body shops, muffler shops, wrecking yards, sheet-metal shops, duct repairmen, street rodders, race-car builders and fabrication shops. Among the benefits are use of plain shop air-compressor air, no dangerous gasses, no flames, smoother cuts, less heat distortion in the edges you cut, little oxidation of the edges and incredible speed.

In basic principle, the plasma process uses a torch something like a TIG torch, but the electrode is deeply recessed up into the torch, where it cannot contact the work and be contaminated, and the arc is maintained as a needle-like point when the air between the electrode and the work is ionized. The air or gasses around the electrode are heated to such a point that they reach the *plasma* state, in which the gasses themselves can *conduct electricity*. While the gas is ionized and making continuity for the arc process between the electrode and the work, another gas is introduced around the nozzle. In the case of plasma welding, the gas is an inert shielding gas; in the case of plasma cutting, it is compressed air. In either case, welding or cutting, the action takes place in a very narrow stream.

Plasma-Arc welding

The original plasma technology was developed in the laboratories of the Linde Air Products Company (a pioneer in many welding processes, now the L-TEC Company) back in the late Fifties. They and other companies have worked on refining the equipment and the process ever since. You won't find plasma welding equipment at most welding supply stores, but it is in a few industry catalogs. This is the kind of equipment usually sold through a company representative. Most of this equipment is used in high-precision joining of very thin materials. Although, up until the last ten years, both plasma welding and cutting have been virtually reserved for industrial purposes only, and most of the plasma-arc welding equipment is still expensive and for limited industrial usage, the process is worth looking at.

In operation, the plasma torch has a central tungsten electrode tucked up inside a nozzle that is more restrictive than other welding gun nozzles, that is closer to the electrode and increasingly tighter as it gets close to the tip of the electrode, until there is just a hole for the arc to come through **(see illustration)**. An "orifice" gas is forced through this nozzle, and it speeds up like air/fuel mix going through a carburetor's venturi. The gas is usually argon.

Inside the welder's power source is a high-frequency arc-starting system not unlike a conventional TIG machine, and this initiates the arc, since the electrode doesn't stick out and can get close enough to the work metal to start the arc itself. This is called the "pilot-arc" circuitry, and it generally cuts out after the arc is established. The current in the electrode superheats the argon until the gas itself conducts electricity, and a long, extremely hot arc is created that welds the work. A second inert gas is introduced in a large nozzle around the inner one, such that a cone of shielding and cooling gas is formed around the long arc column to protect the weld area from contamination, much as in other electric arc-welding processes.

There are several methods of welding with plasma technology, a conventional method akin to TIG welding where filler rod is added, a needle-arc process where parts are fused without filler rod, and a keyhole method where a weld without filler rod can be made that actually fuses the parent metal on the whole mating surface at the same time, top and bottom. The latter produces as pure and uncontaminated a joint as possible. The benefits of using plasma-arc welding over conventional TIG welding is that it is easier to operate as far as maintaining the arc length exactly and the weldor has a better view of the process.

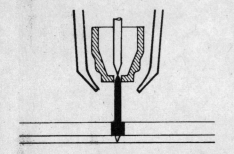

7.3 In the needle-arc version of plasma welding, the narrow-and-tall arc forms a weld that makes 100% penetration, top and bottom. The technique is used mostly in precision industrial applications.

Although you may find one or two PAW units in a catalog, most of the technology is used in industrial situations with mechanized torches and water cooling with amp ranges up to 300 or 400. Most manual-operation plasma welders do not have as much amperage as conventional welders; L-TEC's catalog shows a 110V 15-amp unit, and a 100-amp 220V three-phase machine weighing some 730 pounds that only welds up to 1/8-inch plate, although it has a 100% duty cycle at maximum output.

For those reasons, the plasma-arc welding process is probably not for your home/shop. Much more flexible, lighter and more affordable conventional equipment is available for making welds. However, there is no question but that the practical application of the technology in everyday situations is eminently provided by plasma-arc *cutting* equipment.

Plasma-Arc cutting

In plasma-arc cutting, the technology is much the same as welding, but the arc is even more constricted, with the plasma temperature so high that the arc can cut *any* metal. The very restricted arc cuts a pencil-thin line through the metal, and a sharp force of gas through the nozzle blows the melted metal from the kerf **(see illustration)**. The velocity and steadiness of the cutting action is such that the edges of the cuts are kept very straight and clean.

The benefits of plasma-arc technology in cutting metal are many. The cuts are very clean, with little oxidation of the metal as found in oxy-acetylene cutting, the velocity of the action creates smoother edges that need a great deal less cleanup, and in fact, with the industrial units that are mechanized much like a gas flame-cutter or pattern-cutter, the cuts need no cleanup or preparation for welding **(see illustration)**. There is little or no slag found on the bottom edge of the kerf.

Plasma-arc cutting is considered much safer in many work environments than gas cutting. There are no flammable gasses involved, there is no smoke from the cutting action to bother the weldor, he can watch the process much more closely and there is much less spray of sparks coming from under the cut. If you remember the little sparking toys you had as a kid, where you pushed a plunger and a wheel went around, scraping against a tiny flint making sparks, that is a small-scale version of what you see when plasma cutting. This is in high contrast to gas cutting, where there is a lot of heat generated, and blobs of molten metal are constantly falling on the floor under the cut, creating a fire hazard.

There is *some* heating action in plasma cutting, but in a short time, depending on the thickness of the material you have cut, the parts are ready to be handled for further work. With a gas cutting torch, the parts are still red-hot. Some have described the plasma process as almost "cold cutting." Another benefit of the cooler cutting action is that much less heat is induced into the parent metal, so when working on thin materials there is greatly reduced warpage.

This is what has made the plasma cutter so popular with automotive bodymen and sheet-metal workers. Thin materials can be cut with virtually no distortion. The cuts can be made, as one bodyman described it, "as fast as you could draw a line with a pencil." A few minutes with a file or sandpaper and the edges are ready for some other work, whether to be welded or left as a finished edge. Because of the lower heat and reduced sparks, panel-cutting on cars is much easier, even if there is a secondary panel on the other side because there is less damage to what's on the other side like other painted surfaces that need to be left untouched. Bodymen also like the fact that you can make a cut, lay down the

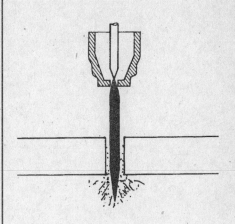

7.4 In plasma-arc cutting, there is usually only one gas (in all but the biggest machines), and that is air from the shop's air compressor, which is forced around the electrode to blow the kerf out neatly.

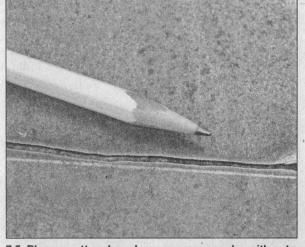

7.5 Plasma cutters have become very popular with auto bodymen for the cleanliness and speed in cutting body panels. These sheet-metal edges need very little prep, and a plasma cutter can cut painted or rusty metal just as easily.

torch, do something and pick up the torch again and start cutting with no other functions to perform other than putting your safety helmet down and pulling the torch trigger. With a gas cutting torch, there is always the danger of what to do *between cuts* with a torch flaming full-bore. If you keep shutting it off each time, you have to go through the process of re-lighting and adjusting it every time.

The last reason is why plasma-arc cutting has become the tool of choice now in wrecking yards across the country. In a yard full of discarded cars with flammables like upholstery still in them and various pools of oil, gasoline and other fluids soaked into the ground all around, oxy-acetylene cutting on cars in wrecking yards has always been a hazardous job. Also, the torches and bottles are a heavy setup and had to be hauled around to various parts of the wrecking yard. With a good plasma machine, the 220V cutter can be plugged in a small shed central to the yard, while a plasma torch cable as long as 234 feet could be used to cut almost anywhere with a lot less fire danger and much faster speeds, 10 or 20 times faster than with acetylene equipment.

Because the plasma machine has arc-starting circuitry built-in, most plasma torches do not need to contact the metal to get started, which is a decided advantage in body work. Once the arc is started and the gas is ionized and conductive, a plasma torch can cut through rusty metal, painted metal, even sections of a car body that have Bondo or undercoating on them. When using an oxy-acetylene torch to cut painted sheet metal, the cut edges are blackened, scarred and blistered, while with plasma the edges have a gray discoloration near the edge and that's it.

In fabricating shops, one of the biggest advantages of plasma-arc cutting equipment is the fact that all metals can be handled equally, from steel to aluminum, to stainless and plated or galvanized metals. It is the nonferrous metals like aluminum and austenitic stainless steel, which are normally hard to cut cleanly with other methods, that make the plasma machines appealing to shops. The author remembers his first experience with a plasma cutter some years back. An aluminum motor plate was being made for a race car, and we needed to cut a 14-inch hole out of the center to clear the flywheel. The material was 1/4-inch-thick aluminum and 7075-T6, which is so hard you can have difficulty even drilling it unless you have a fresh bit. The idea of using a sabre saw or band saw seemed tedious and out of the question. We took it to a shop that had a plasma cutter and within minutes of making a plywood circle template to run the torch around, we had our hole cut with very little heat and perfect edges. It was eye-opening, and when you try one you may be similarly amazed.

When plasma-arc cutting equipment first came into wider, less-industrial usage, some traditional fabricators and bodymen were intimidated. The technology wasn't widely understood, and the term "plasma" seemed to indicate some highly-technical process akin to esoteric lasers. Once the machines got out into the field, they quickly became accepted for their speed, cleanliness, lack of maintenance, lower fire hazards and the ease with which a weldor can operate them. It's almost a pull-the-trigger-point-and-shoot kind of process.

Perhaps one of the bigger attractions of plasma cutting equipment we haven't mentioned yet is the type of gasses used in the process. While the big industrial plasma machines do use traditional shielding gasses, like argon for the arc "pilot" gas and hydrogen, nitrogen or a gas mixture (like 35% hydrogen/65% argon) as the cutting gas, most portable plasma units today use nothing more than *compressed air* from a shop air compressor **(see illustration)**. There are no expensive bottles to buy or periodically refill.

This is how the shop-air works. When the gas in the arc

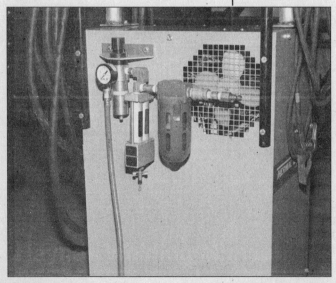

7.6 Shop air-compressor air is all that's required to run most plasma cutters. Here on the back of a Thermal Dynamics machine is the air filter and pressure regulator.

column is ionized, it becomes the arc medium between the work and the electrode. Nitrogen happens to ionize well and makes for a hot arc, and also happens to make up about 75% of the air around us by weight. Most plasma cutters use a high velocity of shop compressed air to become the ionized arc gas, the cutting gas that blows the material out of the cut, and the cooling medium. It can be assumed that all shops already have a heavy-duty air compressor on hand for operating other equipment, so using shop air greatly simplifies the use of a plasma cutter and keeps expenses down. In industrial situations, pure nitrogen or hydrogen or a mix is used for totally clean cuts in precision work, but the shop-air cuts are more than good enough for any automotive or fabricating-shop usage.

Choosing plasma cutting equipment

The large, expensive and heavy industrial plasma cutters and welders are for specific purposes in high-precision and high-production mechanized work, often requiring two gas bottles, three-phase power for 200-600 amps, and use water cooling for the torch as well. For these reasons, we'll concentrate on the wide array of more portable plasma cutters that are available for home and shop use, most of which operate on 220V, single-phase current and use only shop compressed air for cutting and cooling.

At the most basic level, where a home/shop user might be interested, there's a number of domestic and imported plasma cutters that weigh 75 pounds or less and are capable of cutting material thicknesses that an automotive user would come across. If you are comparing plasma cutters to welders, don't be alarmed at the amperages on the smaller plasma machines. Units with 50-amp capability can cut steel up to 3/4-inch thick. An area where there is a comparison with welders is that smaller plasma machines have lower duty-cycles and their cutting speed slows down when thicker materials are cut.

In the 110V category, Daytona Mig offers the Pocket Plasma , which puts out 25 amps at a 20% duty-cycle and cuts sheet metal at 100 inches per minute, though it is said to cut up to 3/16-inch steel material. It requires 70psi air input at a rate of 4-6 cubic feet per minute (cfm). Miller makes several 110V units, with the Spectrum 187D cutting up to 9/64-inch steel material and weighing 47 pounds. Thermal Dynamics starts their extensive line off with the DynaPak 110, which cuts up to 3/16-inch steel, uses all solid-state circuitry, sequential status lights, and has an amazing 80% duty-cycle at 20 amps **(see illustrations)**. With all of the machines available, the maximum cutting thickness is usually given for mild steel, while aluminum and other non-ferrous material take more amps and the same machine can only cut a lesser thickness of these metals. On some machines, a figure may be advertised that gives a maximum thickness for cutting

7.7 The compact end of the plasma cutter market is represented by 110V machines such as this Plasma Pocket from Daytona MIG. It puts out 25 amps, weighs 55 pounds, and requires 4-6 cfm of air at 70 psi.

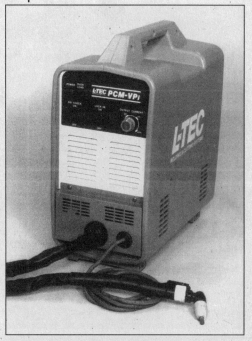

7.8 Another quite-portable plasma machine is the PCM-VPi from L-TEC, which offers cuts up to 5/8-inch in steel, variable amps from 10-40, and a 60% duty-cycle at its rated maximum. It operates on 220V current.

7.9 One of Miller's smallest plasma cutters, the Spectrum 187D weighs only 47 pounds, yet cuts up to 9/64-inch materials, and runs on 110V house current.

7.10 The popularity of plasma-arc equipment has really jumped in the last five years. Now imported units are sold here, and tool companies like Matco have them, as well as the traditional welding equipment manufacturers.

7.11 HTP's entry-level plasma cutter takes 220V current, but weighs only 56 pounds and is said to cut up to 1/4-inch steel. It has a 100% copper-wound transformer.

and another, higher figure for severing. The severing action is a short cut, such as when cutting a length of material.

Beyond the 25-amp range that seems to be the limit for 110V equipment, there are machines for 220V input that are still quite portable. HTP America offers affordable plasma cutters from their Micro-Cut 250 that cuts up to 3/16-inch steel, to the Micro-Cut 375 which can be used on 110V, 220V or 460V input and offers 7.5-35 amps, cutting up to 3/8-inch steel, as well as larger shop units **(see illustration)**. L-TEC has a popular unit, the PCM-VPi, which weighs only 46 pounds with its plastic case and carrying handle, but is said to cut up to 5/8-inch steel with its 50 amps of power, and features a 60% duty-cycle at 40 amps output **(see illustration)**. It is a good choice for any automotive shop, and can sever up to 3/4-inch material such as re-bar for construction sites. Lincoln's entry-level plasma cutter is the Pro-Cut 40, with a 60% duty-cycle at 40 amps, 220V input, cuts up to 3/8-inch steel, and offers a timed pilot arc and timed post-flow. Daytona MIG's medium-sized lineup includes a 35-amp, 220V Plasma Prof 35 that is said to cut up to 3/8 steel quickly, and 1/2-inch steel at 15 inches per minute.

Above the 50-amp range, plasma-arc cutting equipment is in the serious shop equipment arena. Most of these machines are for 220V, *three-phase* power input, which you won't have at most home garages or small shops. Within this large group of choices though, there are cutters with total amperage ranging from 50 amps to 150 amps or more. In this category, you'll find the Lincoln Pro-Cut 125, with 125 amps, 60% duty-cycle, a microprocessor-controlled overshoot limiter, and "Drag-Detect" circuitry that is said to prevent consumable damage. In this machine, let's look at the duty cycles for a professional-grade plasma cutter. Rated at 60% duty-cycle at its highest 125-amp output, it has an 80% duty-cycle at 110 amps, and a 100% duty-cycle at 100 amps or less. At its highest output, this machine can cut 1 1/4-inch steel, and for ordinary 1/2-inch plate, it can cut all day long. That's the difference in the heavier professional machines; they have stronger components to work heavy materials not just a few times a day, but all day, which is why they are overbuilt and too expensive for the home/shop market, even disregarding the three-phase input power required.

Other powerful plasma-arc cutters include: HTP's PCA 65, with 60 amps (220V single-phase), cuts up to 3/4-inch steel (clean cuts on 5/8-inch steel), a 50% duty-cycle at 60 amps, and a weight of 180 pounds. HyperTherm has their 100-amp MAX 100, that will cut 1 1/4-inch steel on 220V or 440V three-phase power, with CC (constant-current) transistorized output, ESAB offers the PCS-90 that cuts up to one-inch steel with three-phase 220V or 440V, and has air pre-flow, post-flow and a low-air-pressure sensor. L-TEC has the PCM-1000i, which can cut one-inch steel at production speeds with its 80 amps, and a 70% duty cycle at that maximum amperage, yet weighs only 80 pounds. Daytona MIG has a full line of heavy-duty plasma cutters, with the Plasma Prof 120 being near the top with 120 amps (220V three-phase), cuts up to 1 1/8-inch steel and 7/8-inch aluminum, with quick-disconnect torches so you can switch to a mechanical torch for a cutting table **(see illustrations)**.

Most of these machines offer such features as infinitely-variable output control, which means that you can dial in the exact requirements for a job, say cutting through an outer skin on a vehicle without cutting panels on the other side. Of course, you can cut thin materials with more power than

7.12 The bigger-amperage machines are all in the 220V category, and many, like this Daytona MIG Plasma Prof 50, require shop-type three-phase current, too. This one has a 35% duty-cycle at its rated max of 50 amps and 100% at 30 amps.

7.13 Still light and portable, but powerful enough to cut 3/4-inch steel, The L-TEC PCM-750i has 50 amps with a 40% duty-cycle at that setting, and has its own torch storage spool and spare parts storage compartment.

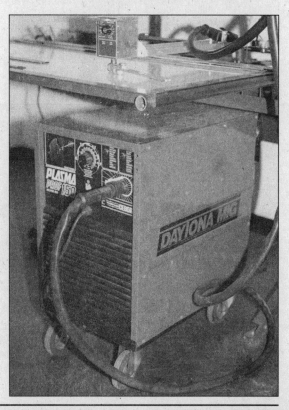

7.14 The larger plasma-arc cutting machines are all in the three-phase power category, like this Plasma Prof 150 from Daytona MIG. It weighs 317 pounds, has a range from 20-150 amps, and can cut 1 1/2-inch steel and 1-inch aluminum at 30 inches per minute.

7.15 **Larger machines are usually offered with an optional 180-degree (straight) torch for use with shape-cutting machines for industrial work.**

is required, but using just the right amount means you have the least danger from flying sparks. On the less-expensive end of the plasma cutter spectrum, some of the machines offer only a knob with several predetermined positions.

Beyond the 80-120 amp range of plasma cutters, where really large plates are cut all day long, the equipment offered is no longer usable with shop air, requiring two inert gas supplies and water-cooling for the torch. However, they offer from 100 amps to as much as 600 amps (the higher amperages are usually found on machines built to be used with mechanized torches), and all with 100% duty-cycle. Obviously, that kind of power doesn't arrive at your doorstep without a hefty invoice.

Using a plasma cutter

If you thought the modern MIG welder brought great advancements in ease of the learning and operating curves, wait until you try plasma-arc cutting. It's as much of an improvement over gas-torch cutting, in both learning curve and reduced maintenance. We watched as a race-car mechanic in a large shop was being trained by another worker to utilize their plasma cutter. The newcomer to the technology made his first 4-inch by 6-inch part from 3/8-inch steel plate after only fifteen minutes of instruction. After experimenting with different speeds, power levels and materials, he was ready to do real jobs after an hour. You can't learn everything there is to know about the process in your first day, but this story is typical of first-time users.

Unlike welders, most plasma cutters of the shop-type variety are ready to use when you uncrate them. Their power cord is ready to plug in (you don't have to put on your own plug), the torch is usually already hooked up to the front of the machine, and all you have to do is connect your shop air supply before making your first cuts.

Although the risk of fire or injury is less with a plasma cutter than with a welder or oxy-acetylene cutting torch, you must still take every precaution before starting. Read over the instruction manual that came with your machine before doing anything. When you are familiar with all the controls, take the torch apart, so you'll understand how it works. Specific design of electrodes and other parts may vary from make to make, but, whatever the make, you'll notice that the electrode is like no other you've seen. Instead of a six-inch-long rod of tungsten as with a TIG torch, the plasma electrode is a machined part.

Although it never comes in contact with the work, the plasma cutter's electrode should still be considered a "semi-consumable" item. Electrodes can last a long time, but keep several spares on hand because they do get worn and contaminated with material blown back from the cutting **(see illustration)**. Besides the electrode, you'll find several other pieces inside the plasma torch, including the nozzle (also called a shield cup, retaining cup, and gas diffuser), and a cutting tip, which is what converges the airflow past the electrode **(see illustration)**. Different brands of torch may have small springs, insulators or swirl rings, but the basic principle is the same for all brands.

There is much less danger with a plasma cutter than other equipment, yet there are still hot sparks generated. There is also ultraviolet radiation. Because the process doesn't seem as bright or intense as welding, some users

7.16 **Eventually, enough material will blow back from cutting to cause a building of slag on the exposed nozzle and orifice of the torch, requiring periodic maintenance.**

7.17 The main components of a typical plasma-arc cutting torch are, from left: torch body with o-ringed and threaded extension, the swirl ring, the electrode, the cutting nozzle, and the retaining cup. Some brands have a slightly different arrangement of parts inside.

7.18 Hot rodders never leave anything alone. Rugged Thermal Dynamics 50-amp plasma cutter used in a rod shop has been modified with the addition of a tubing rack and box on top to hold nozzle dip and plasma consumables.

are tempted to perform plasma cutting without proper safety wear, but your skin can still be burned. So wear long-sleeved shirts with the collar and cuffs buttoned up, and wear leather welding gloves and a full-face shield. If you ever have to work on your machine, it should be unplugged, even if all you are doing is changing the electrode. The machine's output is high enough voltage to cause severe shock and injury. Also, if you are cutting any painted, plated or galvanized metals, ensure that you have adequate ventilation. The plasma process doesn't create fumes by itself, but what's on the surface of the metal can.

On most machines, there is a high frequency arc-starting circuit that makes it unnecessary to touch the work with the torch to initiate the arc. Set your output voltage at the machine, depending on the thickness of the metal you are cutting. On some of the smallest machines, there may just be an on/off switch, or a switch with two or three amperage positions. Most machines have a variable knob spanning from the machine's minimum amperage to its maximum.

Use a guide of some kind to make straight practice cuts **(see illustration)**. Place the torch so that the outer cup rides on your guide with the nozzle the suggested distance from the work and just push the button. The arc will start, it will

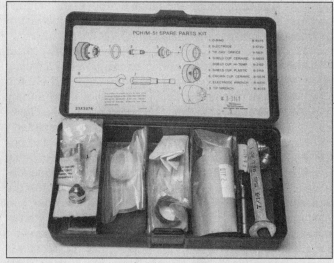

7.19 You'll need to keep on hand some spares of each of the torch components, including wrenches for changing the tip and the electrode.

7.20 The plasma cutter makes very clean cuts, so any raggedness on yours means your hand wasn't steady. Use a sturdy guide whenever possible. With a piece of tubing as a straightedge, here a dry run is being made to ensure the torch follows the correct cut line.

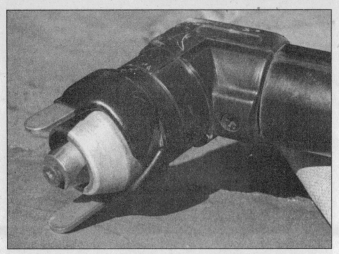

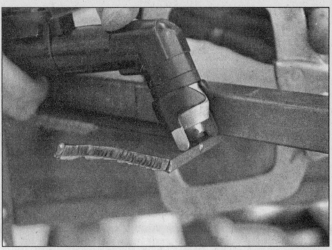

7.21 This clever tool snapped onto a Miller plasma torch holds the torch just the right distance away from the work, so if you have this and a sturdy guide, your cuts should be almost as good as machine-operated torches.

7.22 Same tool as the previous photo, showing how it holds the tip away from the work, and provides a good surface to lightly drag against your pattern or straightedge.

7.23 At top here are two cuts made with a hand-held plasma cutter. In the top one the torch was moved too fast and with not enough amperage. The middle plate had the speed more correct. The bottom plate for comparison only was oxy-acetylene cut with a machine, so this is the smoothness you are trying to duplicate. Only a gas torch cut would have this discoloration of the metal showing.

pierce the metal (no need to go to the edge of a plate to get the cut started) and begin blowing the slag out the bottom. Move along at a steady speed and you're *cutting*. You'll develop a feel for the correct cutting speed for various materials, but the instructions with your machine should tell you the recommended speeds for various thicknesses and materials. Practice moving the torch a few times without the arc, just to see how fast or slow 15 inches per minute may be, and what 100 inches per minute feels like.

Examine the cut edges of the material. If the lines in the cut are not straight up and down, your speed was off **(see illustration)**. If the lines turn to the direction the cut was made from, your cutting speed was too fast. You can also have someone else observe you from a short distance while you are cutting. They will tell you if the sparks went straight down (proper speed), or sprayed more to the direction the torch came from (too fast). Moving too fast can cause premature failure of the nozzles.

When the part you have cut is cool enough to pick up, examine the kerf. If your cutting speed and amperage was right, the small amount of slag at the bottom of the kerf can be easily clipped off with wire-cutter pliers, and the rest of the metal should take minimal cleanup.

In cutting shapes, you can use plywood patterns to cut repeated shapes such as round or square holes or anything else. Just make the template the right size for the torch head to follow. For basic circles, most welding supply shops have a circle-cutting tool (sometimes called a circle-cutting "compass") that can be used with a plasma cutter.

By far the most important thing to maintaining and operating your plasma-arc cutter is the condition and quantity of the air it runs on. Read the manufacturer's recommendations for the size of compressor you need and the pressure and cfm requirements. If you try to make a cut when you don't have enough air, most machines will either not start or make a grinding-like noise inside. Besides having *enough* air, plasma cutters also require *clean, dry* air. Most will come equipped with a drier/regulator right at the air-line connection on the back of the machine, but you also need a good drier on your compressor. And, if your compressor is

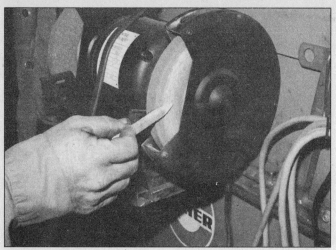

7.24 As with traditional torch cutting, soapstone is useful to mark your cut lines because it won't burn off. With the reduced heat of plasma, you could also use a marker pen. Sharpen the soapstone before drawing.

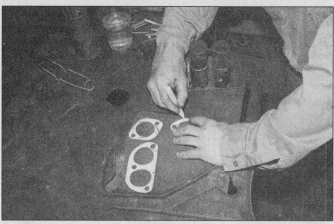

7.25 Here an exhaust gasket is being traced to make thick header flanges from a piece of 3/8-inch steel plate.

very far from where you hook up the flex line to the plasma cutter, it's a good idea to install one on the wall just ahead of the connection for the flex line **(see illustrations)**. Your compressor and the driers should all be drained every night to remove dirt and moisture. Moist air will rapidly deteriorate the electrodes and nozzles.

Cutting too fast or trying to cut too thick a metal for the size machine you have will cause some slag buildup inside the nozzle of a plasma cutter, not unlike the buildup inside a MIG gun. In fact, you may use the same anti-spatter spray or dip in your plasma cutter as you use on your MIG torch to make the slag buildup easy to remove. Eventually, even if you take care of your plasma torch, you will have to replace nozzles and electrodes because usage will enlarge the holes, making for a less-concentrated arc. If any slag is "fried" onto the nozzle or electrode, sand it off by holding the part squarely against sandpaper on a flat surface, and then clean out any orifice holes.

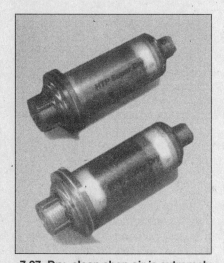

7.27 Dry, clean shop air is extremely important to extending the life of your plasma nozzles and electrodes. These HTP Super-Dry air driers have a bronze filter and desiccant inside that changes color when it needs to be changed.

7.26 The 50-amp plasma cutter makes short work of cutting out the patterns and can easily pierce the center of a pattern to cut out internal holes and shapes.

7.28 In most applications the HTP Super-Dry disposable filter/driers can be screwed right onto the rear of your machine.

7.29 You can't have the air too dry for use with a plasma cutter. If your compressor is outside or a long distance away, use an extra filter/drier on the wall where the hard line switches to the flexible hose for your plasma cutter. Drain daily.

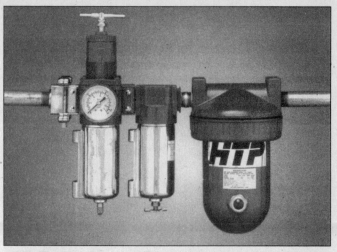

7.30 The Max-Dry from HTP is a three-stage system. Stage one is a self-draining 5-micron filter, stage two is a "coalescing" filter, and the final stage is another filter with a large amount of desiccant. The desiccant changes color when it can't absorb any more humidity, but can be dried out in an oven for reuse.

You'll find there isn't too much to discuss further about how a plasma cutter operates. They are at the same time technologically advanced, and yet simple to operate and maintain. They perform exactly as they are claimed to, in terms of speed, cleanliness of the cuts, lack of cleanup required and the minimal heat induced into the adjacent parts. Plasma-arc cutting is most definitely the preferred modern method of cutting metals, in situations ranging from an air-conditioning duct repairman or an automotive bodyman working on gauge metal to industrial plants where shapes are cut from thick plates all day long. To most automotive enthusiasts and race-car shops, the modern shop combination is a good MIG gun for welding and a companion plasma machine for cutting **(see illustration)**.

7.31 Daytona MIG offers several air filters, from left: the disposable filter element, a wall-mount filter housing, machine-mount filter housing, and in front a small disposable filter.

7.32 Given his preferences, today's hot rodder, race-car builder, farmer or fabricator would like to have one of each - a reliable, easy-to-use MIG welder, and a safe, clean and equally easy-to-use plasma cutter.

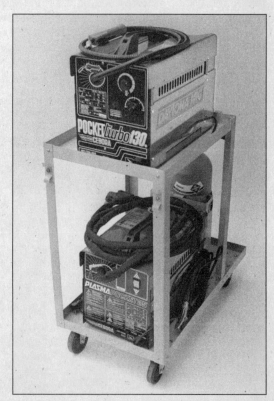

8 Safety & shop equipment

When it comes to equipment for working with metals, there's a lot more required than just a means of cutting metal and fusion-joining it. Many automotive enthusiasts are "tool addicts" to begin with and welding just adds another dimension to the want list.

Other than your welding/cutting equipment itself, the two main requirements for a good environment are the proper safety gear, particularly the goggles or helmet, and a clean, safe, well-designed welding work area or table. As you'll see, there's a wide variety of helmets available. Choose one that you are comfortable with and that meets your budget. You may have gotten a basic helmet with your welding machine, and you can use that until you save up for one of the more advanced models. Other personal safety equipment would include steel-toed industrial safety shoes (available at most shoe stores), good leather gloves, fire-resistant long-sleeve shirts or, if you are arc-welding, a leather welding jacket and/or apron.

A clean, safe welding table setup is of paramount importance. While you are learning, there will be a lot more sparks and slag generated than when you are advanced, and your welding table should be heavy steel, positioned well away from all stored

8.1 You'll find most of your welding safety gear and clothing at your local welding supply store, such as helmets, leather protective wear, gloves and safety shields or goggles.

8.2 This Hunstman welding helmet offers full face and chin protection, and features a flip up welding lens. When you are setting up to weld, the helmet can be down on your head and you look through the clear lens, then flip down the dark lens just before welding. Some weldors find these better than fixed lenses where you have to shake your head to flip the whole helmet down.

8.3 This L-TEC helmet from ESAB, called the Liftorama, features a lift-up safety lens, and underneath a shatter-proof clear lens that can be used when grinding a weld.

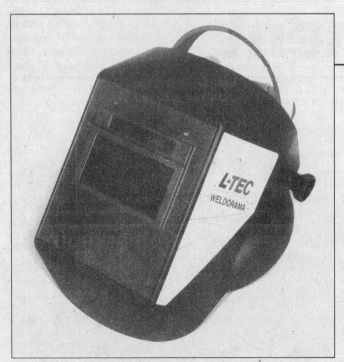

8.4 Another L-TEC helmet, the Weldorama offers a clear sight plate above the welding lens, so the weldor can keep the helmet down, and then just shift his eyes to the dark lens when he is ready to weld.

flammables and with a clear area underneath for any sparks or molten slag to be safely contained without having them scooting across the shop or lodging on top of your shoes. For metal cutting, you need a good "grate" setup as pictured in Chapter 3. You will also need some firebricks, which are helpful to practice welds on because the work won't stick to them. Do not just cover your old wooden work bench with a piece of sheet metal and call it a welding table. Invest in a piece of plate from a scrap yard. When you put a lot of heat into welding projects on a tin-covered wooden surface, enough heat can go through the metal to start the wood smoldering, perhaps even starting a fire after you have left the shop. Also, you must have proper fire extinguishers on hand, preferably an ABC type or halon, that can put out all kinds of fires.

Much of the work of sizing and joining metals for home/shop projects will involve tools you already have, such as a drill press, grinders and sanders, clamps, measuring equipment, squares and levels. A common hacksaw can be used to sever lengths of material but can be tedious on heavier-wall stock. Sheet metal can be cut with aircraft tin-snips, manual or electric nibblers, or a plasma cutter.

Many of the tools shown here are special-purpose tools that you may not have already, and which perform special functions that relate to improving welding work or holding materials to be welded. All of them are useful when the time comes. We all wish we could just put one of each in our home garage, but you may have to collect them over the years as your projects get more involved.

We also show here some tools and equipment that were made by fabricators

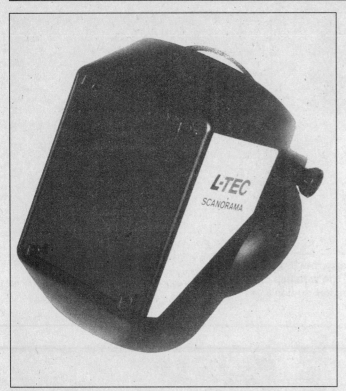

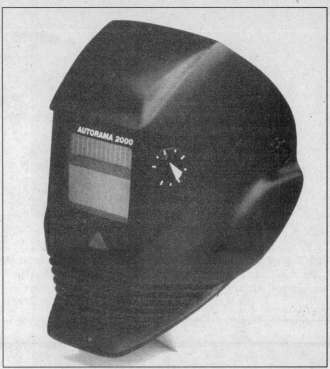

8.5 The Scanorama helmet was designed for MIG and TIG-welding applications, with a large shade 5 filter disc surrounding the welding lens. You can see most details through this area, but your skin is still protected from radiation. You look through the darker portion when welding.

8.6 This Darth Vaderish design from ESAB is the Autorama 2000, which one of a modern breed of welding helmet with an automatically-darkening lens. The lens is powered by solar cells, and turns dark as soon as the welding arc begins. These are considered by many weldors to be much easier to use than flipping a helmet up and down to set up each weld.

8.7 Daytona MIG offers a variety of modern safety helmets, and a special, clip-on lens (foreground) that attaches to your MIG gun. It allows you to set up a weld, then look through the lens when making spot-welds without the bother of a full helmet.

8.8 A good pair of leather welding gloves will last you for many years, but if you are using oxy-acetylene equipment, keep an extra-clean pair for use with this equipment. A spurt of oxygen on a dirty glove could cause combustion, so don't use these good gloves for handling hot or dirty parts.

8.9 From HTP is this Super Spark Guard welding blanket. It can take up 2300° F, and can be used when working on a car to protect the window glass, dash or interior. It measures 37 inches by 50 inches.

8.10 A clean, safe welding table area promotes good work. Your home shop won't need a steel-plate table this big, but note how uncluttered and organized things are here in a professional shop. A rack under the table holds all the C-clamps.

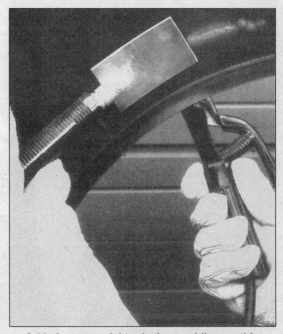

8.11 A very useful tool when welding on thin materials such as newer-car body metal is a copper "spoon." The heat-absorbing spoon can be used to back up butt welds or when filling holes in sheet metal. The welds will not stick to the copper.

and hot rodders for their own use. These are typical of projects you can do once you have practiced your welding skills, and some represent considerable involvement, though on the part of someone who has already "been there."

Sources for the commercial products in this and other chapters can be found in the Sourcelist at the end of this manual.

8.13 This welding shop has a dedicated grinder for sharpening tungstens mounted right on the side of the TIG machine. The rubber bungee cord kills the vibration noise when the grinder is slowing down.

8.12 If you get into a race-car project, you might invest in one of these tubing notchers. Available from Eastwood, Williams Low-Buck Tools, Speedway Motors and other sources. It fits in your drill press and allows precise fish-mouthing of tubing via a captive hole saw.

8.14 Eastwood offers this magnetic quick-clamp which functions to hold parts in alignment at various angles for tack-welding.

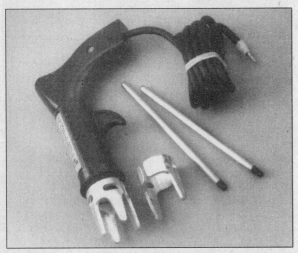

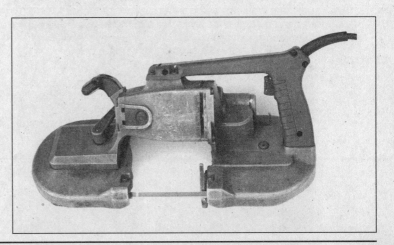

8.15 This unique spot-welding gun for sheet-metal work has a power lead that clamps into the electrode holder of your arc welder. Use the trigger to make the electrode touch the work, pull up for 5 seconds, then pull all the way to break the arc. Get it from Eastwood.

8.16 One of the handiest shop tools we have ever used is the Milwaukee "Porta-Band", which as the name implies is a portable bandsaw. It cuts fast and straight and is very helpful in cutting tubing at angles and other chores associated with welding projects.

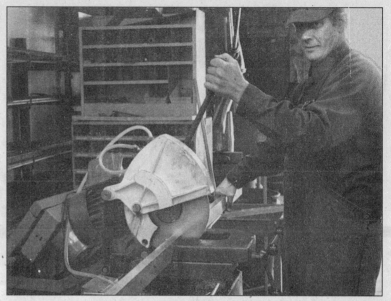

8.18 Other kinds of metal-cutting power saws include this type, which uses a bi-metallic toothed blade, here being used to cut clean through aluminum tubing.

8.17 A "Radiac" or cutoff saw with an abrasive blade is very fast and secure when cutting large amounts of tubing. The work is held in a moveable vise so angle-cuts can be made. This one is cleverly mounted on a 55-gallon drum to capture all the sparks and debris.

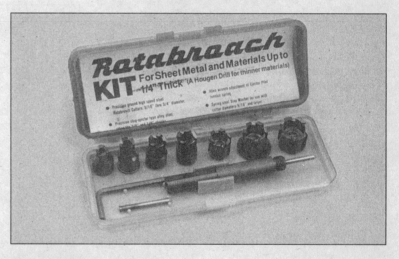

8.19 In auto bodywork, a tool like this can be used in your electric drill to cut out factory spot welds to remove panels for replacement.

8.20 For Eastwood offers a similar tool for removing spot welds which features a hex-sided drive end, so it can't slip in your drill chuck.

8.21 Weldor Bill Maguire made up this electrode rack for his TIG machine from a rolling platform holding 15 plastic plumbing pipes with caps, each marked for the size and type of electrode. A bungee cord holds them in the rack. Tubes keep the rods clean and dry.

8.22 You never know when you'll find something that comes in handy in the shop. This huge and hefty round plate was found at a metal yard and bought at the per-pound price. It's dead flat and cannot warp, and has mounting holes in it for clamping work to it.

8.24 A disc sander with at least 1/2 horsepower is very handy around the shop for squaring edges of flamecut parts, and taking sharp edges and corners off work.

8.23 If you plan to do any ornamental iron work or make a lot of brackets, an ironworker like this is very handy, It can bend solid round, square or hex stock, as well as bend round tubing and flat stock into repeatable shapes.

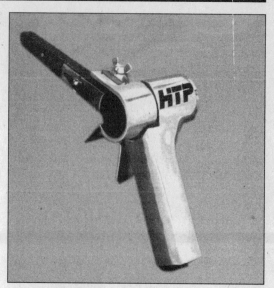

8.25 Ideally, you would have both a disc sander and belt sander for a variety of metal finishing needs. There are combination units, but beware of weak-powered sanders. When you put the rough edge of a 3/8-inch plate up there to sand, they stall easily.

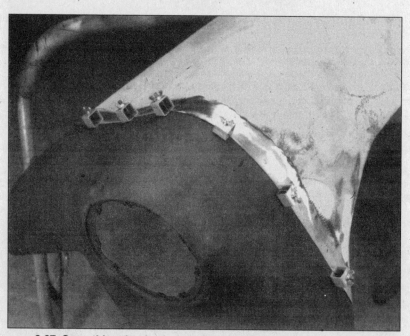

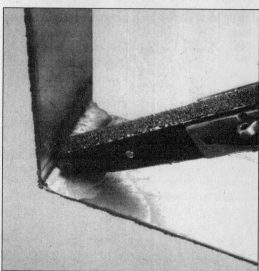

8.26 HTP is marketing this clever belt-sander that can get deep into corners and places where regular sanders and grinders can't reach. The belt guide rotates 160 degrees, and the sander uses 3/8-inch belts.

8.27 Something that is always a problem in body work when replacing panels is getting parts aligned properly before making a butt-weld. Eastwoods Intergrip clamps space the two parts .040-inch apart for full penetration. After tacking the panels, you can disassemble the clamps.

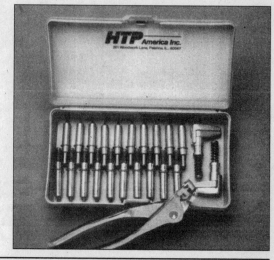

8.28 Nothing beats the original Cleco clamps and pliers for test-assembling sheet-metal parts. Originally developed for aircraft use, these operate like reusable, temporary rivets. In blind holes you insert the fastener with the pliers and the two parts are held together, but come apart easily with the pliers again. HTP offers this set.

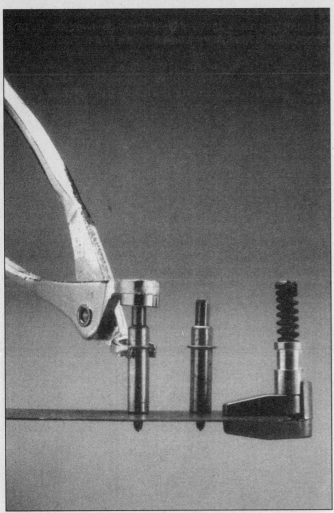

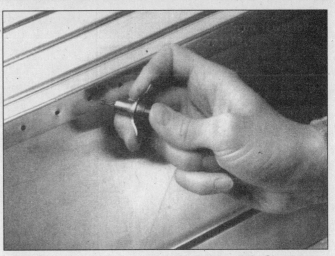

8.30 For small jobs, Eastwood offers these little Cleco-type panel holders that you operate with your fingers. No tool is needed. They have a range of up to 1/4-inch for thickness and fit a 1/8-inch hole.

8.29 You can see here how the pliers extend the tip of the Cleco fastener through a set of holes. When the tool is released, the Cleco grips the parts. Also available are Cleco mini-clamps (right) that exert a temporary hold while you tack-weld small parts together.

8.31 When you want to spot-weld sheet-metal panels that didn't have them originally, like new parts or repair panels you have made , a manual flange punch like this is a real help. This one is from Daytona MIG.

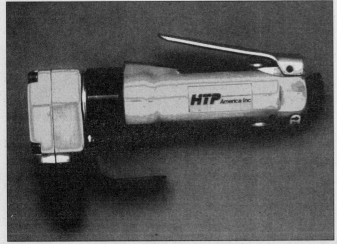

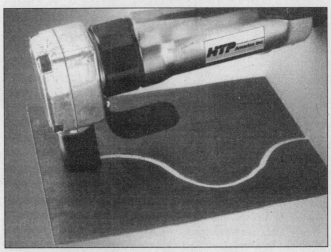

8.32 An air-powered "panibbler" is a fast, clean way to cut sheet metal up to 3/64-inch in steel or 5/64 in aluminum. It will follow a pattern or cutline very closely, and you control the speed with the throttle. This one is from HTP.

8.33 The HTP stud setter is a great boon to bodymen, who used to have to pull out creases and dents by drilling holes and using slidehammers that distorted the metal even further. This 110V tool saves considerable time and labor.

8.34 Small-headed copper-plated "studs" are inserted into the magnetic head of the stud setter.

8.35 On a dented area that has been ground to clean metal, the tool is pushed in contact with the metal and the trigger is pulled for a half-second.

8.36 The suds are spot-welded in place, and a special slide hammer is used to pull out the dent or crease. Studs hold 500 pounds of pull.

8.37 On this dent, the first three studs pulled out the bulk of the damage, and two more are in place to pull the last bit out. Note how the first three studs have been clipped off with cutting pliers.

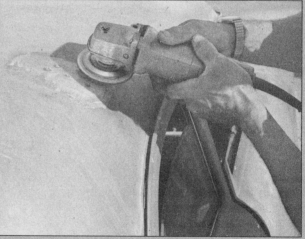

8.38 After the pulling, the stud heads are easily ground off without distorting the metal, and there are no holes left to fill in, as with conventional methods.

8.39 Visit most street rod shops, fabrication shops and race-car facilities, and you'll find that a lot of the shop equipment they have is homemade, and these are the kinds of things you'll be able to do once you have welding and cutting equipment.

8.40 A simple steel materials rack like this is great for keeping tubing, bar stock and flat stock out of your way, and is easily constructed. In front of this one is an electric, automatic bandsaw great for making unattended cuts. This one was purchased inexpensively at a tool auction. Watch your newspapers for industrial auctions and shop foreclosures.

8.41 An old truck rim, a length of round pipe and a piece of scrap plate are combined with welding to make a perfect small welding table or mount for a grinder or sander.

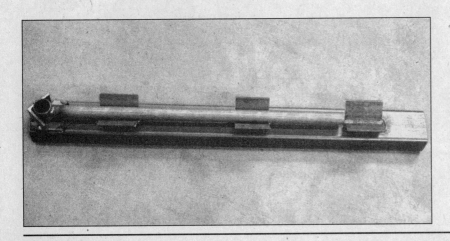

8.42 Leftover pieces of tubing and other stock should be saved in a barrel. You never know when you need a short piece. This fixture for making up a street rod four-link rod is made from short pieces of angle-iron and a length of rectangular tubing.

8.43 Ideal for holding small brackets onto tubing for tacking are these magnetic blocks, available at most welding supply stores.

8.45 Another type of angle fixture from HTP is this type, which clamps the two parts at a perfect 90 degree angle for tack-welding.

8.44 HTP and other companies offer these strong magnetic holders that can secure two pieces of tubing for angles of 45 degrees, 90 degrees, and 135 degrees. Tack the parts then move the magnets to the next joint.

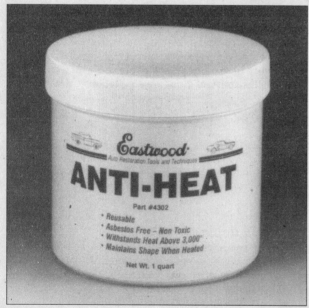

8.46 The Eastwood anti-heat is a putty-like paste that can be formed around heat-sensitive parts when you are welding near them. The paste absorbs heat and can be used to protect auto glass when welding near it.

8.47 Daytona MIG sells this handy spot-sandblaster. It is useful for cleaning paint and rust away from a spot your have to weld, like a recess where a regular sander won't reach. Three-quarters of the blasting media is returned to the gun, so it won't make your shop a "sandpit."

9 Building a utility trailer

One of the most common home/shop projects for welding equipment is a trailer of some kind, Which can be used for carrying a race car or off-road vehicle or 0n a smaller scale, can function as a utility trailer. Each of these is easily within the realm of the hobbyist, though a trailer of any size should not be your *first* welding project. Hone your cutting, fitting and welding skills on other, less critical projects first, like a metals storage rack, a wrought-iron front gate, a fireplace grate, barbecue grille or a rolling cart for your welding equipment. Frankly, the latter is usually the first welding project after the practice sessions. Many are the accomplished weldors we have met who say they welded up their oxy-acetylene equipment cart some 20 years ago and are proud to be still using it.

Since the trailer project is something to be used on public roads and at highway speeds, you want your welding quality to be good before you get started because the welds here have to be strong, not just good-looking. The basic construction details of any trailer are fairly similar, whatever the size. You assemble a rectangle of steel tubing or angle-iron, attach a sus-

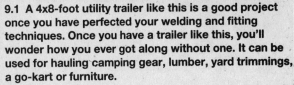

9.1 A 4x8-foot utility trailer like this is a good project once you have perfected your welding and fitting techniques. Once you have a trailer like this, you'll wonder how you ever got along without one. It can be used for hauling camping gear, lumber, yard trimmings, a go-kart or furniture.

9.2 Find a good trailer supply store in your area, where you can browse for suspension parts, wiring, lights and hitch components.

9.3 We purchased this Chevrolet Sprint solid rear axle and springs at a do-it-yourself wrecking yard very inexpensively. New trailer axles and springs can be expensive, but you can often find used ones at swap meets, or you can buy an old, small boat trailer that you can rework into a utility trailer.

pension and axle system, add a floor and sides, taillights, safety chain and a hitch in the front. Most smaller trailers, from 4x8-foot size and down, can be constructed of 2x2 tubing, or 2x2 angle-iron, depending on the hauling requirements. A trailer such as we are illustrating here is capable of carrying motorcycles, a go-kart, personal water-craft, garden tractor, camping equipment, building materials, firewood or landscaping dirt. With a few simple poles and some canvas, you could actually use it to camp in, like a homemade pop-up camper. We built this one of 2x3 tubing and 2x2 tubing of 1/8-inch wall thickness, which is somewhat overbuilt, but these were the materials that were accessible, and the cost of building such a trailer is entirely dependent on your materials. If you were building a car-hauling trailer, you would use two axles, preferably with brakes, and use diamond-plate steel for the floor, with some very sturdy ramps.

If you can get much of the steel from the scrap or remnant pile at your local metal source, scrounge used plywood or surplus diamond-plate steel and get your axle and suspension from a donor car at a wrecking yard, such a trailer can be built for 1/3 to 1/2 the cost of a newly purchased trailer of the same size. You'll need some kind of metal cutting equipment beyond the basic hacksaw or your arm is going to get tired. There's a lot of metal to cut to build even a simple trailer. You could lay out your plan on the driveway or garage floor, mark all your materials and bring them to a shop for cutting if you have to, then bring them back home to weld. Welding such a project can be done with any of the equipment we have discussed in this book, but it goes together fairly quickly with either arc-welding or MIG-welding.

We used inexpensive-grade plywood for our trailer sides, which we made two feet high, and a better grade of 3/4-inch plywood for the floor bolted to the frame with carriage bolts so the floor would remain smooth enough for easy rolling of a furniture dolly into the trailer. Once you have built such a trailer, it's like having a new truck. Everyone you know will want to

9.4 Bolt your springs, U-bolts, spring plates and shackles together, making sure the springs are square to the axle centerline and measuring the same distance apart front and rear.

9.5 Attach a hitch to the ball on your tow vehicle, and mock up the assembly, using 2x4s to simulate the rails. This should give you an idea of what size and layout of trailer you want, and where to locate the axle and wheels. Keep more trailer frame in *front* of the axle than behind, to insure you have enough tongue weight.

9.6 In our case, we determined that the Sprint axle was too narrow for our purposes, since we wanted a full 4x8-foot sheet of plywood as a floor. This meant widening our tubular axle 7 inches.

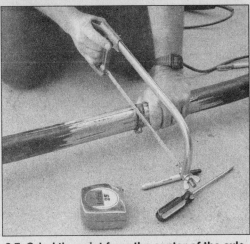

9.7 Grind the paint from the center of the axle, mark a straight centerline across the axle for lining-up purposes later on and cut the axle with a hacksaw. A hose clamp around the axle is used as a saw guide to keep the cut straight.

borrow it to move something. Our tailgate was made from a frame of one-inch-square steel tubing, .063-inch-wall, and we tack-welded to it a section of steel mesh such as is used for barbecue grilles. The hinged tailgate allows wind to flow through the tailgate on the road, reducing fuel consumption from the drag of a solid tailgate.

For our project, we used a solid rear axle and suspension from a compact FWD Chevrolet Sprint, which has single-leaf rear springs. We found later on that we had to add helper springs to accommodate heavier loads with the trailer. The 4x8-foot size allows for a fairly heavy load. We just bought two more Sprint rear springs at the local do-it-yourself wrecking yard, cut the eyes off each end with a friend's plasma cutter and used these as an extra leaf on each side. This increased the load capacity without making

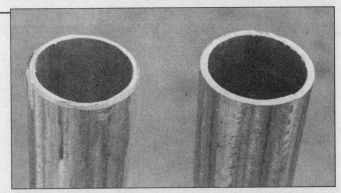

9.8 This axle is heavy-wall tubing, and, since we wanted good weld penetration for strength, the cut ends were beveled with a grinder. Tube at left has been beveled to about half its thickness.

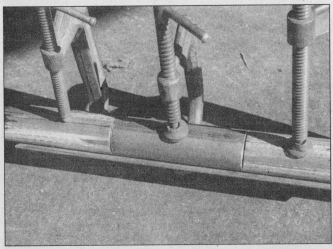

9.9 With the remains of your original centerline in alignment, clamp the axle ends together with a piece of new heavy-wall tubing the same size and keep them all in alignment with a length of wide angle-iron.

9.10 Here the assembly is tack-welded at several points around each joint with a MIG welder.

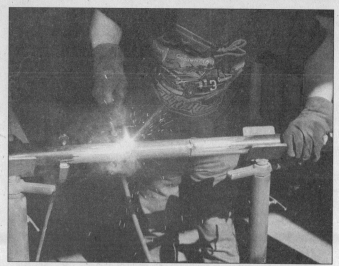

9.11 When the axle is securely tacked at several points, remove the angle-iron and make a strong weld bead all around the axle at each joint. Check for straightness after it has cooled off.

9.12 If your driveway or shop floor is flat enough, lay out your pieces of tubing on the ground and check all your measurements. Cut your joint angles carefully, and, with the pieces laid out, measure diagonally from corner to opposite corner to see if the frame is square. Check this again several times during the tacking and welding phase, too.

9.13 We used what materials we had, with 2x3-inch tubing for the two main rails and 2x2-inch tubing for the rest. When joining tubing of different sizes, cut one to a standard 45-degree angle (here the 2x3), then lay the next piece in, square it and mark along the second tube for the correct angle to cut it.

9.14 You can cut tubing and angle-stock with a hacksaw, but it is tedious. We borrowed a Milwaukee Port-A-Band hand-held bandsaw that made short, accurate work of fitting our tubing.

it too stiff when unloaded. Since you are using an automotive axle, it comes with brakes and all, and you *could* hook these brakes up to your tow vehicle with parts available from a trailer supply store. For our loads, like firewood, furniture and camping equipment, it didn't seem necessary. You could also buy a regular trailer axle with springs and brakes, but they are rather expensive if purchased new. There's a number of straight rear-axle assemblies available from front-wheel-drive cars in wrecking yards at reasonable prices.

There are few hard-and-fast rules in building a trailer, except that you should design it with the suspension and axle located in the rear 50% of the basic frame, not in the center, to maintain good tongue weight up front. Your tongue weight should be roughly 10% of your total trailer weight statically at ride height. The one thing that will certainly make a trailer handle badly is not having a long

9.15 The flattest spot we could find for our frame was a friend's muffler hoist. You could also set your pieces up on stands and use a level to make it flat. Use a big steel carpenter's square often during your setup and tacking, and keep making diagonal measurements for squareness.

9.16 There are special clamps for holding two pieces of tubing square while you are tack-welding, but you can also just clamp something to one tube that can then be drawn into the other tube with another big clamp.

9.17 Tack-weld all of your pieces together as you go. Don't make any full welds until the whole frame has been securely tacked together and is square.

9.18 Once the frame has been well-tacked, on the sides and top, flip the whole assembly over, square it up flat again and tack weld the other side. Note how the main center tube goes all the way to the center of the trailer.

9.19 With the frame fully welded, put it on jackstands, level it and roll your axle, springs and wheels under it. It is starting to look like a trailer.

9.20 Put bushings in the front spring eyes and use cardboard to make up a template for four front-spring-eye mounting plates to be welded to the frame.

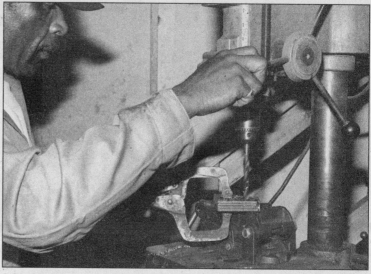

9.21 After flame-cutting, torching or plasma-cutting your plates, sand the edges smooth and stack them together with a vise-grip clamp. You can drill all four plates at the same time, saving time and ensuring that all have the spring-bolt holes in the same place.

9.22 The front spring-mounting plates are bolted onto either side of the front spring eye, squared to the rails and clamped lightly in position for tacking.

9.23 After some solid tack-welding, pull the springs out so the bushings don't melt, and fully-weld the four front spring mounts. Here the springs are bolted back in.

9.24 At the rear, short lengths of heavy-wall tubing, with an inside-diameter that fits the spring bushings, are welded to the underside of the rails (tack first, then remove the bushings to finish welding). Tubes should be positioned to have the spring shackles straight up and down. When the weight of the whole trailer is put on, they will arc to the rear enough for easy spring action.

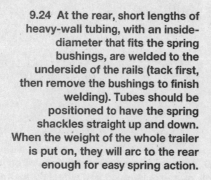

9.25 In our case, the frame was built just the right size to use an uncut 4x8-foot piece of 3/4-inch plywood for the trailer's floor.

9.26 Locate where your tubes are and drill through the flooring and tubing, then bolt the floor down with carriage bolts, with the round heads on top so the floor is relatively smooth and a furniture dolly will go over the floor easily.

enough tongue on the front and, therefore, not enough tongue weight. When loading your utility trailer, try to load the heavier items toward the front of the trailer.

When making joints in tubing, angle and other materials, get as tight a fit as you can before welding. A tight joint will always weld up as a stronger unit than something with gaps to be filled. If you are cutting with a hacksaw, use a carpentry miter-box to start your 45-degree cuts at the right angle. When you're done, give the whole thing a coat or two of rust-resistant paint, get an assigned registration number and license plate at your local Department of Motor Vehicles, and you're on your way.

When your trailer is complete, have a qualified weldor/metals expert inspect it for strength and safety. Then find some things to move!

9.27 Four posts of heavy 1x2-inch angle-iron were welded on, one in each corner, as supports for the plywood sides. After welding, all were checked with a square.

9.28 Having metal around for welding projects can pay off when working with wood, too. Use an extra length of straight angle-iron or tubing to clamp down on a piece of plywood as a saw guide, for perfectly straight cuts.

9.29 The front panel is attached with carriage bolts through the angle-iron posts. The posts were pre-drilled before welding on, because they are much easier to drill in a drill-press than once they are welded in place.

9.30 Short strips of 1/8-inch thick, 2-inch-wide strap metal (pre-drilled) were welded along the floor edges to help attach the bottom of the side panels. When MIG welding outdoors with argon gas shielding, use pieces of plywood around you to form a wind barrier to keep the gas from blowing away as you weld.

9.31 Plywood sides are bolted to the end pillars and the side plates.

9.32 At the local trailer supply store, we found a wide variety of lights, wiring harnesses, plugs and hitch parts to complete our utility project.

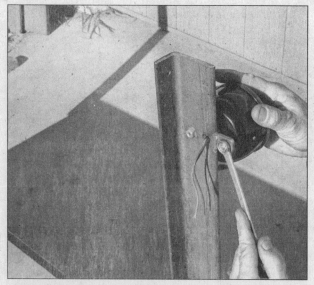

9.33 The taillights were bolted to the rear angle posts, but with a short extra piece of steel added on to move the lights further outboard to clear the tailgate.

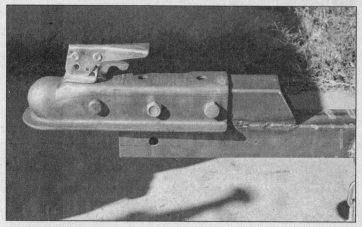

9.34 We originally had the hitch bolted to the main tongue, but found we had a better tongue weight with the tongue down another two inches. Simply welding on another piece of 2x2-inch, heavy-wall tubing set the trailer just right.

9.35 Every trailer needs a safety chain, check with your local DMV to see if your trailer qualifies for just one, due to light weight, or needs two to be legal. Take one end link, grind it clean of any plating and weld it to the trailer tongue (at top here). Below you'll see the removable snap-link that hooks to our tow vehicle.

9.36 Our metal tailgate will save fuel because air flows through it on the road, cutting wind resistance. The frame was made of 1x1-inch tubing, to which was added steel mesh. Hinges (bottom arrows) were welded to the tailgate and bolted to the trailer. Top arrows indicate where tabs were welded to the gate for bolting with wingnuts to the trailer structure.

9.37 With the wingnuts undone, the hinged tailgate folds down as a ramp for furniture dollies, lawnmowers, etc. The trailer should be hooked up to the tow vehicle before you step on the tailgate/ramp, or the lightweight trailer could tilt quickly.

9.38 A 4x8x2-foot utility trailer actually hauls a lot of "stuff". We've known people who built a simple trailer just to make a long-distance household move, then sold the trailer when they got there, saving considerably on what a rental trailer would have cost.

Notes

Glossary of welding terms

AC Current - Alternating current, such as in homes and businesses. Polarity switches at 60 cycles per second (US).

Acetylene - A highly flammable gaseous hydrocarbon fuel used with oxygen in gas torch welding/brazing/cutting.

Alloy - A modified metal made by combining a base metal with other metals or chemicals to produce a metal with different properties.

Amperage - A measure of electrical power. In electric welding, such as TIG, MIG and arc, the higher the welding amperage, the more heat is generated at the arc.

Annealing - A process of heating a metal and slowly cooling it to soften it and make it more workable.

Arc Welding - An electrical welding process in which a consumable, flux-coated electrode rod makes an arc with the work. Also called stick welding. Arc welding deposits a coating of slag over the seam, which must be chipped off after it cools.

Acetylene bottles

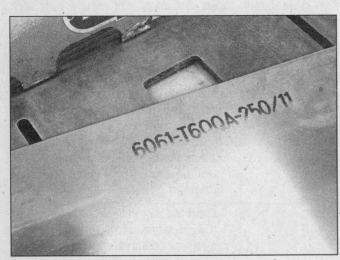
Alloy numbers on aluminum

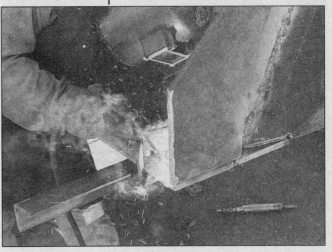
Arc welding

Argon bottles

Arc Blow - A phenomenon in electrical welding where the magnetic forces in the work can cause a wind-like force that blows shielding gasses away. Usually happens in corner welding and can be avoided by switching polarity or moving the ground clamp.

Argon - A colorless, odorless inert gas often used as a shielding gas in TIG and MIG welding.

Backfire - A loud pop heard at the torch in oxy-acetylene welding that indicates combustion has backed up into the torch. A potentially dangerous phenomenon caused by holding the torch too close.

Base Metal - In alloying, this is the pure metal before alloys are added. In welding, this refers to the work metal, as opposed to the filler metal melted in.

Bead - The seam between two pieces of metal that have been fused by welding. The bead usually looks like a tight series of overlapping circles or ovals of metal.

Brazing - A type of metal-joining where the parent or base metal isn't melted but is heated only enough to melt a filler metal such as brass, which holds the parts together after cooling.

Butane - A fuel gas sometimes used with oxygen for brazing or soldering. Butane does not produce as much heat as acetylene.

Burn-Through - When the welding flame or arc is too hot for the material, holes develop in the seam.

Butt Weld - The most common joint in home/shop welding, where the two edges to be joined are lying flat in front of the weldor.

Carbon - A non-metallic basic element that is a key ingredient in alloying of steels. Higher amounts of carbon in a steel make it tougher.

Carbon-Arc - A type of welding in which two carbon rods are brought together to create an arc independent of the parent metal. A process virtually obsolete in home/shop welding today.

Carburizing - In welding, an oxy-acetylene flame that is rich in acetylene, used to coat parent metals with soot before annealing. In metal work, a process of treating a surface such as a tool or knife edge by adding carbon to a hot metal, increasing surface hardness.

Cast Iron - A common metal, formed of steel with very high carbon and silicon content, in which soft graphite flakes appear throughout. The graphite makes the material hard to weld, but it is commonly used in large castings such as automotive engine blocks, heads and crankshafts, as it is inexpensive to manufacture and resists vibration damage.

Clad Metals - Usually mild steel alloys coated with another metal, such as galvanized steel, or sandwiched with another metal such as

Brazing

- The welding current is too high.
- The gap between the metal is too wide.
- The speed of the gun is too slow.
- The gun to base metal distance is too short.

Burn-through

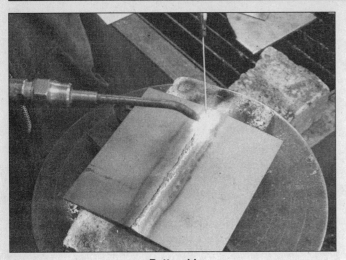

Butt weld

Deposit

kitchenware that has mild steel sandwiched between two layers of stainless-steel.

Copper - A reddish basic metal that is relatively soft, malleable and is one of the best conductors of heat and electricity.

Current - The flow of electricity, usually described by its direction of flow (alternating or direct) and strength (amperage and voltage).

Deposit - The addition of new metal to a welding seam by melting in a filler rod.

Deposition Rate - How fast filler metal is added to a welding seam. Determined by the wire-feed speed in MIG welding, and by the movement of the hand-held filler rod in gas, arc and TIG welding.

Ductility - A property of a metal that indicates how well it can be hammered out thin or drawn into a wire. A welded joint that passes a bending test without breaking is said to have good ductility.

Duty-Cycle - In electric welding processes, this is a way of gauging how long a particular machine can weld before it must be cooled off. It is expressed as a percentage of a ten-minute test period. At a 40% duty-cycle, a welder can be operated for four minutes, then must be cooled for six. At 100% duty-cycle, such as industrial equipment, the welder can be operated all the time.

Electrode - In electric welding, a conductive element that makes the final connection with the work to create an arc of electrical energy. In arc-welding, it is the rod or stick. In MIG it is the welding wire, and in TIG it is a tungsten rod.

Eye-Flash- A eye problem that occurs from observing a welding arc without protective goggles or lenses. Even brief exposure to the intense ultraviolet and infrared radiation can harm your eyes, causing a burning sensation that may show up 6-8 hours after exposure.

Ferrous Metals - Any of several metals made from iron and other elements. Common ferrous metals include wrought-iron, cast-iron, steel and cast-steel. Magnets attract ferrous metals.

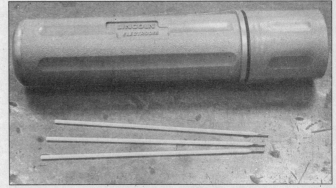

Electrode - arc rods

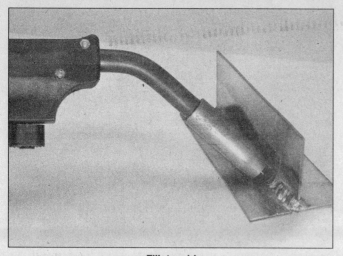

Fillet weld

Firebrick

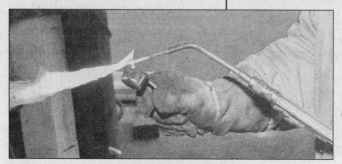

Flame

Flamecutter

Flashback arrestors

Filler Metal - New metal added to a welded joint by melting in a filler rod or wire. Most weld seams require filler metal.

Fillet Weld - A joint such as a 90-degree or T-joint, where the weld bead is filling a triangular-shaped area. Also describes a multiple-pass weld on thick, beveled plates.

Firebrick- Special fire-proof bricks used in welding as a non-conductive base on which to set parts to be welded. Usually larger than common masonry bricks. Do *not* use concrete or red brick to weld on, they will crack or explode from trapped moisture inside.

Flame - The heat-creating, working-end in oxy-acetylene welding/cutting/brazing. The flame, not the torch, contacts the work.

Flamecutter - A mechanized gas or plasma torch that is motorized and follows a pattern, to cut out repetitive shapes from metal.

Flashback - A situation in gas-welding in which combustion goes back into the torch. More serious than a backfire, it is signaled by a loud squeal, and should be stopped immediately by turning off the gasses at their tanks.

Flashback Arrestors - One-way valves installed in oxygen and acetylene hoses to prevent flashback. All gas-welding setups should have these.

Flowmeter - A type of gauge for shielding gasses which indicates the flow via a colored ball floating in a clear glass tube which is easier to read from distance than a dial-type gauge.

Flowmeter

Flux

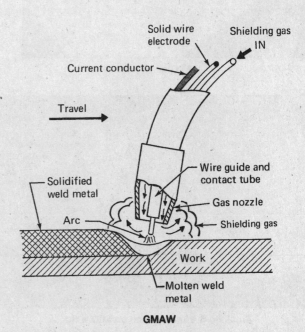

Gas welding

Flux - A chemical compound that cleans base metal under heat. In brazing, flux prepares the base metal for the brass to stick to it. Flux is applied as a coating to arc-welding rods and to wire for flux-cored MIG welding and is consumed in the arc to produce shielding gas.

Forge-Welding - A blacksmithing process where two pieces of metal are heated to the near-molten state and hammered together, resulting in fusion. Until the late 19th-century, all metals were either soldered, brazed or forge-welded.

Fusion Welding - Where the edges of two pieces of metal are brought to a molten state and joined, usually with filler metal of a similar alloy melted in.

Gas Welding - Using a mixture of oxygen and acetylene gasses to form a very hot, concentrated flame to heat and fuse metals.

GMAW - Stands for Gas Metal-Arc Welding, also known as MIG (Metal Inert Gas welding) and commonly called wire-feed welding. The process uses a shielding gas emitted from the torch while the consumable wire is the filler and electrode.

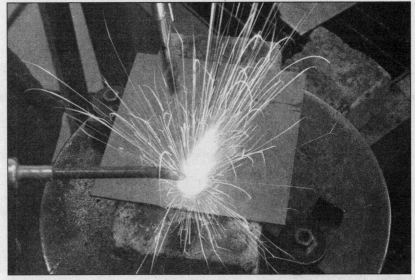

GMAW

GTAW - Stands for Gas Tungsten Arc Welding, also called TIG (Tungsten Inert Gas welding), and may be referred to as heli-arc welding, though this is a tradename. Helium or argon shielding gas emits from the torch, while a non-consumable tungsten electrode makes the arc, and filler is added from a hand-held rod like in gas welding.

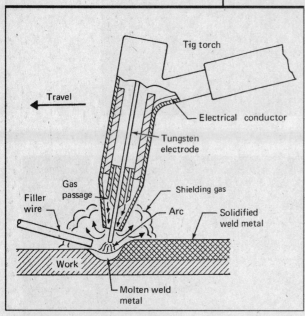

GTAW

Ground Clamp - In electrical methods of welding, this is a heavy cable from the welding machine that clamps to the work or the conductive metal work table, completing the circuit from the electrode to the work and back to the machine.

Gun - In welding, this usually refers to the "torch," particularly in the MIG welding process. The similarity to a gun is that the wire "shoots" out of it into the weld bead.

Hardness - A metal property that can be tested by the ability of the metal to scratch another surface or be scratched. Sensitive equipment is used to measure metal hardness, and the alloy number of a metal is used as a hardness indicator.

Hard-Surfacing - In arc-welding, a procedure in which many weld beads are made overlapping, covering a large area. Using special rods, a very hard, abrasion-resistant face can be added to tools or farm implements.

Heat-Affected Zone - This is the area along either side of the weld that has been changed by the fusion heat. On ferrous metals, it is indicated by a discoloration. In some cases the metal in this zone may have become weaker than the joint itself.

Heat Sink - Something used behind or around an area to be welded, to protect adjacent areas from heat. Wet rags and moldable, heat-resistant clays are often used around welding on thin sheet metal.

Heat-Treating - Changing a metal's characteristics of strength and formability by scientifically heating and cooling it. The term usually implies making a metal harder.

Heli-Arc - A tradename of the L-TEC company (formerly Linde), for their TIG welding equipment. The original process began with Helium as the shielding gas, and the tradename

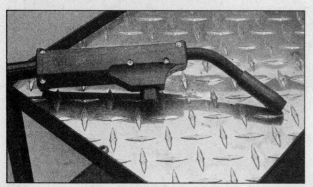

MIG gun

Small heat-affected zone on MIG weld

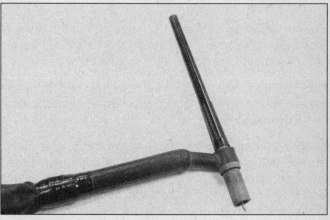

Heli-arc torch

came into such wide usage that it is now generic when used by weldors.

Helium - An extremely light, colorless, nonflammable gas, used in welding as a shielding gas and in everyday use to fill balloons.

Hydrogen - Atomically the simplest of all atoms, hydrogen in its normal state is a colorless, odorless light-weight gas that is extremely flammable. In small amounts it is used in some industrial welding/cutting applications.

Jig - A device used to keep parts in alignment or position during welding.

Joint - Where two parts are joined by welding, or where two sides of a crack are welded.

Kerf - The width of the cut in metal cutting by torch or plasma cutter.

Lap Weld - Where two pieces of metal are overlapped before welding, rather than butted together. Commonly used in brazing, and to stiffen a joint in thin sheet metal.

Lead - Another term for an electrical cable, such as a ground *lead*.

Machine - The power supply for an electrical welding setup.

Machine Welding/Cutting - When the torch or welding/cutting gun is moved by motorized equipment rather than by hand, resulting in a more precise weld or cut.

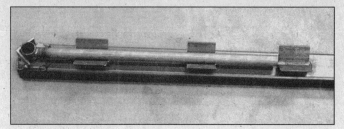

Jig

Brazed lap joint

TIG machine

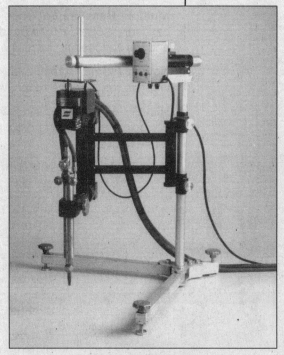

Machine welder/cutter

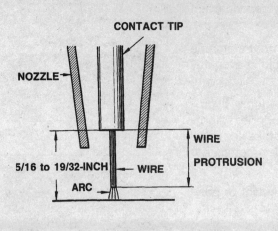

MIG

Multiple-pass weld

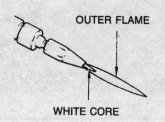

Neutral flame

Malleability - A metal quality indicating how well the material responds to being shaped by a hammer or forming tools.

Manifold System - Where a number of welding torches are fed by a common source of gasses, such as in an industrial situation or a welding school.

MIG - Stands for Metal Inert Gas welding, more commonly called wire-feed welding because the consumable electrode is a metal wire machine-fed through the gun from a roll.

Mild Steel - Synonymous with low-carbon steel, the most commonly found and highly useful material, easy to weld, heat and form.

Molybdenum - A modern metal used in alloying, to make steels and stainless steels stronger and more resistant to corrosion. A well known steel alloy is 4130 chrome-moly which contains molybdenum and chromium and is a strong material used in aircraft and race cars.

Multiple-Pass Weld - When welding thick plates or repairing large cracks in castings. more than one bead must be made. The joint is usually beveled first and the succeeding passes have wider beads until the joint is filled.

Neutral Flame - In oxy-acetylene welding and cutting, this is the desired adjustment of the torch flame, with equal amounts of each gas.

Nickel - A metal used in alloying steel and stainless steels chiefly to increase corrosion resistance and suitability for both very low and very high temperature extremes.

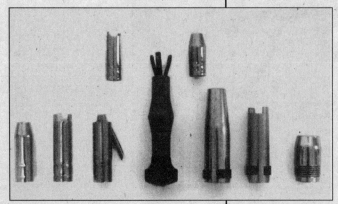

MIG nozzles

Nitriding - A metal treatment process to surface-harden certain steels, castings and forgings.

Nitrogen - The main component (75%) of the air we breathe, nitrogen is an inert gas that can be used as a shielding gas in welding copper, or as the cutting gas in plasma equipment.

Normalizing - A heat-treating process that refines the grain structure in hard steels. It is used when high-strength steels have been welded, to remove stresses.

Nozzle - A component part of the torch in TIG, MIG and plasma welding equipment, designed to focus the shielding gas over the arc.

Out-Of-Position Welding - Welding whenever the parts are not laid flat in front of the weldor, such as welding vertically, overhead or horizontally but perpendicular to the ground.

Oxidation - The deterioration process when metals are exposed to oxygen through air, moisture and natural or manmade harmful elements, On steel it appears as red-brown rust, on aluminum it can be a gray-black. To prevent it, metals must be coated with oils, paints or plating processes.

Oxidizing Flame - In oxy-acetylene welding/cutting, when the flame is adjusted with too much oxygen, identified by a ragged purple outer cone and a hiss from the torch.

Oxygen - A colorless, odorless, tasteless gas that makes up 21 % of the air around us. It is essential to combustion processes, and combined with equal parts acetylene makes a 3315° C flame for welding and cutting.

Penetration - Important in all welding processes, penetration describes how far into the two pieces of a joint the fusing process extends. Maximum penetration makes the strongest joint.

Piercing - In metal cutting, piercing is the technique for starting a cut in the middle of the material (such as cutting an *interior* hole in a piece of plate). It usually requires slightly different torch procedure than starting from an edge.

Pickling - Treating a metal chemically before welding it. For instance, cad plating on bolts, chain and other hardware can create dangerous fumes when welded, plus good contact is hard to make. Plated parts should be stripped in swimming-pool acid before welding.

Plug Weld - Where a piece of tubing fits inside another and is welded to it through holes drilled in the outer tube. Also called a rosette weld.

Polarity - The direction in which electrical current flows in a welding setup. There is AC, which alternates in 60 cycles per second (US), and DC, direct current, which can be either *straight* polarity or *reversed* polarity.

Porosity - An undesirable quality in a weld, with tiny holes caused by welding dirty metal, using damp arc electrodes, or getting a gas torch too close to the metal.

Post-Flow - A setting on a TIG machine allows the weldor to adjust how long after the arc is broken the shielding gas will continue to flow to protect/cool the bead.

Post-Heating - Heating a welded part after the final welding to relieve stresses.

Pre-Heating - When an entire part, or just the weld area, is heated with an oven or torch before welded to prevent thermal stresses and uneven expansion and contraction. Thick metals and aluminum and iron castings are usually preheated before welding.

Propane - A fuel gas commonly used in self-contained torches for heating and soldering plumbing pipes. It can be used with oxygen to perform welding/brazing on thin materials.

Oxygen bottles

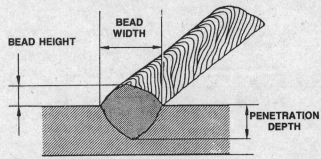

Penetration

Pre-heating

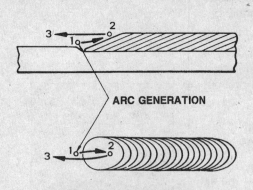

ARC GENERATION

OVERLAPPING BEADS

Puddle

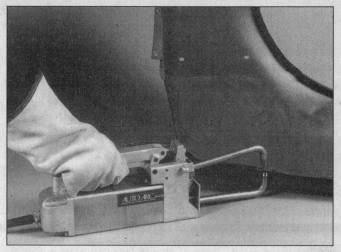

Resistance welding

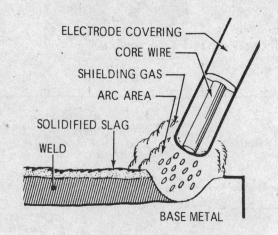

ELECTRODE COVERING
CORE WIRE
SHIELDING GAS
ARC AREA
SOLIDIFIED SLAG
WELD
BASE METAL

Arc welding rod

Puddle - The welding bead in process, as the concentrated area of the parent metal is melted and joined with molten filler rod. The finished bead is a continuous string of overlapping puddles.

Rectifier - A major component of many electric welding machines, the rectifier changes AC input current to DC output.

Resistance Welding - A method of welding where electrodes are placed on either side of the material to be joined, and a brief arc is made, which is enough to fuse the materials together at that point without greatly affecting the area around it. The weld is made by heat and pressure, and the technique is often used as spot-welding on sheet metal.

Rod - The filler rod in welding processes. In arc-welding, rod is another term for the coated, consumable electrode. In gas and TIG welding, the filler rod is usually uncoated and hand-fed into the puddle.

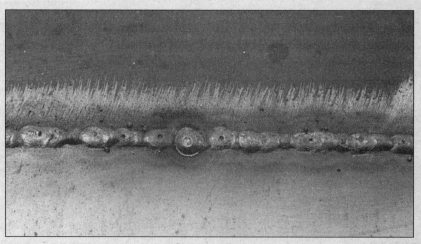

Seam welding

Root - The bottom of a weld bead viewed in cutaway. In multiple-pass welding on thick material, the first bead in the bottom is called the *root pass*.

Reverse Polarity - In electric welding, the term refers to a DC setup where the work is made *negative*, and is called DCRP. It is the opposite of DCSP, or *straight polarity*.

Seam Welding - A procedure used on lighter-gauge metals where the bead is composed of overlapping spot welds. Some MIG machines can be timed to perform seam welds. It is also used on machine-made welds to join long seams in sheet metal.

Sheet metal - Thinner metals, such as found in auto bodies, appliances, heating/cooling ducts. Usually refers to metals from 12-gauge to 24-gauge.

Shielding Gas - An inert (nonflammable, nonreactive) gas forced out around a weld procedure to cover the arc area, excluding air and impurities from the forming weld.

Shielded Metal Arc Welding - Another term for stick or arc-welding, it is abbreviated as SMAW. The flux coating on the consumable electrodes vaporizes into shielding gas to protect the weld.

Short Circuit - In electrical terms, this is what makes the arc when there is an air gap between positive and negative current flow. When you plug an appliance that is already switched on into the wall outlet and there is a tiny spark at the plug's prongs, this is a small-scale version of the short-circuit that makes electric welding possible.

Slag - Oxidized impurities resulting from welding and cutting. In arc welding, the slag forms a thick, hard coating over the seam, which must be chipped off with a pointed hammer. Slag is also found along the bottom of a cut made by a gas torch.

Slope Control - In electrical welding, professional-level welders have controls that adjust the shape of the current waves, to weld better on non-ferrous materials. Slope control can also be used to describe controls that gradually increase current at the beginning of a weld, and taper off current at the end, both to avoid cratering.

Spatter - Tiny balls of filler metal stuck to the parent metal around the weld, spatter is produced mostly by incorrect welding technique, but in arc welding spatter is unavoidable. Spatter is also present in smaller amounts with MIG welding.

Spot Welding - Small circular welds used to hold light sheet-metal panels together. Usually made through a hole in the topmost panel and common in auto bodywork (also see resistance welding).

Slag

Spatter

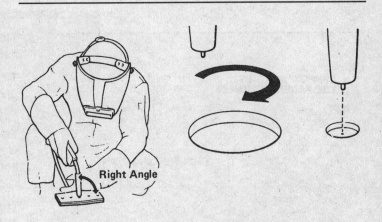

Right Angle

Spot welding

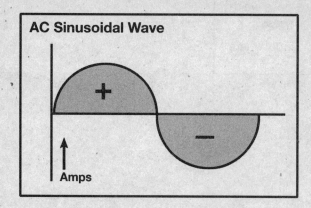

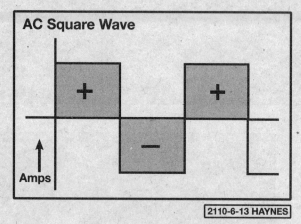

Square-wave technology

Stick Welding - Another term for arc welding.

Stitch Welding - A seam where welding is done only in short strips with gaps in between where full welding isn't required. Better MIG machines have timer controls to easily do stitch welding.

Stud Welding - An option for some types of MIG welders whereby a special attachment to the gun accepts hollow studs. The studs are pressed onto a surface where the arc is made, and filler wire welds the stud to the surface and fills the inside of the stud. A very fast method of replacing broken studs in exhaust system work.

Square-Wave Technology - An electronic method of changing the shape of the AC current wave for improved welding of non-ferrous metals with TIG equipment.

Submerged-Arc Welding - An industrial process where the seam is buried under a long, thin pile of flux material, and a mechanized welder travels along the seam welding *underneath* the flux pile. The arc is not visible, and the technique is used often on heavy plates such as in shipbuilding.

Synchronous Control - A type of electronic control which ensures that each weld will begin at the same point on the wave cycle, particularly important for consistent spot welds in automatic operation.

Tack Welding - Very short welds made at each end and the middle of a seam, to hold the pieces in alignment before a full seam is welded. When designing and building a project, it's important to tack-weld everything first before finish welding. You may want to change something at the last minute and tack-welds can be easily broken off or cut through to make changes.

Tempering - Steels can be hardened by heat-treating but may become too brittle. Tempering heats a metal to some degree below the transformation temperature and then cools it to bring back some toughness in the metal.

Tensile Strength - A measure of a metal alloy's (or welded seam's) ability to resist being pulled apart.

TIG Welding - This stands for Tungsten Inert Gas welding (see heli-arc).

Titanium - An expensive, strong, lightweight material used in aerospace and race cars. Special techniques are required to weld titanium.

Transformer - A major electronic component of electric welding machines, it turns high-voltage, low-amperage line current into low-voltage, high-amperage welding current.

Tungsten - The non-consumable electrode used in TIG welding. It is resistant to corrosion and doesn't melt until 6170° F.

Tack welding

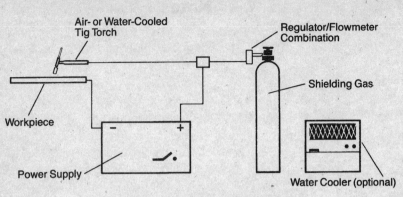

Air- or Water-Cooled Tig Torch

Regulator/Flowmeter Combination

Shielding Gas

Workpiece

Power Supply

Water Cooler (optional)

COMPONENTS OF A TIG WELDING SYSTEM

TIG welding

Undercut - A weld defect where too much heat was applied and at the sides of the bead the parent metal is eroded. Usually accompanied by too much penetration on the backside of the weld.

Voltage - A characteristic of electrical current that equals the amps times the ohms (resistance). In welding machines, input current is usually described in volts, while welder output is usually measured in amps.

Welder - The machine that makes the welded seam.

Weldor - The person who operates the welder.

Wrought Iron - A soft form of iron that includes some slag in its formation. Traditionally the material chosen for making ornate fences, gates and horseshoes because of its shapability.

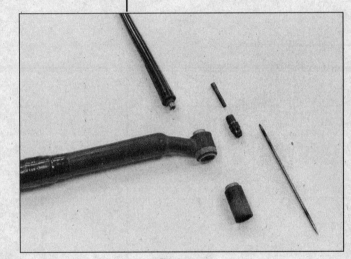

Tungsten

Notes

Index

Haynes Welding Manual

Sourcelist

Airco Gas and Gear
BOC Gasses
575 Mountain Avenue
Murray Hill, NJ 07974

Daytona MIG
1821 Holsonback Drive
Daytona Beach, FL 32117

Eastwood Company
580 Lancaster Avenue
Malvern, PA 19355

HTP America
261 Woodwork Lane
Palatine, IL 60067

Lincoln Electric Co.
22801 St. Claire Avenue
Cleveland, OH 44117-1199

L-TEC Welding & Cutting Systems
The ESAB Group
P.O. Box 100545
Florence, SC 29501-0545

Miller Electric Mfg. Co.
718 S. Bounds Street
Appleton, WI 54911

Haynes Automotive Manuals

NOTE: New manuals are added to this list on a periodic basis. If you do not see a listing for your vehicle, consult your local Haynes dealer for the latest product information.

ACURA
12020 Integra '86 thru '89 & Legend '86 thru '90
12021 Integra '90 thru '93 & Legend '91 thru '95

AMC
Jeep CJ - see JEEP (50020)
14020 Concord/Hornet/Gremlin/Spirit '70 thru '83
14025 (Renault) Alliance & Encore '83 thru '87

AUDI
15020 4000 all models '80 thru '87
15025 5000 all models '77 thru '83
15026 5000 all models '84 thru '88

AUSTIN
Healey Sprite - see MG Midget (66015)

BMW
*18020 3/5 Series '82 thru '92
18021 3 Series including Z3 models '92 thru '98
18025 320i all 4 cyl models '75 thru '83
18050 1500 thru 2002 except Turbo '59 thru '77

BUICK
*19010 Buick Century '97 thru '02
Century (FWD) - see GM (38005)
*19020 Buick, Oldsmobile & Pontiac Full-size (Front wheel drive) '85 thru '02
19025 Buick Oldsmobile & Pontiac Full-size (Rear wheel drive) '70 thru '90
19030 Mid-size Regal & Century '74 thru '87
Regal - see GENERAL MOTORS (38010)
Skyhawk - see GM (38030)
Skylark - see GM (38020, 38025)
Somerset - see GENERAL MOTORS (38025)

CADILLAC
21030 Cadillac Rear Wheel Drive '70 thru '93
Cimarron, Eldorado & Seville - see GM (38015, 38030, 38031)

CHEVROLET
10305 Chevrolet Engine Overhaul Manual
*24010 Astro & GMC Safari Mini-vans '85 thru '02
24015 Camaro V8 all models '70 thru '81
24016 Camaro all models '82 thru '92
Cavalier - see GM (38016)
Celebrity - see GM (38005)
24017 Camaro & Firebird '93 thru '00
24020 Chevelle, Malibu, El Camino '69 thru '87
24024 Chevette & Pontiac T1000 '76 thru '87
Citation - see GENERAL MOTORS (38020)
24032 Corsica/Beretta all models '87 thru '96
24040 Corvette all V8 models '68 thru '82
24041 Corvette all models '84 thru '96
24045 Full-size Sedans Caprice, Impala, Biscayne, Bel Air & Wagons '69 thru '90
24046 Impala SS & Caprice and Buick Roadmaster '91 thru '96
Lumina '90 thru '94 - see GM (38010)
*24048 Lumina & Monte Carlo '95 thru '01
Lumina APV - see GM (38035)
24050 Luv Pick-up all 2WD & 4WD '72 thru '82
Malibu - see GM (38026)
24055 Monte Carlo all models '70 thru '88
Monte Carlo '95 thru '01 - see LUMINA
24059 Nova all models '69 thru '79
24060 Nova/Geo Prizm '85 thru '92
24064 Pick-ups '67 thru '87 - Chevrolet & GMC, all V8 & in-line 6 cyl, 2WD & 4WD '67 thru '87; Suburbans, Blazers & Jimmys '67 thru '91
24065 Pick-ups '88 thru '98 - Chevrolet & GMC, all full-size models '88 thru '98; C/K Classic '99 & '00; Blazer & Jimmy '92 thru '94; Suburban '92 thru '99; Tahoe & Yukon '95 thru '99
*24066 Pick-ups '99 thru '01 - Chevrolet Silverado & GMC Sierra '99 thru '01; Suburban/Tahoe/Yukon/Yukon XL '00 & '01
24070 S-10 & GMC S-15 Pick-ups '82 thru '93
*24071 S-10, GMC S-15 & Jimmy '94 thru '01
24075 Sprint '85 thru '88, Geo Metro '89 thru '01
24080 Vans - Chevrolet & GMC '68 thru '96

CHRYSLER
10310 Chrysler Engine Overhaul Manual
25015 Chrysler Cirrus, Dodge Stratus, Plymouth Breeze, '95 thru '98
25020 Full-size Front-Wheel Drive '88 thru '93
K-Cars - see DODGE Aries (30008)
Laser - see DODGE Daytona (30030)
25025 Chrysler LHS, Concorde & New Yorker, Dodge Intrepid, Eagle Vision, '93 thru '97
*25026 Chrysler LHS, Concorde, 300M, Dodge Intrepid '98 thru '03
25030 Chrysler/Plym. Mid-size '82 thru '95
Rear-wheel Drive - see DODGE (30050)
*25035 PT Cruiser all models '01 thru '03
*25040 Chrysler Sebring/Dodge Avenger '95 thru '02

DATSUN
28005 200SX all models '80 thru '83
28007 B-210 all models '73 thru '78
28009 210 all models '78 thru '82
28012 240Z, 260Z & 280Z Coupe '70 thru '78
28014 280ZX Coupe & 2+2 '79 thru '83
300ZX - see NISSAN (72010)
28016 310 all models '78 thru '82
28018 510 & PL521 Pick-up '68 thru '73
28020 510 all models '78 thru '81
28022 620 Series Pick-up all models '73 thru '79
720 Series Pick-up - NISSAN (72030)
28025 810/Maxima all gas models, '77 thru '84

DODGE
400 & 600 - see CHRYSLER (25030)
30008 Aries & Plymouth Reliant '81 thru '89

30010 Caravan & Ply. Voyager '84 thru '95
*30011 Caravan & Ply. Voyager '96 thru '02
30012 Challenger/Plymouth Saporro '78 thru '83
Challenger '67-'76 - see DART (30025)
30016 Colt/Plymouth Champ '78 thru '87
30020 Dakota Pick-ups all models '87 thru '96
*30021 Durango '98 & '99, Dakota '97 thru '99
30025 Dart, Challenger/Plymouth Barracuda & Valiant 6 cyl models '67 thru '76
30030 Daytona & Chrysler Laser '84 thru '89
Intrepid - see Chrysler (25025, 25026)
*30034 Dodge & Plymouth Neon '95 thru '99
*30035 Omni & Plymouth Horizon '78 thru '90
30040 Pick-ups all full-size models '74 thru '93
30041 Pick-ups all full-size models '94 thru '01
*30045 Ram 50/D50 Pick-ups & Raider and Plymouth Arrow Pick-ups '79 thru '93
30050 Dodge/Ply./Chrysler RWD '71 thru '89
30055 Shadow/Plymouth Sundance '87 thru '94
30060 Spirit & Plymouth Acclaim '89 thru '95
*30065 Vans - Dodge & Plymouth '71 thru '03

EAGLE
Talon - see MITSUBISHI (68030, 68031)
Vision - see CHRYSLER (25025)

FIAT
34010 124 Sport Coupe & Spider '68 thru '78
34025 X1/9 all models '74 thru '80

FORD
10355 Ford Automatic Transmission Overhaul
10320 Ford Engine Overhaul Manual
36004 Aerostar Mini-vans '86 thru '97
Aspire - see FORD Festiva (36030)
36006 Contour/Mercury Mystique '95 thru '00
36008 Courier Pick-up all models '72 thru '82
*36012 Crown Victoria & Mercury Grand Marquis '88 thru '00
36016 Escort/Mercury Lynx '81 thru '90
36020 Escort/Mercury Tracer '91 thru '00
Expedition - see FORD Pick-up (36059)
*36024 Explorer & Mazda Navajo '91 thru '01
36028 Fairmont & Mercury Zephyr '78 thru '83
36030 Festiva & Aspire '88 thru '97
36032 Fiesta all models '77 thru '80
*36034 Focus all models '00 and '01
36036 Ford & Mercury Full-size '75 thru '87
36040 Granada & Mercury Monarch '75 thru '80
36044 Ford & Mercury Mid-size '75 thru '86
36048 Mustang V8 all models '64-1/2 thru '73
36049 Mustang II 4 cyl, V6 & V8 '74 thru '78
36050 Mustang & Mercury Capri '79 thru '86
*36051 Mustang all models '94 thru '03
36054 Pick-ups and Bronco '73 thru '79
36058 Pick-ups and Bronco '80 thru '96
*36059 Pick-ups, Expedition & Lincoln Navigator '97 thru '02
*36060 Super Duty Pick-ups, Excursion '97 thru '02
36062 Pinto & Mercury Bobcat '75 thru '80
36066 Probe all models '89 thru '92
36070 Ranger/Bronco II gas models '83 thru '92
*36071 Ford Ranger '93 thru '00 & Mazda Pick-ups '94 thru '00
36074 Taurus & Mercury Sable '86 thru '95
*36075 Taurus & Mercury Sable '96 thru '01
36078 Tempo & Mercury Topaz '84 thru '94
36082 Thunderbird/Mercury Cougar '83 thru '88
36086 Thunderbird/Mercury Cougar '89 thru '97
36090 Vans all V8 Econoline models '69 thru '91
*36094 Vans full size '92 thru '01
*36097 Windstar Mini-van '95 thru '03

GENERAL MOTORS
10360 GM Automatic Transmission Overhaul
38005 Buick Century, Chevrolet Celebrity, Olds Cutlass Ciera & Pontiac 6000 '82 thru '96
*38010 Buick Regal, Chevrolet Lumina, Oldsmobile Cutlass Supreme & Pontiac Grand Prix front wheel drive '88 thru '02
38015 Buick Skyhawk, Cadillac Cimarron, Chevrolet Cavalier, Oldsmobile Firenza Pontiac J-2000 & Sunbird '82 thru '94
*38016 Chevrolet Cavalier/Pontiac Sunfire '95 thru '01
38020 Buick Skylark, Chevrolet Citation, Olds Omega, Pontiac Phoenix '80 thru '85
38025 Buick Skylark & Somerset, Olds Achieva, Calais & Pontiac Grand Am '85 thru '98
*38026 Chevrolet Malibu, Olds Alero & Cutlass, Pontiac Grand Am '97 thru '00
38030 Cadillac Eldorado & Oldsmobile Toronado '71 thru '85, Seville '80 thru '85, Buick Riviera '79 thru '85
*38031 Cadillac Eldorado & Seville '86 thru '91, DeVille & Buick Riviera '86 thru '93, Fleetwood & Olds Toronado '86 thru '92
38032 DeVille '94 thru '02, Seville '92 thru '02
38035 Chevrolet Lumina APV, Oldsmobile Silhouette & Pontiac Trans Sport '90 thru '96
*38036 Chevrolet Venture, Olds Silhouette, Pontiac Trans Sport & Montana '97 thru '01
General Motors Full-size Rear-wheel Drive - see BUICK (19025)

GEO
Metro - see CHEVROLET Sprint (24075)
Prizm - see CHEVROLET (24060) or TOYOTA (92036)
40030 Storm all models '90 thru '93
Tracker - see SUZUKI Samurai (90010)

GMC
Vans & Pick-ups - see CHEVROLET

HONDA
42010 Accord CVCC all models '76 thru '83
42011 Accord all models '84 thru '89

42012 Accord all models '90 thru '93
42013 Accord all models '94 thru '97
*42014 Accord all models '98 and '99
42020 Civic 1200 all models '73 thru '79
42021 Civic 1300 & 1500 CVCC '80 thru '83
42022 Civic 1500 CVCC all models '75 thru '79
42023 Civic all models '84 thru '91
42024 Civic & del Sol '92 thru '95
*42025 Civic '96 thru '00, CR-V '97 thru '00, Acura Integra '94 thru '00
Passport - see ISUZU Rodeo (47017)
*42040 Prelude CVCC all models '79 thru '89

HYUNDAI
*43010 Elantra all models '96 thru '01
43015 Excel & Accent all models '86 thru '98

ISUZU
Hombre - see CHEVROLET S-10 (24071)
*47017 Rodeo '91 thru '02, Amigo '89 thru '02, Honda Passport '95 thru '02
47020 Trooper '84 thru '91, Pick-up '81 thru '93

JAGUAR
49010 XJ6 all 6 cyl models '68 thru '86
49011 XJ6 all models '88 thru '94
49015 XJ12 & XJS all 12 cyl models '72 thru '85

JEEP
50010 Cherokee, Comanche & Wagoneer Limited all models '84 thru '00
50020 CJ all models '49 thru '86
*50025 Grand Cherokee all models '93 thru '00
50029 Grand Wagoneer & Pick-up '72 thru '91
*50030 Wrangler all models '87 thru '00

LEXUS
ES 300 - see TOYOTA Camry (92007)

LINCOLN
Navigator - see FORD Pick-up (36059)
*59010 Rear Wheel Drive all models '70 thru '01

MAZDA
61010 GLC (rear wheel drive) '77 thru '83
61011 GLC (front wheel drive) '81 thru '85
61015 323 & Protegé '90 thru '00
*61016 MX-5 Miata '90 thru '97
61020 MPV all models '89 thru '94
Navajo - see FORD Explorer (36024)
61030 Pick-ups '72 thru '93
Pick-ups '94 on - see Ford (36071)
61035 RX-7 all models '79 thru '85
61036 RX-7 all models '86 thru '91
61040 626 (rear wheel drive) '79 thru '82
61041 626 & MX-6 (front wheel drive) '83 thru '91
61042 626 '93 thru '01, & MX-6/Ford Probe '93 thru '97

MERCEDES-BENZ
63012 123 Series Diesel '76 thru '85
63015 190 Series 4-cyl gas models, '84 thru '88
63020 230, 250 & 280 6 cyl sohc '68 thru '72
63025 280 123 Series gas models '77 thru '81
63030 350 & 450 all models '71 thru '80

MERCURY
64200 Villager & Nissan Quest '93 thru '01
All other titles, see FORD listing.

MG
*66010 MGB Roadster & GT Coupe '62 thru '80
66015 MG Midget & Austin Healey Sprite Roadster '58 thru '80

MITSUBISHI
68020 Cordia, Tredia, Galant, Precis & Mirage '83 thru '93
68030 Eclipse, Eagle Talon & Plymouth Laser '90 thru '94
*68031 Eclipse '95 thru '01, Eagle Talon '95 thru '98
68040 Pick-up '83 thru '96, Montero '83 thru '93

NISSAN
72010 300ZX all models incl. Turbo '84 thru '89
72015 Altima all models '93 thru '01
72020 Maxima all models '85 thru '92
*72021 Maxima all models '93 thru '01
72030 Pick-ups '80 thru '97, Pathfinder '87 thru '95
*72031 Frontier Pick-up '98 thru '01, Xterra '00 & '01, Pathfinder '96 thru '01
72040 Pulsar all models '83 thru '86
72050 Sentra all models '82 thru '94
72051 Sentra & 200SX all models '95 thru '99
72060 Stanza all models '82 thru '90

OLDSMOBILE
*73010 Cutlass '74 thru '88
For other OLDSMOBILE titles, see BUICK, CHEVROLET or GM listings.

PLYMOUTH
For PLYMOUTH titles, see DODGE.

PONTIAC
79008 Fiero all models '84 thru '88
79018 Firebird V8 models except Turbo '70 thru '81
79019 Firebird all models '82 thru '92
79040 Mid-size Rear-wheel Drive '70 thru '87
For other PONTIAC titles, see BUICK, CHEVROLET or GM listings.

PORSCHE
80020 911 Coupe & Targa models '65 thru '89
80025 914 all 4 cyl models '69 thru '76
80030 924 all models incl. Turbo '76 thru '82
80035 944 all models incl. Turbo '83 thru '89

RENAULT
Alliance, Encore - see AMC (14020)

SAAB
*84010 900 including Turbo '79 thru '88

SATURN
*87010 Saturn all models '91 thru '02

SUBARU
89002 1100, 1300, 1400 & 1600 '71 thru '79
89003 1600 & 1800 2WD & 4WD '80 thru '94

SUZUKI
90010 Samurai/Sidekick/Geo Tracker '86 thru '01

TOYOTA
92005 Camry all models '83 thru '91
92006 Camry all models '92 thru '96
*92007 Camry/Avalon/Solara/Lexus ES 300 '97 thru '01
92015 Celica Rear Wheel Drive '71 thru '85
92020 Celica Front Wheel Drive '86 thru '99
92025 Celica Supra all models '79 thru '92
92030 Corolla all models '75 thru '79
92032 Corolla rear wheel drive models '80 thru '87
92035 Corolla front wheel drive models '84 thru '92
92036 Corolla & Geo Prizm '93 thru '02
92040 Corolla Tercel all models '80 thru '82
92045 Corona all models '74 thru '82
92050 Cressida all models '78 thru '82
92055 Land Cruiser FJ40/43/45/55 '68 thru '82
92056 Land Cruiser FJ60/62/80/FZJ80 '80 thru '96
92065 MR2 all models '85 thru '87
92070 Pick-up all models '69 thru '78
92075 Pick-up all models '79 thru '95
*92076 Tacoma '95 thru '00, 4Runner '96 thru '00, T100 '93 thru '98
*92078 Tundra '00 thru '02, Sequoia '01 thru '02
92080 Previa all models '91 thru '95
*92082 RAV4 all models '96 thru '02
92085 Tercel all models '87 thru '94

TRIUMPH
94007 Spitfire all models '62 thru '81
94010 TR7 all models '75 thru '81

VW
96008 Beetle & Karmann Ghia '54 thru '79
*96009 New Beetle '98 thru '00
96016 Rabbit, Jetta, Scirocco, & Pick-up gas models '74 thru '91 & Convertible '80 thru '92
96017 Golf, GTI & Jetta '93 thru '98, Cabrio '95 thru '98
*96018 Golf, GTI, Jetta & Cabrio '99 thru '02
96020 Rabbit, Jetta, Pick-up diesel '77 thru '84
96023 Passat '98 thru '01, Audi A4 '96 thru '01
96030 Transporter 1600 all models '68 thru '79
96035 Transporter 1700, 1800, 2000 '72 thru '79
96040 Type 3 1500 & 1600 '63 thru '73
96045 Vanagon air-cooled models '80 thru '83

VOLVO
97010 120, 130 Series & 1800 Sports '61 thru '73
97015 140 Series all models '66 thru '74
97020 240 Series all models '76 thru '93
97025 260 Series all models '75 thru '82
97040 740 & 760 Series all models '82 thru '88

TECHBOOK MANUALS
10205 Automotive Computer Codes
10210 Automotive Emissions Control Manual
10215 Fuel Injection Manual, 1978 thru 1985
10220 Fuel Injection Manual, 1986 thru 1999
10225 Holley Carburetor Manual
10230 Rochester Carburetor Manual
10240 Weber/Zenith/Stromberg/SU Carburetor
10305 Chevrolet Engine Overhaul Manual
10310 Chrysler Engine Overhaul Manual
10320 Ford Engine Overhaul Manual
10330 GM and Ford Diesel Engine Repair
10340 Small Engine Repair Manual
10345 Suspension, Steering & Driveline
10355 Ford Automatic Transmission Overhaul
10360 GM Automatic Transmission Overhaul
10405 Automotive Body Repair & Painting
10410 Automotive Brake Manual
10415 Automotive Detailing Manual
10420 Automotive Eelectrical Manual
10425 Automotive Heating & Air Conditioning
10430 Automotive Reference Dictionary
10435 Automotive Tools Manual
10440 Used Car Buying Guide
10445 Welding Manual
10450 ATV Basics

SPANISH MANUALS
98903 Reparación de Carrocería & Pintura
98905 Códigos Automotrices de la Computadora
98910 Frenos Automotriz
98915 Inyección de Combustible 1986 al 1999
99040 Chevrolet & GMC Camionetas '67 al '87
99041 Chevrolet & GMC Camionetas '88 al '98
99042 Chevrolet Camionetas Cerradas '68 al '95
99055 Dodge Caravan/Ply. Voyager '84 al '95
99075 Ford Camionetas y Bronco '80 al '94
99077 Ford Camionetas Cerradas '69 al '91
99083 Ford Modelos de Tamaño Grande '75 al '87
99088 Ford Modelos de Tamaño Mediano '75 al '86
99091 Ford Taurus & Mercury Sable '86 al '95
99095 GM Modelos de Tamaño Grande '70 al '90
99100 GM Modelos de Tamaño Mediano '70 al '88
99106 Nissan Camionetas '80 al '96, Pathfinder '87 al '95
99118 Nissan Sentra '82 al '94
99125 Toyota Camionetas y 4-Runner '79 al '95

Nearly 100 Haynes motorcycle manuals also available

8-03

Listings shown with an asterisk (*) indicate model coverage as of this printing. These titles will be periodically updated to include later model years - consult your Haynes dealer for more information.

Haynes North America, Inc., 861 Lawrence Drive, Newbury Park, CA 91320 • (805) 498-6703